D0049122

SISTERS

LIVES OF DEVOTION

AND DEFIANCE

SISTERS

LIVES OF DEVOTION
AND DEFIANCE

JULIA LIEBLICH

BALLANTINE BOOKS   NEW YORK

In chapter 4 all names and locations have been changed.
Elsewhere in the book, some names and identifying
details have been changed.

Grateful acknowledgment is made to the following for
permission to reprint previously published material:
HEREFORD MUSIC: lyrics from "The Rock Will Wear Away"
words and music by Meg Christian and Holly Near. Copyright
© 1976 by Hereford Music. All rights reserved.
W.W. NORTON & COMPANY, INC.: Excerpt from
"Who Said It Was Simple" from *Chosen Poems,
Old and New*, by Audre Lorde. Copyright © 1968, 1970,
1973, 1974, 1976, 1982 by Audre Lorde.
WILLIAM L. RUKEYSER: Excerpt from "Kathe Kollwitz"
from *Speed of Darkness: Poems by Muriel Rukeyser*,
published by Random House, Inc., 1968.

Portions of chapter 4 appeared in "The Cloistered Life" by Julia
Lieblich, *The New York Times Magazine*, July 10, 1983.

Library of Congress Cataloging-in-Publication Data
Lieblich, Julia.
Sisters: lives of devotion and defiance / Julia Lieblich.—1st ed.
p. cm.
Includes bibliographical references.
ISBN 0-345-37299-9 : $20.00
1. Dame, Mary Aileen. 2. Quinn, Donna. 3. O'Reilly, Catherina.
4. Nicgorski, Darlene. 5 Nuns—United States—Biography. I. Title.
BX4670.L49   1992
271′.9′00092273—dc20
[B]   91-55505
                                                              CIP

Text design by Holly Johnson

Manufactured in the United States of America

First Edition: March 1992
10 9 8 7 6 5 4 3 2 1

To my parents,
Beverly and Malcolm Lieblich,
and my Aunt Fannie Bakst

If the first woman God ever made was strong enough to turn the world upside down all alone, these women together ought to be able to turn it back, and get it right side up again.

SOJOURNER TRUTH

CONTENTS

ACKNOWLEDGMENTS

Four nuns and a journalist are a little grayer since this project began. The hundreds of hours of interviews and conversations were enough to make the most vocal nuns consider a vow of silence. I am grateful to Mary Aileen Dame, Donna Quinn, Darlene Nicgorski, and a woman I call Catherine O'Reilly for taking the risk to tell me their stories.

The friends, colleagues, and family members who shared their reminiscences are too numerous to name. In particular I want to express my gratitude to Sisters Joan Chittister, Judy Connolly, Connie Driscoll, Lillanna Kopp, Rose McMahon, Marie Augusta Neal, Anne Taveirne, Margaret Ellen Traxler, and the late Sister Bea Desmairis; to Margarita Barrios, June Erlick, Helen Girard, Renny Golden, Clara Graham, Father Andrew Greeley, Michael McConnell, Annie Lally Milhaven, Bertha Noble, Mary Bernice Percy, Sally Schwartz, Shirley Tung, and the late Penny Lernoux; to attorneys Michael Altman, William Risner, Ellen Yaroshefsky, and all the other lawyers and defendants at the sanctuary trial; and to the sisters' immediate family members: Mary Aileen Dame, the late Edgar Dame, Prudy Dame, Louisa

Dame, Edgar Dame, Jr., Chester Dame, Joyce Quinn, Bill Quinn, Clementine Nicgorski, and the late John Nicgorski.

I wish to thank the archivists of the School Sisters of Saint Francis, the Sinsinawa Dominicans, and the Sisters of Mercy of New Hampshire for providing historical data.

My professors at Harvard Divinity School helped enormously. I am indebted to Harvey Cox, for his encouragement and invaluable guidance in placing the sisters' stories in a larger political context; to Margaret R. Miles and Bernadette J. Brooten for sharing their vast knowledge of early Christian women's history; and to Diana Eck for teaching me to appreciate the rich diversity of religious traditions in this country.

I could not have completed this book without the counsel and good humor of four remarkable women in my Monday night writers' group in New York: Mary Ellen Donovan, Lesley Dormen, Shelley Levitt, and Judith Stone. I thank Renata Rizzo-Harvi, Daniel Quinn, and the members of the Writers Room in Greenwich Village for providing me with a sanctuary while I wrote a portion of this book. I am also indebted to Nancy Day, Phyllis Karas, Carolyn Toll Oppenheim, Caryl Rivers, and Paula Sline for welcoming me into their writers' group in Boston.

My own spiritual community of sorts sustained me through this project. I am particularly grateful to Amy Bizzigotti, David Kirkpatrick, Jeanne McDowell, Colleen Murphy, Frances Reidy, Elena Sisto, and Stephen Westfall for their unwavering love and support; to Aimee Garn and Gene Holtzman for their generous readings and suggestions; to Miriam Davidson, Melissa Everett, and Jane Redmont for their spiritual depth and political vision; and to Marlene Adelstein, Jane Butts, Kyle Crichton, Sarah and Chris Gant, Steve Gelberg; Cooky Gerson; Pamela White Hadas; Lee Hourihan; Andrew Kupfer; Tim Jenkins; Robert Kempf, Jeannie Mandelker, Doug McNeish; Joe Neel; Tracy Ronvik; Sue Shapiro; and Nina, J.R., Dylan, Lucas, and Cali Simpson, who provided me with a home away from home in Chicago.

Special thanks to my former colleagues at Time Inc., particularly Roy Rowan, who showed me how to write a book; to Marie Cantlon, who has devoted her life to nurturing feminist writers, and whose editorial guidance is reflected throughout this project; and to my agent, Charlotte Sheedy, a warm and wise woman who helped bring this book to fruition.

I am particularly indebted to my editor at Ballantine, Joanne Wyckoff, whose enthusiasm and quick wit helped me through the rough times, and whose unerring critical judgment turned a book about four nuns into the story of progressive sisters.

Lastly, I want to thank my parents, who encouraged me to write, and my eighty-eight-year-old aunt, Fannie Bakst, who inspired me with her courage.

PREFACE

Growing up in the 1960s, I had no interest in singing sisters or flying nuns. I preferred ethereal sisters in films like *The Song of Bernadette*. Bernadette may have been a little simple, but her eyes glowed with the confidence of a woman with a vision. She had that cosmic connection with God that eludes us mere mortals.

Among novels I loved Henry James's *The American*. Forbidden to marry her American suitor, a French heiress runs off to a cloister to wear the hairshirt habit of the Carmelites. The suitor is turned away from the convent. The only trace of his beloved is the eerie sound of chanting voices echoing from within the chapel. I imagined the heiress pacing the halls of the cloister, the memories of lost love fading as she immersed herself in prayer. It seemed a calm, wistful fate.

I did not meet any nuns until 1982, when I spotted a newspaper advertisement that piqued my interest:

Rap session for former nuns.
What have we learned from our experience?
Let's get together and compare notes.

I cut out the item and pinned it to my bulletin board. For days I couldn't stop thinking about these former nuns. What had possessed them to join a religious order? Why had they left? I called and asked if I could sit in on the meeting.

The seven former sisters didn't seem to object to a voyeur among them, a Jewish one at that. They were used to women like me, who romanticized their vocation. They knew the black habits and the secret rituals were the stuff of romance and had been for seventeen centuries. Many had harbored the same fantasies when they were younger.

Their reasons for leaving the convent varied. Some felt that religious life proved too stifling intellectually and emotionally. They resented the subservient role of women in the church. Others fell in love. While all acknowledged the positive aspects of convent life, not one regretted having left.

Most of my illusions were dispelled during the course of the evening. For every Bernadette it seemed there were vast numbers who felt beaten by the system. Sixty thousand nuns in the United States had left the convent since the mid-1960s. Many had chosen a religious vocation before they were mature enough to make intelligent decisions about their futures. As they became better educated, they began questioning their psychological motivation for entering an enclosed society. Some left because they could no longer rationalize earlier choices. Others stayed in convents for the same pragmatic reasons women remain in bad marriages. Yet neither complacency nor financial security could explain why more than 100,000 highly educated women decided to stick it out.

There's a classic saying among nuns: "It doesn't

matter why you entered the convent, it's why you stay."
During the next four years I tried to discover why
women continued to find fulfillment in religious life. I
interviewed scores of nuns in several countries, from Is-
rael to Nicaragua. At first I was fascinated with the tra-
ditionalists in their long habits, who had resisted the
dramatic changes loosed by the Second Vatican Council.
Elderly sisters with Irish brogues told me stories of the
early days in the convent, living "in this world but not
of it."

Gradually I became more interested in women who
were of this world. I understood how otherworldly nuns
could live without lovers, but I wanted to know why
modern women would choose to give up exclusive relationships to join a community. I could find out how
traditional nuns viewed God by reading Church doctrine, but I had to talk to progressive sisters to learn
about their evolving spirituality.

What impressed me most about these nuns was a
commitment to social justice rarely equaled in secular
life. Whether expressed in a war zone or a monastery, it
was the intensity of this commitment that continued to
draw me to nuns long after I lost interest in wimples
and veils. A life of absolute dedication was more alluring
than any childhood fantasy. If I could not live the life,
perhaps I could learn from it.

It has been more than ten years since four Maryknoll
and Ursuline missionaries were raped and murdered in
El Salvador by government-sponsored security forces. I
still remember the explanation offered by Jeane Kirkpatrick, then United Nations ambassador designate.
"The nuns were not just nuns," she said. "The nuns
were also political activists." These were not the women
who taught your children and nursed your sick, she

seemed to say. They were political and thus somehow deserving of their fate.

This book is about four Catholic sisters who are also more than just nuns.

Like the Maryknolls, Sister of Mercy Mary Aileen Dame worked among the poor in the barrios of Latin America. Political revolution was the catalyst for her own revolution from obedient sister to activist nun. The Vatican's oppression of women moved Dominican Sister Donna Quinn to reclaim a church rooted in the radical principles of Catholicism. Contemplative Sister Catherine fought from the cloister to save a community that nurtured her spirit. School Sister of Saint Francis Darlene Nicgorski defied her government to aid men and women fleeing persecution. In the end she played a prophetic role that transcended the boundaries of church.

From different orders and regions of the United States, each sister has grappled with tough questions about faith and morality while challenging the church hierarchy at a crucial time in history. One sister made headlines when she questioned the Vatican on reproductive rights, another when she was arrested for defending the rights of refugees. The story of how these women evolved from handmaidens to heroines, however, has not been told. It's an important chapter in the history of the women's movement. It's a far cry from *The Song of Bernadette*.

SISTERS

LIVES OF DEVOTION
AND DEFIANCE

CHAPTER 1

SISTERS:

THEN AND NOW

I am in the world to change the world.
MURIEL RUKEYSER

She usually didn't deliver babies after dark. She left that to the granny midwives, or she would never get any sleep. But Jorge, a farm worker from Campo Alegre, had lost his first wife in childbirth and was frightened that his second wouldn't make it through the night.

It was September 1967 in Cartago, Colombia. At seven P.M. Sister Mary Aileen Dame finished rounds at the *consulta*, the clinic she had run since leaving her nursing job in Manchester, New Hampshire, two years earlier. A Sister of Mercy since 1950, she looked much younger than her thirty-four years. Her light blond hair, pale Irish skin, and freckles gave her a girlish appearance, accentuated by the ankle-length habit that dwarfed her slender five-foot-one-inch frame. Even her sisters had to admit she looked awkward under the yards of white serge, like a child wearing her mother's dressing gown.

She drove her old Jeep along the muddy roads to Jorge's bamboo shack, her habit hiked to her knees so that she could shift gears. Inside the house, the dirt floor was slippery from rain that had seeped through the thatched roof. She couldn't help grimacing when she saw two chickens scurrying around the cramped room. ("I know that in my lifetime it will be too much to ask them to keep the dirty chickens out of their houses," she had written to a sister back home, "but we will work toward getting them to keep the pigs out anyway.")

Jorge had just returned from the hacienda, where he picked bananas for fifty cents a day. A slight man in his early thirties, he sat at a table listening intently to the evening news on his radio, a rare possession in the barrio. When he and Mary Aileen talked at the *consulta*, she often wondered how a simple campesino knew so much about politics. Now she understood.

Jorge's three children from his first marriage lay on a cot they shared each night with their grandmother. Ana, the two-year-old, wore a soiled cloth wrapped around her like a diaper. She whimpered softly. "Ana has diarrhea," Jorge told Mary Aileen apologetically. "I had to wrap her in my shirt so she could sleep with the others."

"How long has she had it?" Mary Aileen asked, stroking the child's head as she pressed her bloated stomach.

"Since yesterday," he said.

"I'll bring her something from the *consulta*."

On a second cot lay Jorge's wife, Margarita. Mary Aileen examined the young woman and wiped the perspiration from her face. "You'll be fine," Mary Aileen assured her. "I'll be right here when you're ready." Comforted by the *madrecita* draped in white, Margarita shut her eyes.

Over an open fire in the corner, Margarita's mother, Doña Maria, boiled water in a large black pot. Mary Aileen watched her pour the hot liquid into a bowl containing a handful of black beans. Soupy beans to feed six people, Mary Aileen thought, or was it seven. Undoubtedly Doña Maria would insist on sharing the family's meager offerings with her.

Mary Aileen asked Jorge to help her hang sheets of newspaper across the room to give Margarita the illusion of privacy. Together they strung the pages from one end of the shack to the other. While attaching the last sheet, Mary Aileen slipped on the mud and kicked over a pan of urine by Margarita's bed. Jorge turned away. "I'm very sorry, Sister," he said.

"No, no, it's my fault," Mary Aileen insisted, wiping the bottom of her habit, already caked with mud. "Let's sit while Margarita rests."

Slouched over the table, Jorge looked more gaunt than she remembered. Nerves, probably, and lack of sleep. Every morning at three o'clock he piled on a truck with forty other campesinos for the long drive to the hacienda. He and Mary Aileen sat silently, staring at the chickens walking across the room. Finally Jorge spoke.

"You know, Sister," he said, "if I could give my life so that my children wouldn't have to live like animals, I'd die tomorrow.

"Don't get me wrong. I know you sisters mean well. But you come to our country and bring us some food, a little medicine. We're so worried about losing the few scraps we get, we're afraid to fight.

"And where does that leave us?" he asked, glancing at Ana in his soiled shirt. "My children are still worse off than my chickens."

Mary Aileen stared blankly at Jorge. She had no idea what to say. She had come there to help him. Couldn't he see that? She had come there to help them all.

• • •

"I just remember feeling hurt," Sister Mary Aileen Dame told me two decades later. "It would be years before I understood what Jorge was trying to tell me."

We sat on a wooden bench outside the National Palace in Managua, Nicaragua, the fifth Latin American country in which she has worked. Now a doctor, she practices internal medicine at a clinic and a prison on the outskirts of the city. In the late sixties she abandoned her habit and black lace-up "nuns' shoes" for button-down oxford shirts, cotton pants, and rubber-soled loafers. Her fine blond hair, once hidden under a veil, is cut short around her ears. Large tortoise-shell sunglasses hide her bright brown eyes.

I had learned of Mary Aileen from a nun in Boston. I wanted to know what led sisters to live in war-torn countries, and what gave them the strength to endure year after year. "You want to meet a missionary?" she asked. "Track down Mary Aileen Dame."

Mary Aileen bought two beers from a vendor, who poured the foamy liquid into plastic bags. When I fumbled with mine, she pierced the corner and held it above my mouth, letting the cool beer trickle down my throat.

"You'll learn," she said, her thick Boston accent unaltered by years of Spanish. "Bottles are scarce."

As we drank our beers, Mary Aileen talked about her tour of Colombia. In five years she and two nuns had built three clinics and a school. They had fed and vaccinated thousands. But knowing what she did now, she would never work there again.

"Why not?" I asked.

"Because the Colombian government didn't care for its own people. It left the job to private charities. Jorge knew that for all our good intentions, we were just putting Band-Aids on ulcers. For every child we fed, thousands more starved. Now, Nicaragua is different," she told me, her face becoming animated. After the revolution the government opened free clinics and sponsored nationwide health campaigns. Life expectancy increased and infant mortality was cut in half. But Mary Aileen's mood turned somber as she recounted the devastation wrought by almost a decade of war.

It is ironic, I thought. Twenty years earlier Mary Aileen and thousands of other nuns had come to Latin America to save the region from "Godless Communism." Now some critics accused them of spreading the very ideology they were supposed to contain.

"We've been called everything," she said flatly. " 'Sandinista sisters. Communists. Naïve nuns.' If people call us Communists or women who don't understand politics, it's easy for them to dismiss what we have to say. Members of Congress have come here for twenty-four-hour tours and gone home to testify before subcommittees as experts. But those of us who have lived with the poor, how often are our voices heard?"

Dominican Sister Donna Quinn lit a candle as soon as we arrived at her office in downtown Chicago. "It's my vigil," she said. "It gives the room a quiet, prayerful feeling." The flickering does have a calming effect. Somehow the steep pile of mail and the twelve messages on the telephone answering machine seem less daunting.

While Mary Aileen Dame has spent most of her working life in Latin America, Sister Donna Quinn has stayed close to her home turf. Born and bred in the

Windy City, she is executive director of Chicago Catholic Women, a 1,500-member group dedicated to giving
women an equal voice in the Church.

Despite the papers strewn across her desk, the room
is homey, more like a living room than an office. Against
the wall are a couch and coffee table, tucked in a corner
a gold metallic statue of the Vatican. "It's a joke," Donna
explained. A friend had given it to her after the Vatican
had threatened to expel her for signing a *New York Times*
advertisement calling for dialogue on abortion. Plugged
in, the statue lit up in red, revealing a pope in the window. It is an apt symbol: Donna versus the Vatican. For
more than two decades she has taken on one of the most
powerful institutions in the world.

I had first read about Donna Quinn when she made
headlines as one of twenty-four nuns who signed the
Times ad. She had captivated reporters with her pithy
pronouncements on everything from teenage pregnancy
to the pope. I wanted to meet this intrepid nun who had
meshed feminism with Catholicism and who had replaced the self-effacing humility espoused in the convent
with a healthy self-regard.

While her public persona is fearless and angry, the
private woman took me by surprise. At five feet two
inches she is proper and soft-spoken, like the convent
girl she was raised. Wiry gray curls frame a round face
with delicate features. She speaks with the thick nasal
accent of a White Sox fan.

Her ongoing battle with Rome strikes many progressive nuns as a waste of time. They prefer to ignore
the pope and his coterie and identify with what they call
the church of the grass roots. "Well, that's fine," said
Donna, "but if they belong to a canonical community,
their life is affected by the governing institution. I don't

work at IBM. I am a nun, and nuns are the pillars upon which this sexist church rests. That's why I have to work so hard to change it."

Many sisters, she contends, are afraid to challenge the institution closest to their hearts. "They have no problem signing a peace proposal. But if a sister takes a pro-choice position, she can be thrown out of her community."

"Are you afraid of that?" I asked.

"Sure I'm afraid," she said, staring at the flickering candle. "I've been part of the Sinsinawa Dominican community for twenty-six years. It's my family. How can a bunch of men I've never met throw me out of my family?"

"The goal of our life isn't to be cloistered," said Sister Catherine O'Reilly, relaxing in the monastery dining room. "It's a means to an end. Enclosure provides the silence and solitude necessary for contemplation. Most people would find it too confining. A woman came here recently for a three-month trial live-in, and by the end of the fourth week she was climbing the walls."

Dressed in a crisp white cotton blouse and blue skirt, Catherine looked cool and comfortable on a hot August afternoon. Her straight brown hair is cropped short. A fringe of schoolgirl bangs brushes her roundish face. "I never lost my baby-fat cheeks," she said. "I'm forty-three years old and people still pinch them."

There is nothing particularly "nunny" about Catherine, her word to describe overly pious or docile women. When she speaks, she speaks loudly and clearly, avoiding the hushed tones and religious jargon favored

by some contemplative nuns. "That is the language of
angels," she said. And Catherine does not identify with
angels.

We had met two years earlier, when I was writing
an article about contemplative nuns. I was captivated
by the seeming contradiction of her strong social
conscience and her yearning for solitude. While she
shared Mary Aileen and Donna's commitment to social
justice, she expressed her passion in quiet contemplation.

For almost two decades Catherine has lived inside
the cloister. Despite images of monasteries as dark for-
tresses, her home is bright and inviting. Situated in a
suburb of well-kept homes and manicured lawns, the
red-brick building with the white French doors looks
more like a prep school than a cloister. The convent
and the adjacent chapel are visible from the road, but a
ten-foot-high serpentine wall hides the grounds in
back.

The monastery has been home to most of the resi-
dents for more than two decades. Thirty-four-year-old
Sister Jane is the newest member, who joined the previous year after giving up a successful teaching career.
Eighty-eight-year-old Sister Monica is the matriarch, the
only nun who still wears the traditional floor-length
brown robe and flowing black veil. With the white linen
collar framing her finely lined face, she is a picture of
serenity.

Most people would rather see a nun in a habit than
in a polyester pantsuit, the author Walker Percy once
suggested. "Men and women are comforted when they
see nuns dressed as nuns," Monica explained. But most
people, Catherine points out, have never ironed yards
of white serge or worn scratchy wool habits in ninety-

degree heat, a prospect that takes some of the romance out of the regalia.

Catherine prefers casual clothes and rubber-soled sandals so that she can walk the hardwood floors in silence. Her gait is unmistakable. She takes short, rapid steps, holding her hands to her chest. Sister Monica has been imitating Catherine's distinctive walk for years. When the mood strikes her, Monica sneaks up behind Catherine, mimicking her rabbitlike gestures. Catherine breaks into laughter.

"We have lots of fun together," Monica told me. "We click, you see, though we don't always agree. I tell Sister Catherine that she runs around too much. She's always leaving the convent to go to some meeting or other."

The matriarch furrowed her brow, revealing a more intricate pattern of wrinkles. "And I don't see why she can't wear the habit. The Holy Father has asked all nuns to wear the habit. Why can't she listen to the Holy Father?"

I could not imagine Sister Darlene Nicgorski dressed in the habit of the School Sisters of Saint Francis. Indeed, she told me, she had worn a modified blue dress and veil only a few months before Vatican II turned the order upside down. At five feet eight inches she is built like an athlete, strong and sturdy, with wavy brown hair, green eyes, full lips, and the firm, square jaw of her Polish ancestors. She looked comfortable in jeans and a T-shirt. Her only adornment was a pair of gold hoops, a present from a Guatemalan sister who had convinced her to pierce her ears.

We sat on a worn plaid couch in a home I am be-

ginning to recognize as the new convent. The mis-
matched furniture had been found on street corners, at
yard sales, and in friends' attics. Unframed posters from
Guatemala decorated the living room walls. In a corner
stood a simple shrine: a picture of Our Lady of Guadalupe, a candle, and a Spanish Bible.

Darlene looked tired as she sank into the sofa. Her
friends, she told me, had been urging her to take some
time off all summer. They worried that she was headed
for a breakdown with the sixteen-hour days she was
working arranging transportation and housing for refugees who had fled the violence in El Salvador and Guatemala.

She had resisted for months. More and more Central
Americans were flooding into Phoenix. They needed
places to go; they needed transportation to the churches
and temples throughout the country that had agreed to
offer them sanctuary. They didn't get a vacation. Why
should she?

By winter she acknowledged that the strain was getting to her. She was irritable, exhausted, no good to
herself or the refugees. She agreed to sign up for a retreat for returning missionaries in Adrian, Michigan.

Three days after she arrived in Michigan, she was
returning from an afternoon walk along the snow-
covered grounds when a sister handed her an urgent
message. That morning, she learned, federal agents had
broken into her apartment. They had arrested Margarita,
a young Salvadoran woman staying there, and had confiscated dozens of files, her passport, her diaries and letters, and photographs. Darlene was indicted on six
felony counts, including conspiracy to violate U.S. immigration law. If convicted, she could face up to thirty
years in prison.

For a day and a half Darlene felt numb. She just kept moving—returning phone calls, packing her things. It wasn't until she spoke to Margarita on the telephone that she cried.

She did not have much time to think. News of the indictment thrust her into the public eye. Although unaccustomed to the media, she responded readily with simple statements that reflected her faith.

"In my heart I feel I have done nothing illegal. I don't think it's the government's role to tell us which stranger we can welcome, or which person we can feed. If I am guilty of anything, I am guilty of living out the gospel."

I had written to Darlene to ask if I could spend time with her during the sanctuary trial and after the media flurry died down. What kind of faith inspired a nun to defy her government to aid refugees fleeing persecution? Like the three other nuns, she was a woman of conviction, and, I suspected, a prophetic voice in the Catholic church. I wanted more than an interview. I wanted to hear the story of her life.

II

Just who is the modern nun, I wondered, and where did Mary Aileen, Donna, Catherine, and Darlene fit into the spectrum of traditional nuns in full regalia and radical sisters in T-shirts and jeans? What percentage of the more than 100,000 sisters in the United States had abandoned their habits? Did the majority believe in classical notions of poverty, chastity, and obedience? How many were questioning the central tenets of the Catholic church?

I put these questions to a former nun, who

shrugged her shoulders. "I always wondered the same things," she said. "I'm not sure even sisters know who they are. And the public believes what it sees on TV." Indeed, for every person I met who associated the word *nun* with the missionary sisters killed in El Salvador, dozens more mentioned Sally Field in "The Flying Nun."

Nuns, it seems, are the stuff of fantasy. Movies present sisters as silly schoolgirls (*The Trouble with Angels*) and starry-eyed saints (*The Song of Bernadette*). Pornographic novelists write of habited whores in leather and chains. Activist nuns are beginning to play cameo roles in television shows, but it is still the old-fashioned sister who captures the public's imagination. The nun in the recent series, "Father Dowling Mysteries," may be a first-rate sleuth, but her childlike manner and flyaway habit earn her a place among the singing nuns of prime-time TV.

Nuns' saccharine stories of convent life only reinforce stereotypes of humble handmaidens of the Lord. Many books by former sisters are just as misleading. Although some chronicle the often devastating abuses nuns have suffered at the hands of authoritarian abbesses and clerics, most tell only half the story of convent life. In historical accounts nuns are all but invisible. Only in the past two decades have scholars pieced together the role that sisters have played since the early days of Christianity.

The first celibate sisters, I learned, were a far cry from the habited nuns of Catholic-school lore. During the first three centuries of the Church, groups of virgins and widows in the Christian East and West opted for a celibate life of prayer and good works. They lived in their homes or in small communities. Some even worshiped side by side with male celibates, much to the chagrin of the bishops, who feared that these mixed communities might form an order resistant to Church authority.

Celibacy was not imposed on women in the beginning. Many chose an ascetic life when church fathers disapproved of the unmarried state. While Paul advocated celibacy, the first-century theologian, Clement of Alexandria, was among those who regarded virgins with contempt. It was not until two hundred years after the first Christian women's communities appeared that church fathers, such as Tertullian, lauded virginity as a model of Christian perfection.

Like today's progressive nuns, these independent women were hardly the model the men had in mind. Many virgins and widows did not equate devotion with dourness, and it is doubtful they took vows of poverty and obedience. Some enjoyed wearing fancy clothes and jewelry, attending bawdy wedding parties, and making frequent trips to the public baths. The North African bishop Cyprian warned virgins to stop disrobing at public baths lest their bodies arouse the male bathers. "Without perhaps losing your own soul, you nevertheless ruin others," he wrote. But the virgins refused to comply.

Tertullian urged virgins to wear a veil to conceal their beauty and to identify themselves as brides of Christ: "Be veiled, virgin, if virgin you are! . . . you are wedded to Christ. . . . Act as becomes your husband's discipline." This mystical marriage to Christ was taken so literally that unfaithfulness was punished as adultery. Clerics must have liked this bridal imagery. As self-proclaimed representatives of Christ on earth, they could claim authority over his brides. But some virgins rebelled against this attempted control by leaving the Church.

The late third century marked the beginning of formal convent life for women. Pachomius, the founder of communal religious life in Egypt, established a convent in the Egyptian desert near Thebes across the river from his male monastery. He placed his sister Mary in charge of the women, who spent their days in private and communal prayer, memorizing Scripture, and sewing clothes.

Most of these new nuns were daughters of the aristocracy. Some chose the monastic life; others were shipped off as young girls by their families. Widows often joined their daughters in the monastery, and some intrepid women fled to convents while their husbands were still alive.

The celibate life provided an attractive alternative to arranged marriages at tender ages and protection from the dangers of childbirth. By the fourth century, nuns could pursue studies, travel, and strive for a degree of influence in the Church. But women achieved this freedom at the price of their sexuality. Only by giving up their capacity to reproduce did they transcend the "weakness" of their sex in the eyes of the Church fathers. These honorary males, however, could not teach beside their brothers nor hold positions of leadership in the Church.

Still, women flocked to convents in the Christian East and West. Between A.D. 500 and 1099, some three hundred monasteries for women were founded in France, Belgium, and Britain alone. The growth in monasteries corresponded with an increase in missionary activity, particularly on the rural frontiers. Clerics recruited noble families to found churches and endow monastic communities. Unmarried daughters and widows were often installed as abbesses, some of whom ruled over double monasteries of nuns and monks located on countryside estates far from the gaze of urban bishops.

The most powerful abbesses, usually of royal lineage, rivaled queens in influence. They ruled their own lands, decreed punishment, and sent their own knights into battle for the king. They performed quasi-clerical functions in the convent, hearing confessions, granting absolution and benediction, and giving communion in rituals known as "masses without priests," until such practices were suppressed by clerics.

Religious houses in northern France and in the German lands of Saxony were renowned centers of learning that provided nuns with an education unavailable to their lay sisters. Convents served as boarding schools for the sons and daughters of the aristocracy until the ninth century, when Charlemagne ruled that the sexes be segregated.

The glory of many convents, however, was short-lived. After the death of a founder, some convent property reverted back to family ownership. Monasteries were destroyed by fire and flood, and several communities of nuns in Britain succumbed to the plague of A.D 686. Even more devastating were the Viking, Saracen, and Hungarian invasions during the eighth through the eleventh centuries. In 870 the Danes destroyed Barking Abbey, burning the nuns alive in the convent. The nuns of Whitby took refuge in the fortified monastery of Tynemouth, but the Danes managed to destroy the church and massacre the nuns.

To ward off Viking rapists, Saint Ebba and the nuns of Coldingham resorted to self-mutilation, cutting off their noses and lips with razors. Horrified by the women's appearance, the invaders fled, but only after setting fire to the convent. The nuns perished with their virginity intact, thus ensuring their place in heaven. Rape was a fate worse than death for women defined by their virginity.

The late Middle Ages saw a decline in the status of religious life. The nobility began to use monasteries increasingly as a dumping ground for their rebellious daughters, discarded mistresses, and enemies' widows. Wealthy women without vocations had little use for nuns' habits. They wore their own clothes and brought their servants to the convent. These renegade nuns thought nothing of leaving the cloister to attend weddings and of entertaining men in the convent parlor. Although tales of sexual depravity in medieval convents were rampant, the deterioration of religious life had more to do with high living than with low morals.

In an attempt to restore discipline, reformers of the eleventh and twelfth centuries issued decrees forbidding the continuation of double monasteries of nuns and monks. In 1298 a papal bull was issued to "provide for the perilous and detestable state of certain nuns . . . [who] have shamelessly cast aside the modesty of their sex." The decree mandated perpetual enclosure for all nuns. Women who had wanted to serve the community were confined to the cloister.

Strong women, however, emerged in the strictest of cloisters. The German abbess Hildegard of Bingen, a bold sister unafraid to criticize Church authorities, was an important intellectual of the twelfth century. Well versed in Latin, Scripture, and the natural sciences, she wrote highly regarded scientific treatises. She corresponded with popes, emperors, and kings, as well as with Eleanor of Aquitaine and Thomas à Becket. Even the renowned Cistercian monk Bernard of Clairvaux, no fan of females, recognized the significance of her work.

Some women sought an alternative to enclosed convents. Groups of Christian laywomen in the twelfth century, known as the Beguines, lived in their homes or Beguine houses under their own rule. The women attended Mass daily, led by supportive priests, and observed a regular schedule of prayer. They set up infirmaries, visited the sick in their homes, and taught impoverished children. Although they did not take a vow of poverty, they were expected to live modestly. They promised to remain celibate only while living as Beguines and were free to leave the community at any time.

As the movement grew, the Beguines gained in number and prestige throughout Europe. From 1250 to 1350 one hundred Beguine houses sprang up in Cologne, northern Europe's second largest city. The movement initially received papal approval and boasted such illustrious patrons as Louis IX of France. But many clerics opposed the women, who were often outspoken critics of the Church. Priests feared female independence and distrusted the Beguines' mystical spirituality, which often took the form of prolonged fasts accompanied by ecstatic visions.

In 1311 the Council of Vienne condemned the Beguine movement. "We have been told that certain women commonly called Beguines, afflicted by a kind of madness . . . express opinions on matters of faith and sacraments contrary to the catholic faith." Clerical persecution followed, and by the fifteenth century this early European women's movement had been all but wiped out.

Not until the sixteenth century did the traditional convent provide nuns with more of the options enjoyed by the Beguines. "Semicloistered" convents were established. Women who wanted to combine prayer with caring for the poor and sick were allowed to leave their convents, as long as they maintained a regular schedule of communal devotion. In 1544 Angela Merici founded an uncloistered Ursuline community to teach and minister to the poor. But its freedom was brief. In 1545 the Council of Trent attempted to counter Protestant charges of laxity in the convent by forcing women back into the cloister. "No nun shall after her profession be permitted to go out of the monastery," the council ruled, "even for a brief period under any pretext whatever."

Despite the decree, in 1634 Saint Vincent de Paul allowed a new order of religious women, the Daughters of Charity, to live outside of convents in hospitals and asylums. The sisters, he wrote, would have "no cloister, but the streets of the town; for a grille the fear of God, for a veil, holy modesty." To circumvent the council's ruling, the women wore simple gray dresses instead of habits. And they were called daughters of the parish rather than nuns. Within three decades this unconventional order received papal approval.

The eighteenth century brought the first nuns to the United States. In 1790 American women who had joined a Belgian Carmelite community returned home to found a convent in Charles County, Maryland. During the next century, thousands of other nuns, eager to escape a hostile religious climate in Europe, made the same journey.

Many communities retained the class consciousness of their European motherhouses, admitting two types of nuns—educated "choir sisters," and "lay sisters" from the lower classes, who performed manual labor. American bishops, who needed nuns to staff schools, resented strict European rules that forbade nuns from coming into contact with male students and orphans and from traveling any distance to work.

"They will not concern themselves in the business of female education," John Carroll, the first American bishop, lamented of the cloistered Carmelites. In reality the Carmelite way of life was in keeping with a Vatican decree that had mandated the law of enclosure for all nuns. The Church would not recognize semicloistered sisters until Pope Leo XIII issued the bull *Conditae a Christo* in 1900; and not until 1950 would the Vatican clearly distinguish between *nuns*, who devoted their lives to prayer in the cloister, and *sisters*, who ministered outside the convent, terms used interchangeably today.

Some immigrant clerics were determined to retain a strict rule over the nuns they supervised. In Kentucky Father Charles Nerinckx, the Belgian founder of the Sisters of Loretto, insisted that his teaching nuns observe total silence except during recreation. They were barefoot from March through November and slept in their clothes on straw mats on the floor. Within eleven years twenty-four sisters under the age of thirty had died, many from tuberculosis. The stringent rule was not revised, however, until after the *priest's* demise.

The first American-born saint, Mother Elizabeth

Bayley Seton, a Protestant convert and widow with five
children, founded the first indigenous American wom-
en's order, the Sisters of Charity, in 1809. She resisted
emigré priests who tried to pressure her to adopt a strict
French rule and instead chose a more liberal one that
allowed sisters to teach and travel. In addition to caring
for orphans and the sick, she and her sisters opened both
free and "pay" schools, laying the foundation for the
country's parochial-school system.

While nuns in Europe could depend on dowries and
endowments, the American nuns were left to their own
resources. Some communities ran farms. Others earned
money by charging tuition and taking in sewing and
laundry. One creative group of Poor Clare nuns sold a
tonic, Excellent Waters, for curing sore eyes.

Most of the communities that survived the early
nineteenth century depended on the labor of slaves,
brought to the convent by novices as part of their dowries. "Be not scandalized at it," a nun wrote to her father, "for it is the fashion of the country; we are taking
a Negro to wait on us." The superior of the Sisters of
Loretto sold a slave to finance the founding of the congregation in 1812. Twelve years later the order accepted
its first black postulants. The first black community of
nuns, the Oblate Sisters of Providence, was founded in
Baltimore in 1831. But due to the prevailing racism, it
was difficult for them to find priests to administer the
sacraments.

During the nineteenth century, 119 new congregations were established, twenty-eight of them by Americans. The number of nuns increased from forty to more
than forty thousand, and by the end of the century sisters outnumbered priests four to one. Many women
were attracted to the relative freedom religious life of-

fered, including the opportunity for leadership positions, friendship with women, and stimulating work.

Their work, however, was hindered by anti-Catholic sentiment fueled by Protestant clerics. Veiled women were an easy target for propagandists, who delighted in spreading tales of the alleged secret goings-on inside the cloister, from lurid sexual practices between nuns and priests to infanticide. Readers reveled in stories inspired by the hairshirts nuns wore in acts of penance and the "discipline"—knotted whips sisters used to flagellate themselves to atone for their sins.

Books about ex-nuns were the acceptable pornography of the day. In 1836 Maria Monk, a Canadian woman who claimed to be an ex-nun but had only spent a brief time in the convent, scandalized the country with her biography, *Awful Disclosures by Maria Monk of the Hotel Dieu Nunnery of Montreal*. The book included a grisly murder of a nun by gleeful priests and sisters. It sold 300,000 copies in twenty-four years.

Believers in the "Catholic threat" taunted nuns in public and desecrated convent property. In 1834 a mob destroyed an Ursuline academy in Charlestown, Massachusetts. Some states introduced bills requiring inspections of convents. Nuns in Roxbury, Massachusetts, and other towns were often subjected to surprise visits by bands of rowdy men.

But the nuns persevered. By the end of the century sisters had managed to set up 3,811 schools and 663 girls' academies in cities and remote rural areas. Nuns ran day-care centers, maternity homes, and homes for the aged. They staffed mental institutions and residences for delinquent girls and unwed mothers and worked to improve conditions for prisoners. At a time when nursing was considered a daring profession for women, nuns ministered to the sick in more than two hundred hospitals, as well as in private homes and almshouses. During the cholera and yellow-fever epidemics they tended patients no one else would touch.

It was their nursing during the Civil War that won them the respect of the masses. Some 640 sisters, 20 percent of all war nurses, cared for wounded soldiers. The Sisters of the Holy Cross dug wounded men from frozen mud and carried them to safety. A Sister of Mercy searched the battlefield at Shiloh by lantern, raising each head to make sure that no living man had been left for dead. A soldier reflected the sentiment of the day when he described a nursing nun in his diary: "Amid this sea of blood, she performed the most revolting duties for those poor soldiers. She seemed like a ministering angel and many a young soldier owes his life to her care and charity."

Sisters had become a formative influence in the nineteenth-century immigrant Church. By the early twentieth century, however, they would lose their clout. The pattern was familiar. Just as nuns gained ground, a new code of canon law was written that limited their activity on every front. Although the Church had formally recognized "active" sisters in 1900, the 1917 code called for the reimposition of the cloister in all convents. Some nuns protested this new wave of repression, but it would be half a century before sisters rose up again in rebellion.

III

Sister Marie Augusta Neal, a professor of sociology at Emmanuel College in Boston, spoke to me about today's rebellious nuns. A diminutive woman with short gray hair, Sister Marie Augusta has the gentle, self-effacing manner of a more traditional nun. But she is hardly traditional. In 1963 she was among the first eight women to receive a Ph.D. in sociology from Harvard University. Since then she has studied the attitudes of the women she knows best. Under the sponsorship of the Leadership Conference of Women Religious, she surveyed sisters in the United States on everything from how they interpret their vows to whether they read *Vogue*. An unheard of 88 percent of nuns responded to her first questionnaire. Her latest study, completed in 1989, focused on sisters and social justice.

The more than 100,000 Catholic sisters in the United States account for less than one-eighth of the nuns throughout the world. The majority of the 893,000 sisters—465,000—are from Europe; 179,000 are from North and Central America; 103,000 from Asia; 91,000 from South America; and 14,000 from Oceania. Some 41,000 reside in Africa, the continent showing the fastest increase in vocations. At the close of 1988, sisters worldwide outnumbered priests more than two to one.

Marie Augusta Neal's research shows that while the majority of the nuns of yesteryear were daughters of the upper classes, most of today's sisters are from working-class Irish- and German-American families. Less than 5 percent are women of color. Among the most highly educated women in the country, more than half have master's degrees, and 7 percent hold doctorates.

It is no secret that nuns are advancing in years. Fifty percent of sisters are over the age of sixty, and young entrants are a rarity. More surprising is the progressive attitudes of today's nuns. Forty percent define themselves as liberal, as opposed to the 20 percent who call themselves conservative. Based on a series of questions,

70 percent say women should participate in all levels of decision making in the Church. Seven percent have even considered the possibility of ordination for themselves. More than 80 percent said they view social justice as their primary mission in religious life. And more than half would back a sister's right to dissent in conscience on justice issues even if it conflicts with the wishes of a superior or bishop.

Still, words do not necessarily translate into action. The term *liberal* for a nun steeped in tradition may simply mean abandoning trappings such as the habit. When Sister Marie Augusta asked "Has involvement in action for justice and peace drawn you more toward prayer or away from it?" 54 percent of sisters said they weren't involved enough in social-justice issues to answer the question, although about 80 percent had already stated it as their primary mission. And despite sisters' claims that they support the right to dissent, many dissenters, particularly those taking a pro-choice stand on abortion, have been deeply distraught by the silence of their sisters in times of crisis.

Based on her research, Sister Marie Augusta concludes that 30 percent of sisters can be counted on to work toward eradicating social injustice, whether it's malnutrition in South America or homelessness on the South Side of Chicago. She believes that the four women about whom I am writing are part of an even smaller cadre. "They're among the five percent of prophetic sisters on the radical rim," she said. "They go in and get things ready for the rest of us."

This book, then, is about four women on the rim. As prophetic sisters they are among the strongest voices of devotion and defiance in the Roman Catholic church. Although they are white North Americans, their values and commitments have been shaped by encounters with women and men of all nationalities, colors, and classes. Their struggles are emblematic of the larger issues facing today's Church: the effect of Third World liberation movements on "First World" Catholics, the influence of the women's movement on nuns and the laity, the development of new forms of feminist spirituality that resist dogma, and the emergence of communities of resistance that challenge the institutional Church at its very core.

The Vatican can hardly ignore this challenge from North American sisters at the forefront of change. As the number of priests dwindles, sisters are becoming the unofficial leaders of parishes, running churches, hospitals, and schools. Nuns such as Donna Quinn, whose administrative and leadership skills were nurtured in the convent, can mobilize thousands of women around issues of justice. Rather than viewing these women as a resource and engaging them in dialogue, however, the Vatican sees them as one of the dominant threats to its hierarchical model. Although the Second Vatican Council liberated nuns from many repressive customs, the conservative hierarchy is once again attempting to turn back the clock in an attempt to reassert its dominance. It has repeatedly thwarted nuns' efforts to bring feminism into churches, religious orders, and schools. It has vehemently opposed sister-led movements for the ordination of women.

Although nuns do not have official clerical status—according to Rome they live in a kind of limbo between laity and clergy—they are subject to the whims of the Vatican. In 1983 the Vatican issued a revised code of canon law that included a section on religious life. The pope is called the highest superior to whom the vow of

obedience should be ultimately addressed. Nuns are required to wear religious clothing as a sign of consecration and live in their own religious houses rather than
apartments. Sister Marie Augusta's most recent survey
indicates, however, that only 5 percent of sisters think
they should still wear the habit. Thus many sisters are
ignoring these decrees, or interpreting them so liberally
as to render them meaningless, until they are forced into
a confrontation with Rome.

During the past three decades there have been his-
toric confrontations. In 1968, for example, the Immaculate Heart of Mary Sisters in Los Angeles refused their
cardinal's demand that they retract the reforms they ini-
tiated after Vatican II. Under pressure the sisters left their
congregation en masse. In 1982 the pope gave Sister of
Mercy Agnes Mary Mansour an ultimatum to give up
her position as Michigan's director of the Department
of Social Services, which involved handling public funds
for abortion. She left her congregation instead. In 1985
Sister of Mercy Arlene Violet, the Republican nominee
for attorney general in Rhode Island, was told that as a
nun she could not run for office. She took a "temporary
leave" from her congregation. The crackdown in the
United States is not limited to women. Confrontations
between the Vatican and "dissidents," such as Father
Charles Curran, who was ousted from his theology
post at Catholic University because of his liberal stance
on contraception, divorce, and homosexuality, show
that the conflict is only escalating. He joins his European and Latin American brothers, such as Brazilian
theologian Leonardo Boff, who was silenced by the
Vatican for criticizing the way the hierarchy uses its
authority.

The questions remain: How will Rome respond to

ongoing challenges from the grass roots? Will sisters stay in canonical congregations, or will they turn their back on the hierarchy? What new models of authority are emerging as sisters assert their power and form new alliances with the laity? What will emerge as the new definition of the Church?

Perhaps the most important question is the one that could render the others moot: Are we entering a golden age of progressive nuns or witnessing the final chapter in the history of Catholic sisters?

I thought the best way to answer these questions was to examine the lives of four women. How did Mary Aileen, Donna, Catherine, and Darlene evolve from obedient nuns to progressive sisters? What is their mission in religious life? How do they discern what is holy? How do they interpret their vows? To whom are they accountable? To whom do they pray? And then there is the question I am asked most often: Why did they enter religious life in the first place? This is a good place to begin.

CHAPTER 2

REVOLUTION OF THE HEART:
A MISSIONARY COMES OF AGE

The greatest challenge of the day is: how to bring
about a revolution of the heart, a revolution which
has to start with each one of us?

DOROTHY DAY

It was the summer of 1950 when seventeen-year-old
Mary Aileen Dame arrived at the gates of the motherhouse in Manchester, New Hampshire. She stared at the
red-brick building surrounded by a high wrought-iron
fence. The size of the convent was overwhelming. How
would she ever learn the maze of corridors and crannies?

Packed in her steamer trunk were the clothes she
would need to make the transition from teenager to nun:
half a dozen corsets designed to flatten womanly curves,
ankle-length cotton petticoats—black—to hide shapely
legs, heavy black stockings, and baggy nightgowns, all
ordered from a store in Boston that specialized in attire
for nuns.

The mistress of postulants, a stately nun charged
with training new sisters, escorted her to the novitiate
quarters. She would live here with twenty-five other
women in a long room divided into cubicles shrouded,
like hospital beds, by white curtains suspended from the
ceiling. Cells. Her cell contained an army cot, a metal
chair, and a bedstead holding a china bowl and pitcher.
In the center of her pillow lay a plain wooden crucifix,
the focus of her committed life.

She had told her parents she was entering the convent just two months earlier. She knew they'd be startled, because she had never expressed any interest in religious life. Her first passion as a girl had been speed skating. Three nights a week she raced at the rink in her hometown of Revere, just north of Boston. By age thirteen she was traveling to meets with her older brother to compete with other nationally ranked contestants. She won a gold medal in the Boston American Silver Skates race in 1950, and brought home a silver in the North American Speed Skating Championship. In her high school she excelled at gymnastics and performed on the tumbling team during halftime shows at football games. She especially loved the human formations. Light and agile, she was always climbing on top.

During her senior year she was voted Most Athletic. Her mother was not pleased. It was a dubious achievement for a girl in a working-class New England town. But her real vocation was nursing. From the time she was eight years old, Mary Aileen wanted to be a nurse like her Aunt Clara. Mary Aileen and her sister regularly brought home sick cats and birds from the school coal bin. As soon as she was old enough, Mary Aileen volunteered as a candy striper at a local hospital.

Although the Dame family considered themselves religious, they were not the kind of Catholics who discussed the meaning of the Trinity or critiqued the Sunday sermons. In the Dame household religion was something you did. Mary Aileen's mother, a trained soprano, sang in the church choir and performed at weddings and funerals. Her father, a part-time inventor who worked as a machine operator for the local lighting company, was a convert to Catholicism who embraced his religion with the fervor of a new believer. He was a pillar in the Holy Name Society. In the evenings he taught his children the rosary.

Edgar Dame regretted that he couldn't afford to send his two sons and three daughters to parochial school, but he made sure they didn't lack for instruction. They went to Christian-doctrine classes twice a week, sang in the church choir, and attended Mass daily. At twelve, Mary Aileen was picked to be a sacristan, the coveted honor of laying out the priest's vestments for Mass. In the early-morning stillness of the chapel she felt a sense of awe and reverence. Before the others arrived, she knelt before the altar to thank the Blessed Virgin for choosing her.

Mary Aileen didn't get to know any nuns until she volunteered to be a teacher's helper at the church summer school. She assisted a Sister of Mercy who taught during the school year in East Boston. She was impressed by the independent woman who had a career and wasn't burdened with a houseful of children. Young and energetic, she seemed to love her vocation. Mary Aileen thought that convent life must be fulfilling if it attracted such vibrant women. The life of a housewife, even one who sang on the side, was beginning to seem hopelessly dull.

By the end of the summer Mary Aileen had decided to enter the convent. She hadn't spent much time pondering her calling. Between candy striping and skating she had had little time to date. It was true she was not as pious as some of the girls who were entering the convent, the ones who spent hours kneeling before the stations of the cross. She had no visions, no signs of a calling. But if she wanted to be a nun, she assumed it was God's will. Without telling her parents, she contacted the Sisters of Mercy, which a friend had mistakenly told her was a missionary order that sent nurses to exotic places. To be a nurse and a missionary seemed the best of all possible worlds.

Two weeks after contacting the order Mary Aileen took a bus to Manchester, New Hampshire, to visit the motherhouse. She met with Reverend Mother Grace, a gentle woman in her late seventies. Mary Aileen told her she wanted to go to nursing school, and the reverend mother said it was a possibility. (The community had never trained a nun to be nurse.) When the reverend mother said a nun was "on mission," Mary Aileen thought she meant in Africa or South America. (The farthest Mercy mission was in upstate New Hampshire.)

Like many young women enamored of the convent, Mary Aileen didn't know the first thing about religious life. And like many religious orders, the Sisters of Mercy did not seem concerned about informing candidates what awaited them. The process that brought young women to their doors was a mysterious one, they believed. Only the committed deserved to learn the rules of convent life.

When Mary Aileen said good-bye to her family at the convent gate, she didn't cry like some of the others. She had no idea that once she entered, she could never go home. She hugged her brothers and sisters and told them not to worry. Come Christmas, she'd be back in Revere.

At 5:20 the morning bell rang throughout the motherhouse. Mary Aileen jumped out of bed and pulled open her curtain. She filled her bowl with water from the pitcher and washed her face with plain, unscented soap. She dressed quickly, saying a short prayer as she buttoned the black cotton shirt with the crisp white collar and zipped up the long black serge skirt that hung limply on her slender frame. She placed the black cap in the middle of her head and smoothed the net veil over her fine blond hair. She wasn't used to dressing without a mirror, but she would learn.

Hands folded, eyes lowered, she walked silently to the chapel. This was called custody of the eyes. Nuns, she was instructed, should focus on their inner lives and not on the world around them.

The old chapel filled her with a familiar reverence. Light filtered through the stained-glass windows, illuminating the white altar. She took her seat on one of the benches across from the rows of women draped in black, the ninety professed nuns of the motherhouse. After meditating silently, all rose to their feet for matins, the morning psalms and devotions of the Little Office of the Blessed Virgin Mary. In unison they repeated the ancient psalms, just as they had been recited every day for hundreds of years:

> *Creator generis humani, animatum corpus sumens, de Virgine nasci dignatus est; et procedens homo sine semine largitus est nobis suam Deitatem.*

> [The Creator of mankind, taking a body with a living soul, vouchsafed to be born of a virgin; and becoming man without man's concurrence, bestowed upon us his deity.]

Although Mary Aileen didn't understand all of the Latin, she loved the sound of the chants. In the majestic surroundings she felt closer to God than ever before. She could feel Jesus' presence, she could talk to him. He was like an intimate friend who cared about every minute of her day.

The day revolved around the canonical hours of the Office. In her blue notebook Mary Aileen had jotted her schedule:

6:40 Mass
7:25 Breakfast in the refectory
7:50 Spiritual lecture
8:30 Morning chores
10:00 Lecture on performing tasks efficiently
10:30 Spiritual readings
11:40 Noon prayers in the chapel
12:05 Dinner and spiritual reading
1:00 Course in Church history
2:00 Indoor recreation
2:45 Afternoon chores
4:45 Afternoon prayers
5:00 Supper
6:00 Study hall
7:00 Outdoor recreation
7:30 Discussion of daily lesson and next day's schedule
8:30 Night prayer
8:45 Baths
9:15 Lights out

Much of the day was spent in silence. As a first-year entrant, she was forbidden to talk to second-year novices or professed sisters. She could speak with her peers only during the recreation periods. At the morning sewing circle she darned her socks and chatted politely under the watchful eye of the mistress of postulants. A couple of the women seemed particularly nice, but she was careful to avoid spending too much time with any one sister. The mistress had lectured them about the dangers of particular friendships—*P.F.'s*, she called them. No two sisters were supposed to be alone together without the presence of a third. They were forbidden to set foot in one another's cells. To discourage cliquishness was the reason given. The older postulants knew it was to prevent more "intimate" friendships between nuns.

Obeying the rules was Mary Aileen's goal. Above all, she wanted to be a good sister, worthy of Jesus' love. To remind herself of lapses, she wrote daily in the little black book the mistress had given her. Called *The Examination of Conscience*, its pages listed the many rules a sister might break on any given day: missing a spiritual lesson, breaking the rule of silence, speaking to a professed sister, chewing gum, being late for prayers.

Although the community did not impose severe penances, such as self-flagellation, the sisters shared their shortcomings with the rest of the community during an exercise called the Chapter of Faults. Once a month Mary Aileen walked into the chapel and knelt before the altar next to the other sisters. When her turn came, she got up, genuflected, and walked to the prie-dieu.

"I accuse myself of breaking the holy silence," she said. "I accuse myself of running down the corridor. I accuse myself of speaking to a professed sister. I ask God and each of you present to forgive me my faults. During the next week I will work to observe the rules with more vigor." Then she genuflected again and took her place in line.

A teenager used to following orders at home, she adjusted easily to the first year of convent life. Her classmate, Rose McMahon, was different.

A former telephone operator, Rose was twenty-four when she entered. To her the novitiate was like boot camp, something to be endured before her religious life really began. She thought a lot of the rules were childish and ridiculous, unlike Mary Aileen, who followed every rule assiduously. Eventually Rose and the older postulants broke Mary Aileen in. They showed her how to short-sheet beds, and sneak down to the kitchen when everyone was asleep to steal ice cream. They shared pizza smuggled in by a nun who had hidden the box in the drape of her sleeve.

But the schoolgirl antics were not to last. The mother superior decided to send Mary Aileen and a professed nun, Bea Desmairis, to the Mount Saint Mary Sacred Heart Hospital School of Nursing. Mary Aileen was thrilled. She thought she would have to wait years to start nursing school. From that moment her life became different from that of the other nuns. Every morning at 6:30 she and Bea left the convent to catch the bus to the hospital.

Mary Aileen and Bea were test cases, the first nuns to study nursing alongside secular students at Mount Saint Mary. They were told they were holier than laywomen and, to their embarrassment, were not permitted to socialize with classmates, not even eat with them. During breaks, when the other students headed to the cafeteria, the nuns would be whisked up to the sacristy for a glass of milk and a doughnut.

The sisters took a full course load. Although excused from many typical convent duties, they were required to make up missed prayers in the evenings. At 9:30 P.M. they were allowed to study for one hour in the mistress of postulants' office, but this was not always sufficient. Mary Aileen actually broke a rule of her own accord.

After lights out, she would sneak into the bathroom and read in the tub.

Six months passed quickly. It seemed like no time before Mary Aileen was to trade in her postulant's garb for the habit of the holy order.

On a crisp winter morning eight young women lined up outside the chapel. Mary Aileen looked radiant in a flowing white satin wedding dress and a long lace veil. She held a bouquet of roses tied with a ribbon. For the first time since she had entered, she had received permission to curl her hair.

She followed the others into the church and walked silently down the aisle. Out of the corner of her eye she saw her family in the front pew. When she reached the altar, she knelt before the bishop.

"My daughter, what do you wish?" the bishop asked.

"The grace of God and the habit of the Holy Order," she answered.

"You are certain?"

"With all my heart."

"The way of the cross, my child, is not of this world," he said, touching her forehead. "But your reward will be that much greater in heaven."

She rose and walked directly to the community room in the motherhouse. Two nuns helped her off with her bridal dress and into a plain underslip, heavy stockings, and the long black habit of the Sisters of Mercy. A professed sister cut off a lock of her silky blond hair, a sign that she was renouncing worldly vanity to serve God. She was beautiful in spirit, faithful only to him. She could sense Jesus, almost touch him. She felt like a bride; she believed she was a bride of Christ.

The second year, the novitiate, was devoted to cultivating the sisters' inner lives. Annual family visits were limited to four. The novices could attend no outside classes. Canon law required the year to be spent within the enclosure and to be "devoted entirely to formation of character, study of the Constitutions, practice of prayer, instructions on the vows, virtues, and exercises suited to correcting defects, subduing passion, and acquiring virtues." The novices were to learn self-abnegation and humility before God.

Public tongue-lashings were common. Youthful frivolity was no longer tolerated. "This is not college," the novice mistress warned, "this is a convent."

The mistress of novices asked a sister why she liked the canonical year.

"Because of the friendships," she answered. That was the wrong answer. She was supposed to say she loved the silence.

Many loved the serenity of the novitiate year. Mary Aileen hated it. She enjoyed praying in the chapel, but enough was enough. She had never been the contemplative type. She missed her nursing classes and detested the enforced silence and rigorous schedule of manual labor. There were always more walls to wash, floors to wax.

She sought refuge in the infirmary, where she was charged with the care of the elderly sisters. While the novices were at recreation, she delivered meal trays. In the infirmary she could break the deadening silence and listen to the sisters reminisce. She felt a kinship with the aged women, who seemed more spirited than the rigid mistresses. The old niece of the foundress told her about the history of the community, how the reverend mother had crossed the country in the 1800s in a covered wagon, and how she fought with bishops to start schools and hospitals. She had even taken off her habit to travel.

Mary Aileen stayed with many of the sisters during their final hours. She said prayers with them and massaged their soft, cold hands. Sometimes she'd sit by a sister the entire night. She believed that the moment of death was sacred. And that there should always be a companion to send a sister off.

After the novitiate Mary Aileen began a grueling schedule of study and work. She completed her nursing degree and enrolled in Mount Saint Mary College for a bachelor of science degree, juggling seven classes and a new job as school infirmarian. Diploma in hand, she returned to nursing school to work as a supervisor and teach a course in dermatology. She worked from 3:00 P.M. until 1:00 in the morning, rose at 5:45 for Mass, then prepared for the 8:00 class she was instructing. Exhausted and inexperienced, she kept barely one page ahead of her students.

The schedule was relentless, but rarely was a nun permitted to take classes without earning her keep. Nuns were the cheap labor needed to operate schools and hospitals. Having taken a vow of poverty, they worked for a stipend and required no benefits. Self-sacrificing, they rarely complained about the inadequate training or the long hours. Mary Aileen was no exception. When the superior noticed that she looked particularly pale and thin, she sent her to the community's summer home in Massachusetts for a week to recuperate. Mary Aileen spent the entire time caring for a sister recovering from eye surgery.

The director of the Sacred Heart Hospital School of Nursing became ill, and there was no one experienced to take her place. Hiring a layperson was out of the question. Like an understudy, Mary Aileen happened to be waiting in the wings. At age twenty-six she was named acting head.

Running a nursing school under normal circumstances was taxing enough, and the Sacred Heart school was up for state and national accreditation. Mary Aileen had to write course curricula and set up departments that did not yet exist. For months she got by on four hours of sleep a night.

Young and insecure, Mary Aileen ran the school the only way she knew how, like a convent. The rigidity she had resisted during her novitiate had become ingrained. She insisted the students go to Mass every morning. They couldn't be so much as a second late to class. Personal problems were no excuse.

Mary Aileen even expelled a student a few weeks before graduation. Arguably she was the best nurse the school had ever trained, but during her last semester she had lagged behind in her work. Heartbroken, Mary Aileen refused to make a concession. After eight years in the convent, the novice had become a mistress.

II

On the first Friday of every month in the early 1960s, the Sisters of Mercy ended their morning prayers with an impassioned plea: "Please, God, save the world from Godless Communism." The United States had failed to overthrow Fidel Castro, heightening fears of Soviet expansionism. Now the poor in Latin America were considered particularly vulnerable to "Communist-inspired" revolutionary movements. The Catholic church took the offensive. It asked 10 percent of American sisters to volunteer for service in Latin America to evangelize for the faith.

Twenty thousand nuns were dispatched to the region, and Mary Aileen hoped to add herself to the list. She didn't know much about world politics, she hardly read a newspaper, but she prayed to God to finally let her be a missionary, to see something of the world and live among God's poor.

The Manchester Sisters of Mercy sent two teachers to Cartago, Colombia, a city 130 miles from Bogotá. When one sister died suddenly of a cerebral hemorrhage, the community asked Mary Aileen and Rose McMahon to take her place. It was rare for two such good friends to be assigned to work together. Mary Aileen was delighted. Rose was the perfect antidote to her serious side. When Mary Aileen felt overwrought, Rose could be counted on to provide comic relief.

The hot, damp climate was a welcome change from the frigid New Hampshire winters. Mary Aileen and Rose joined Sister Pauline, a teacher from Massachusetts, in a convent the local Colombian bishop had built especially for them. They christened their home Casa Blanca. By local standards it was luxurious: a two-story white house with a spacious patio. Next to it they built a tiny chapel, where they said the Divine Office. While Mary Aileen missed the sound of one hundred nuns' voices chanting in unison, she loved the intimacy of their simple ceremony.

Their convent training had emphasized obedience; it also taught the sisters to take charge. Wearing their white summer habits, they drove through the city in an old Jeep. During the first weeks Pauline taught classes at the parish school, Mary Aileen prepared for patients, and Rose went from door to door in Cartago evaluating the medical needs of the people. She handed out colored I.D.'s to the families—red, yellow, or blue, depending on level of need—so Mary Aileen would know which patients to give preference.

Their fledgling community reminded Mary Aileen of the stories she had heard of the first Sisters of Mercy, the three Irish women who founded their order.

In 1827 three women vowed to visit the sick, provide shelter for the homeless, and educate poor children in Dublin, Ireland. Led by Catherine McAuley, the daughter of a prosperous builder, they formed a loosely organized religious community, the Congregation of Our Lady of Mercy. The neighbors christened them the "walking sisters" because they visited the ill and elderly in hospitals and homes. So as not to be accused of proselytizing, the sisters wore plain dresses instead of nuns' habits.

The community grew slowly. Five women joined in 1829, three in 1830. The sisters followed a regular schedule of prayer and meditation and attended Mass daily. Because they had not received permission from the Vatican to start a new community, they were not technically a religious congregation in the Catholic church. Their home was more a social-service agency than a conventional convent; they shared their quarters with orphaned children and homeless women.

Conservative laymen looked askance at such unorthodox practices. Anonymous letters attacked the new community, and local priests spoke disparagingly of its work. The archbishop insisted that the women either behave and dress as befitted ladies of their station or become a formal religious congregation. Though Catherine McAuley resisted at first, threatening to close her house rather than adopt a "religious" rule, she finally relented. She agreed to re-form her group according to canonical regulations. At the archbishop's direction she and two sisters studied for one year at a local convent, returning to their own community upon completion of formal religious training. Satisfied that his wayward nuns had reformed, the archbishop heard their vows as the first Sisters of Mercy.

Religious training for new entrants was remarkably progressive compared with that of typical nineteenth-century European orders. Although the canonically approved Rule of the Sisters of Mercy was full of regulations, novices were not encouraged to comply passively. "The conscience that proposes questions becomes enlightened," wrote Frances Warde, an original member of the fledgling community. She cautioned sisters not to let regulations interfere with their primary mission: the care of the poor. "It is not necessary that [rules] be strictly adhered to, but only insofar as they tend to facilitate the end."

While most European novice mistresses concentrated on "breaking the wills" of their new charges, Sister Frances encouraged superiors to rule by love rather than reprimands, lest they become "mistress[es] of slaves." She counseled against fostering in novices a false piety "made up of tears and sighs" and encouraged a program of action and charity that would "transform weak women into heroines."

In 1843 the Diocese of Pittsburgh invited Frances Warde to the United States to establish the first Sister of Mercy foundation. She sailed for New York and rode to Pittsburgh with trappers in horse-drawn covered wagons and oxcarts. During the next decade she founded eight convents and three dozen schools, orphanages, and hospitals in five states.

In 1858 she established a foundation in Manchester, New Hampshire. Local Yankees had vowed not to let Catholic sisters enter their state, let alone their town. The day after the nuns arrived, however, they began visiting the sick and, in short order, managed to ingratiate themselves among the natives. Soon the nuns were teaching Sunday school classes at the church. They began night courses in religious and secular topics for children who worked days in factories. They opened a free school for girls in the church basement, marking the beginning of the state's parochial-school system. Mother Warde loved Manchester and made it her home until her death in 1884.

By the time Mary Aileen arrived in Colombia, there were some 14,000 Sisters of Mercy in the United States and more than 27,000 "Mercies" throughout the world.

Like the walking sisters, Mary Aileen set up shop right at the convent. A lab technician from the United States interpreted for her until she picked up enough Spanish to manage on her own. During the day she treated up to sixty patients. Afterward she made house calls in the city and the outlying barrios. In one-room shacks she found adults with typhoid sharing beds with children with mumps. She saw case after textbook case of malnutrition, tuberculosis, diarrhea, parasites.

"The poverty is more widespread than I'd ever imagined," she wrote to her superior. "Yesterday I visited an eighty-year-old lady in a little bamboo mud house without floors or lighting. The poor soul was burning with fever. With the help of antibiotics, thank

God, she is much better today. Her granddaughter came by to pay me the fee: one live chicken."

Defying medical convention, Mary Aileen became intimately involved in her patients' lives. When a widow with cancer died, Mary Aileen assumed responsibility for her young children, caring for them in the convent until relatives arrived from Bogotá for the funeral. It was awful to see children so young crying for their mother. In the United States children were sheltered from death. Here they buried their own mother. They literally piled the dirt on her grave.

While Mary Aileen tended to patients, Pauline started a sewing cooperative, where she showed women how to cut patterns and operate sewing machines. Rose organized a school for eighty children. She trained local women as teachers and convinced them to let her use their homes for classrooms. Each morning the children brought their chairs and a few sticks of wood to build a fire to heat oatmeal for lunch.

Mary Aileen converted a nearby house into a dispensary, complete with a waiting room, laboratory, and examining room. Assisted by a local nurse and a teenage girl she had trained to be a lab technician, she started clinics for pregnant women, infants, and sick adults. She taught the local women basic facts about cleanliness and simple methods for preventing diarrhea. "We realize that health teaching, not mere pill pushing, must take precedence in our work with the sick," she wrote to her sisters.

Every day Mary Aileen and her assistants distributed food donated by a Catholic relief agency. Soon they opened a feeding station for up to forty children. Among their first patients were two young girls from the barrio who had been kept locked in a dark room. Their mother thought they were retarded, but they just lacked food and stimulation. After several visits to the mother's home, Mary Aileen convinced her to bring the girls to the feeding station. The day the first child smiled, Mary Aileen threw a party for the staff.

Mary Aileen was unabashedly delighted with her work in Colombia. In just one month they had treated more than seven hundred people. Life in Cartago had begun to revolve around the clinics and the convent. In the evening neighbors stopped by just to talk or to play their guitars and sing. Some joined the sisters for prayers in the chapel.

Rose liked to say that she felt "inoculated by Latin Americanismo." Mary Aileen felt it too.

"I realize I am passing through the honeymoon of mission life," she wrote to her superior, "but I certainly am enjoying every minute of it."

By the third year the sisters were spending most of their time in the barrio on the outskirts of Cartago. The clinics in the city were just about self-sustaining, while the people in the barrios were in desperate need of medical care. In August Mary Aileen wrote to her superior about her plan for a new dispensary:

> The barrios are the poorest financially and morally of all Cartago. Most of the houses are without lighting and water, and the sewage runs in open gullies behind the houses. I have been counting the pennies we receive from the Motherhouse so we can provide these people with a dispensario and pharmacy; a classroom and small kitchen for teaching mothers; a little room with tables, chairs and sinks for feeding

children one meal a day in order to teach them
how to use utensils, washing hands and teeth
etc.; and a prenatal clinic. Please pray that God
will give us His blessing. . . . If we could do it,
it would truly be a Mercy project.

In a few months the sisters had saved enough to
open their dispensary. Every morning at six o'clock
Mary Aileen left her convent to drive her Jeep to the
barrio. She was grateful to be providing medical care to
people who had never seen a doctor, but she was becoming increasingly uncomfortable about the contrast
between her living conditions and those of her patients.
Rose felt the same way. She taught children who went
home to mud huts while she went home to one of the
nicest houses in Cartago.

The sisters decided to move to the barrio. It would
be difficult leaving their chapel, but they could pray together wherever they lived. Like Frances Warde and
Catherine McAuley, they were a Mercy community;
they didn't need a convent to make it official.

They met with the bishop to inform him of their
plans to leave the convent he had built. A large, imposing man, he listened intently, then tried to discourage
them.

"It's improper," he said. "People expect you to live
comfortably. It's a sign of respect."

Two days later, without informing the nuns, the
bishop flew to the United States to talk to the mother
general of the order about the errant sisters. When Mary
Aileen found out, she was stunned that he would go to
such absurd lengths to stop them, and furious that her
community would receive him. What was the point of
being a nun if they were not free to work with the peo-

ple who needed them? What was the point of being part of a community if it didn't stand by its sisters? She dashed off a letter to her superior:

> To be honest, and at the risk of offending, I wonder just where community support comes in. It certainly leaves one with a feeling of frustration and wondering where one stands. The bishop had opposed all our suggestions for the advancement of the mission. The beautiful convent and the even more beautiful rectory are so far his only accomplishment in three years. If we were not sure that concern for the poor was our ultimate responsibility, it would be easy to stop right now, give in, and live in our present circumstances.

The superior responded with a letter that was vague enough for the sisters to interpret as they wanted. They moved to the barrio.

The sisters rented a small house in back of a store. Living in the barrio gave Mary Aileen more insight into the lives of her patients. When she had no water, she had to struggle to get a bucketful from the well. She stopped yelling at the mothers for their kids' dirty fingernails when they came to the clinic. She had only herself to take care of. These women had five or six children and had to divide up what little water there was.

Many families didn't even have wells. Every week they had to line up in the heat at the local spigot. One morning a fight broke out. A man carrying a machete got so angry, he cut off both arms of another man. The people were so frightened, they didn't call Mary Aileen.

By the time she saw the young man, he was dead. Nineteen years old and killed over a bucket of water.

The bishop visited the barrio only twice while Mary Aileen was in Colombia. The second time, he spoke to the children about the importance of wearing shoes. Mary Aileen thought to herself, "My God, where are they going to get shoes?"

At the church he gave a sermon: How blessed are the poor.

Rose whispered to Mary Aileen, "How blessed are the poor! Mrs. Gomez doesn't have anything to feed her six kids. Isn't that blessed?"

Sheltered in wealthy schools and hospitals, many priests and nuns, Mary Aileen believed, remained oblivious to the needs of the impoverished.

"But the rest of us began to view the world differently," said Mary Aileen. "We started to realize that spirituality separated from the situation in which one lives was impossible. How could we talk about God without thinking of the people around us? And then there was Medellín. Medellín really turned things around. And Colombia was where Medellín happened."

III

In 1968 the bishops of Latin America met in Medellín, Colombia, for their second general conference. Their purpose was to examine the Church in light of the Second Vatican Council convoked by John XXIII (and later Pope Paul VI) from 1962 to 1965. For many of the clergy the week of presentations at Medellín publicly acknowledged what they had privately known all their lives. The upper classes and foreign conglomerates owned and monopolized Latin America's resources and used violence to keep the poor submissive.

For centuries the Catholic church had been used to validate the status quo. Clerics preached that the unequal allocation of earthly rewards was preordained. The poor were appeased with promises of a better life in the hereafter.

Medellín brought the focus back to the present. The bishops issued a call to priests and sisters to compensate for the inequity by showing a "preferential option for the poor." This preference would form the basis of a new theology of liberation, which "looked at the life and message of Jesus through the eyes of those who [had] normally been excluded or ignored." Theology would no longer be "exclusively the province of the privileged social strata."

The conference led to the emergence of Christian grass-roots groups called *comunidades de base*, gatherings of twenty to forty men and women who met on a regular basis to read a biblical selection and reflect on its relevance for their lives. The goal was to help people to understand the roots of their oppression so that they could become the agents of their own liberation.

The reverberations of the Medellín conference radiated throughout Latin America: the age-old alliance of the Church hierarchy with the military and the ruling classes had been ruptured. Not all Latin American religious, however, embraced the conclusions of Medellín. The conference polarized the progressives and conservatives among the region's bishops, priests, and nuns. Those who supported the status quo denounced Liberation Theology as a betrayal of Christian values by a Marxist-inspired doctrine of class analysis. They worried that base communities would resist hierarchical control. Those who embraced Medellín believed that the new theology rejuvenated lost Christian precepts. They saw members of base communities as reminiscent of the early Christians who came together to break bread and pray.

Among those who endorsed liberation theology, there was disagreement on how best to achieve structural change in the rigid, class-conscious Latin societies. While the bishops at Medellín had rejected violence, the more radical were becoming disillusioned with the slow pace of reform. The most famous of the radical priests was Camilo Torres, a Colombian cleric killed in a skirmish with an army patrol.

Mary Aileen had heard about the priest who had taken up a weapon and joined a revolutionary front. ("Can you imagine a priest joining the guerrillas?" she asked Rose.) But Camilo Torres captured her imagination. She tried to find out all she could about him, even talking to people in Bogotá who had known him personally. Some said that he had been crazy, that he acted without thinking. Although Mary Aileen couldn't quite explain it, she felt a tremendous admiration for the man.

Several nuns from Cartago attended classes at a center in the mountains of Manizales, where scholars from all over the world had gathered to analyze the record of the conference. Mary Aileen couldn't leave the clinic, but she and her sisters read all they could get their hands on about the Medellín conference. For Mary Aileen it was a relief to hear bishops saying what she had been feeling for some time. Appeasing a starving family with promises of heaven had always struck her as hollow when Jesus talked of the kingdom of heaven on earth.

While Mary Aileen felt elated, Rose feared the dramatic break with tradition: "People started questioning everything. It was the first time I ever heard anyone suggest that Jesus Christ might not be the son of God. I felt such a pain in my stomach. How could they question that?"

Still, they took the Medellín mandate to heart. Pauline began a discussion group to analyze society in light of the gospel. Mary Aileen met weekly with a group of women to discuss health issues. Until they understood their own bodies, she told them, they couldn't take charge of their lives.

They also began examining issues in their own lives that they had long taken for granted. Nuns back in the States still wore full habits. But Mary Aileen balked at the impracticality of riding around in a Jeep in the tropics wearing a long white dress.

One particularly hot day she made a call to the motherhouse in New Hampshire. The reverend mother was out. Mary Aileen asked her assistant if the sisters could redesign their habits, and she said yes. The only material Mary Aileen could find was twill. She made a dress with pleats down the front. It was wrinkled terribly. She wore it to a meeting in Bogotá, and everyone said it looked awful. When the mother superior found out about the new habit, she was not pleased, but Mary Aileen held firm. She wasn't going to spend another day washing and ironing white serge in the hot sun.

The change in attire wasn't nearly as dramatic as the change in prayer. "Our prayer life had been handed down to us on a platter," said Mary Aileen, " 'Do this and you'll have a wonderful relationship with God.' Prayer was almost like an exercise we learned in school. It started to feel false to say the same words over and over again, almost as if your head wasn't necessary."

While she continued to attend Mass every morning, she no longer raced home every evening to say the Office. She began to experiment with other forms of prayer, using her own words, or sitting silent in meditation.

"And I started to look at ways I could be active and prayerful at the same time. Prayer was still contact with the divine. But I began to see the divine in people."

While Latin America grappled with the changes inspired by Medellín, the Sisters of Mercy struggled with the internal reform advocated by the Second Vatican Council and a papal letter, *Ecclesiae Sanctae*, mandating special assemblies for all religious congregations. The sisters were directed to reevaluate their constitutions, customs, and regulations in light of the life of Christ as presented in the Gospels, the spirit of their order's founder, and the changes in modern society.

Mary Aileen was among the two dozen representatives elected to attend special "chapters" during the summers of 1967 and 1968. Before traveling to Manchester, she changed back to the traditional garb of her community. She checked into a hotel in Bogotá wearing a short blue dress. She came out the next morning in a long wool habit.

Also attending the chapters was a friend from her novitiate class, Helen Girard. Like Rose, Helen was an outspoken woman known for her dry wit. She and Mary Aileen supported the liberal position. They were clearly in the minority that summer. Two-thirds of the nuns had a more conservative agenda.

The sisters elected a new mother general and examined every rule and regulation concerning their common life. They discussed the administration of the community, finances, prayer life, and dress. The habit proved the most controversial topic. Some sisters wanted a modified habit. Most thought a new form of dress would undermine the order. Taking off their habit symbolized personal freedom, and they questioned whether such a sign of freedom was desirable in nuns.

Helen formed a committee of the more progressive sisters to study the vows. The group concluded that the sisters' vows were intended to liberate them. Their poverty was intended to free them from material things. Chastity, they decided, meant not owning or being owned by people. Obedience was a response to conscience.

By the end of the second summer the group had reached a degree of consensus Mary Aileen had not dreamed possible. "People struggled during that summer. There were deep inner struggles. It was painful and beautiful because you could almost feel the Spirit moving." Helen wasn't sure, however, if all the sisters were ready for the changes to which they had agreed.

"Some sisters would assent to a change because philosophically it sounded right," she said. "They approved of our new definition of the vows, for example, but it was not what they really wanted. When some said yes, it meant 'I wish I could be saying yes.' Somebody had always assigned them their jobs and told them when they had been there long enough. They were in the habit of having someone doing their serious thinking for them. They weren't ready to make decisions on their own."

After seven years in Colombia, Mary Aileen made her first independent career decision. She was ready to move on. Another nurse had arrived, and Mary Aileen didn't think she was needed anymore. She considered applying to medical school. She was playing doctor, she might as well be one. But she soon dismissed the idea of attempting the six-year program at the age of thirty-eight. She decided to study midwifery in the United States with the intent of returning to South America afterward. Columbia University in New York awarded her a full scholarship for the one-year program.

To pay for her room and board, she worked as a housemother at a dormitory for nurses. The idea of rules for rules' sake now struck her as pointless.

One evening ten student nurses emptied all the ice machines in the dorm and poured the cubes onto the floor. When Mary got out of bed to see what the racket was about, she saw girls in their bathing suits sliding up and down the hall.

"I told them it would be nice if they cleaned up when they finished, and I went back to bed."

Mary Aileen earned her midwifery degree and set out to find work in a country that cared about providing health care for the poor. She contacted the Panamanian Ministry of Health. She was hired to run a twenty-five-bed hospital on the island of Bocas del Toro and to oversee thirteen health stations on islands along the coast.

"I thought it would be a good change. I had heard that the Panamanian government had instituted some good reforms in health care. And I wouldn't have to answer to priests and bishops."

Bocas was once a flourishing port town dominated by the United Fruit Company. By the time Mary Aileen arrived, it was a ghost town. "Just wooden shacks built on sticks. They had one hospital left. There was no transportation from one village to another, except for an old iron train that left at five A.M. and returned at six at night. All I could think of was prison."

She lived in a cottage across the street from the hospital, where she worked from six A.M. to seven P.M. Once a week she and a local doctor went to visit the island outposts. "We used to take these old vessels that looked like PT boats. Many times we'd leave at two or three in the morning. Sometimes it took thirteen hours just to get there. On weekends I'd take a five-seater plane to the Indian villages on the coast to vaccinate the people."

The conditions in the villages depressed her. The exhilaration, the romance of mission life was gone, and her letters reflected her growing frustration.

"Poverty is still an unbelievable revelation to me," she wrote to her sisters. "The people here have been abandoned for such a long time. It's more proof that the message of Christ still falls on deaf ears. You and I meet it daily, man's denial of the dignity and worth of other men. It's like pecking at marble to try to change things. Yet we have Christ's word that it can be done. The rock will take shape."

A few months after she arrived, her friend Helen Girard came to visit for six weeks. She had left religious life after twenty-three years and needed some time to think.

Bocas was a shock to Helen.

"It's so primitive," she said to Mary Aileen. "I can't believe it's 1972 here."

"Think again," Mary Aileen said. "This is what 1972 looks like in most of the world."

Helen remembers the conditions vividly: "The hospital Mary Aileen worked in was terribly run down. I think she had as many rats as patients. She ran the whole place almost single-handedly. I was really impressed. In the evenings we'd drink warm beer and talk. The days

were short and the nights were long, so we had plenty
of time to catch up."

Like many nuns, Helen felt that the community had
failed to respond genuinely to the call for renewal issued
by Vatican II. While the changes looked good on paper,
the order was still wedded to tradition. "I left out of
loyalty to what I believed in," she said. "I felt our congregation was not what it claimed to be. Our teachers
had taught us that the divine dwells in each of us, but I
found that our community did not respect the worth of
the individual. Individuality was looked at with suspicion. It wasn't that I didn't want to be a nun. In my
letter to the pope requesting dispensation, I wrote, 'I
find it necessary to leave religious life, because I want to
live life religiously.' I guess that sounds arrogant. But I
wanted to be able to follow my own conscience."

When Helen left Bocas, Mary Aileen experienced a
loneliness she had never known before. Although she
was friendly with a couple of Panamanian sisters, she
couldn't talk to them about changes in the Church. The
sisters were ecclesiastically conservative, faithful to an
institution of which she no longer felt a part. Nor did
she feel connected to the sisters back home.

"I felt more separated than ever from my community. One day we had a terrible murder in Bocas. A
sixty-year-old man who thought his thirty-year-old
wife was running around with a younger man took a
gun and shot her and then shot himself. She died. He
lived and had a punctured lung. We had to find an army
plane or boat to get both bodies to Panama City under
police custody. It was just an awful day. When I got
home, I received a mailing from the convent: a list of
rules. I couldn't believe it. It seemed so irrelevant. The

list of dos and don'ts had nothing to do with my life. I began to wonder how I could stay in religious life."

In the midst of her crisis she found comfort in Father Filipe, a Spanish priest. At age thirty-nine she was relatively inexperienced with men. She was surprised at the ease with which she could talk to him. Unlike most priests she had known, he lacked the arrogance that often went with a clerical collar. Young, attractive, passionate about social justice, he worked in a mission on a remote island just off the coast.

"He used to visit Bocas every three weeks. Then we got friendly and he started visiting more often. I admired him deeply. His father had been killed by Franco, and he was involved in the struggle for liberation from a very early age. He was the only person in Panama I could really talk to about changes in the Church.

"One night he came to my office at the hospital at about five-thirty. Then we moved to my house and sat in the kitchen. We had a glass of rum, and then I kept making pots of coffee. We talked about my whole life. His whole life. My problems. His problems. He had thoughts on everything. We talked literally all night without stopping. When I heard the church bells ring, I said, 'My God, it's six in the morning!'

"I don't know if I was in love with him. I thought I was. I was on an island and I was lonely."

For the first time she seriously considered leaving religious life. Perhaps it wasn't necessary to be a nun to do missionary work. Lately her congregation seemed to hinder more than help her. They were more concerned about whether she behaved than whether she was getting her work done.

When she entered, she was just a teenager who didn't

know a thing about religious life. She stayed because she believed it gave her the freedom to devote herself to her passion: medicine. Few married women she had known had pursued careers. How could she have a family and take off for days to vaccinate patients on some godforsaken island?

Helen was gone from the order. But there was Rose and the rest of the sisters from the novitiate, with whom she had spent years developing friendships. They were her community within a community. She loved her sisters. She hoped her congregation would come to see there was more to religious life than regulations. She prayed that they would.

"I guess I didn't love Filipe enough to want to change my life for him. There are so many great things to do and be. One lifetime isn't enough."

Filipe left the priesthood to marry. Mary Aileen decided to apply to medical school.

The Church did not permit nuns who took public vows to become doctors or even to assist women in childbirth until 1936, when canon law was revised. In 1974 the Sisters of Mercy gave Mary Aileen permission to study medicine. At age forty-two she was accepted to the La Salle medical school, run by the Christian Brothers in Mexico City. She received a partial scholarship, and the Sisters of Mercy loaned her the rest of her tuition.

Of the ninety students in Mary Aileen's class, about a quarter were women. "Most of the students were fifteen to twenty years younger than I, but I never really felt my age. I loved studying medicine. I didn't find the work easy, but I didn't find it killing."

She liked the lack of structure at La Salle, the freedom to come and go as she pleased. By the second year she was spending a few nights a week and Saturday afternoons at a prenatal clinic in a local barrio.

Upon graduation she returned to Massachusetts to intern at Boston City Hospital. Her few evenings she spent with family and with old friends from the novitiate who worked in the vicinity. Coming home allayed some of her fears about the community. More sisters, she found, were becoming committed to issues of social justice. At her urging, the community sent sisters to a month-long course in Mexico to introduce them to the politics of Latin America. It was not just stargazing at poverty but real social analysis.

In Boston she could sense the tension heightening between the more progressive and conservative nuns in the community. After a year of discussion the congregation asked the Vatican for permission to divide into two regions, each with its own governing board. The sisters committed to preserving the traditions of the community, particularly the wearing of the habit, gravitated toward region one. Activists, such as Mary Aileen and her friends, joined region two. Although she was saddened by the rift, she was relieved that the voices of the progressive nuns would dominate her region.

After studying in Latin America, she was unaccustomed to the pace of medical training in the United States. Gynecology and obstetrics were her most difficult subjects. As a midwife she had promoted natural childbirth; as an intern she had to insert monitors. Abortion was also problematic. It was simply not an issue in Latin America. If a woman was pregnant, she had her child.

The doctors who worked in obstetrics were assigned to examine women about to receive abortions. Mary

Aileen refused. "It caused a furor in the hospital," she said. "I agreed to see women after they had had their abortions, but not before, because I didn't want to be involved in the whole decision process."

Still, she was ambivalent about her own decision. At a post-abortion clinic she saw a fifteen-year-old girl whose family had put her out when they discovered she was pregnant. She had no place to go and was living under someone's porch. So she had an abortion.

"She was so filled with guilt," said Mary Aileen. "When she saw that my pin said, 'Sister,' I'll never forget the fear in her eyes. She said, 'You're a sister and I told you all this.' I said, 'I think if this had happened to me, I wouldn't just have had an abortion, I would have jumped off a bridge. I don't think I could have handled it as well.' "

Several nuns in her community were becoming active in the women's movement. One sister suggested that Mary Aileen read the work of Mary Daly, a theologian at Boston College. In her 1968 book, *The Church and the Second Sex*, Daly called for the reform of the Roman Catholic church on the grounds that misogynistic church fathers had oppressed women. Four years later, in *Beyond God the Father*, Daly made the leap from "reformist feminism" to "post-Christian" radical feminism. She rejected the use of the term God *"the father,"* replacing it with God *"the verb,"* a deity for the evolving revolutionary consciousness of women.

In *Gyn/Ecology: The Metaethics of Radical Feminism* Daly went even farther. She rejected the word *God* altogether because there was no way to purge it of masculine connotations. She described a world in which women are subjected to numerous abuses, from Chinese foot binding and African genital mutilation to American gynecology. She urged women to flee conventional society and live on the "boundaries of patriarchy."

Mary Aileen was sure of one thing: She wasn't going to live on the edge. "I told the sister I didn't want to hear about this new theology. I was extremely fearful at the time of anything that would question the structures of Church as I knew it. I was afraid it would be like pulling on a wool sweater. I thought my faith would unravel."

IV

Mary Aileen passed her medical boards and returned to Mexico. To get her license required half a year of social service for the government. At the request of a Christian Brother she agreed to spend six months working in a tiny Indian village called Acahualulco.

Just getting there was a challenge. It took eight hours by bus from Mexico City to the nearest large town. Then Mary Aileen rode by horseback four miles up a snowcapped mountain. When she arrived in the village that evening, she was met by a couple of men on horseback. A woman had been in labor since early that morning and couldn't deliver. Mary Aileen was exhausted from the trip, but she agreed to examine the woman.

"They led me along a road that wound around a mountain to a village of twenty houses. It was pitch-black. We ended up at a tiny hospital. The woman was lying on the table. Thank God it wasn't a difficult procedure. There was a bag of water in front of the baby's head. I needled the embryonic membrane and she delivered in about ten minutes. The Indians loved that. They thought it was a miracle."

The villagers were fascinated by this tiny white woman who came to deliver their babies.

"Where are you from?" a woman asked.

"From the United States," Mary Aileen replied.

The woman nodded. "Yes, near Mexico City. I've heard of it."

Mary Aileen lived in a one-room shack near the three-bed hospital. Someone brought her a mattress, and with a few boards she made herself a bed. "There was no water, heat, or electricity. I made a hole in the ground to build a fire and cooked rice and beans in a tin can. Half the room was filled with corn. It attracted these silky black mountain rats with long gray tails. They didn't bite, but I had to cover myself with net at night so that the rats wouldn't walk on me. It was freezing cold and it drizzled all the time, so I slept fully clothed in a great big winter coat inside a sleeping bag. I read by candlelight, with the rats for company.

"Once a month I traveled several hours to the neighboring village to bathe. The rest of the time I would cat-bathe in a stream at the bottom of a hill. It was rotten dirty. Not very enticing. But everybody was in the same boat, so no one would notice if you weren't too clean."

News of a doctor spread quickly throughout the neighboring villages. One night Mary Aileen was awakened by noises outside. When she looked out the window, she saw candles. Scores of them. A man knocked at her door. He said the people from his pueblo had come to see the doctor: 150 men, women, and children. They had walked fourteen hours and would pitch their tents in a field in front of the hospital. One by one she examined the patients. It took her two days, but she saw them all. Malnourished children. Anemic mothers. Alcoholic fathers.

Alcoholism was endemic in Acahualulco. One afternoon an inebriated old man in his late seventies stumbled into a fire and emerged with third-degree burns over three-quarters of his body. Mary Aileen had no bandages or paper, so she powdered his wounds with antibiotics alone. "I kept him in the hospital for a while, but the odor was impossible. I couldn't have him in the same room with women who were delivering. I finally said to the family, 'If you take him home, I'll come every two days.' It was quite a distance. I wanted to send him to a hospital, but the Indians believed that if he died outside of the village, his soul wouldn't go to heaven.

"I couldn't do much. I just watched him and gave him antibiotics, but eventually he got much better. One day I came to see him, and he said, 'I'll say good-bye to you because I'm going to die now.' I said, 'You're not going to die. Don't talk that way. Can't you see your wounds are healing?' But he said, 'I'm very tired and I want to die.' It was eerie. I came back two days later and he was buried.

"The Indians were in touch with the Spirit. They told me their dreams and they'd predict things. There's a closeness to Mother Earth. In the United States, we are bombarded with music, plays, movies. They just worried about getting enough from one day to the next. Those who really live that way are in touch with the Spirit, with their land, with a few people who make up their family. They taught me to appreciate those moments in life that allow you to be close to the Spirit."

In the convent Mary Aileen had been instructed that Catholicism was the one true religion. "I had been frightened to explore. I was only supposed to think about the Ten Commandments and the gospel. I didn't let my mind wander beyond basic Christian beliefs. Indian spirituality helped me to realize that exploring the beauties of other religions didn't take away from my own."

She also decided to give feminist author Mary Daly another chance. A sister had sent her *Gyn/Ecology*. By reducing Christianity to a patriarchal myth, Daly seemed to be rejecting everything Mary Aileen held dear. But if her sisters had made sense of this radical critique, Mary Aileen was determined to get through the book as well. She usually managed to read only a couple of pages before she was called to see a patient.

One Sunday at two o'clock in the morning she was summoned by a woman about to deliver her third child. There was no gas for the lamp, so she examined her patient by candlelight. "The woman pushed and pushed but she couldn't deliver. Within five hours her contractions had stopped completely; her blood pressure was down." Mary Aileen knew the prognosis was bad. "I realized that she was going to have an anencephalic baby, a child without a skull.

"I didn't have the instruments to deliver the baby, but I thought that a private doctor, who lived about three miles away, might. At ten A.M. I talked to the woman's husband, who had a swollen ankle, and her father, who was completely drunk, into letting me take her to the doctor. We made a stretcher out of pieces of wood and carried her."

They began the trek down the mountain and were suddenly encircled by dozens of men. The men had been drinking corn brew since early that morning. They told Mary Aileen she couldn't take the pregnant woman away because if she died in another town, her soul wouldn't go to heaven.

"It was a woman's lot to die in childbirth. There wasn't a family that hadn't lost a daughter or daughter-in-law. However, by pushing and screaming, we were able to get past the crowd. As we walked, it started pelting rain. All of a sudden we saw a truck coming. I couldn't believe it. A local priest had decided to try to make it up the hill so he could give last rites to a dying woman. He drove us to the doctor. The doctor wasn't in. By that time I knew the baby was dead, so we rode to the nearest hospital about three hours away."

At the hospital the doctors delivered the baby, stillborn. "It was an awful scene. It was a Catholic hospital staffed by very traditional nuns. The good sisters dressed the baby. They dressed a dead fetus because that's what you're supposed to do."

Mary Aileen knew that she had to bring the baby back to the village so it could be buried there. She wrapped it in her knapsack and caught a ride to the nearest town. For four miles she trekked up the mountain with the baby strapped to her back.

When she arrived in the village, she broke the news to the family. They stared blankly as she tried to explain the baby's death. How could she make them understand a person born without a skull? It was no use, she realized. "They were sure I had crushed the baby's head."

She prayed to Jesus to give her strength. Her missionary zeal had given way to despair. Never before had she felt so overwhelmed by the conditions that surrounded her, the rampant alcoholism, the complete disregard for the lives of women. She counted the days till her stint in Acahualulco would be over.

Before she left, she spent some time with the Indian

chief. He hadn't liked her when she first arrived. He hadn't wanted a North American coming into his pueblo. But one day he fell ill, and Mary Aileen climbed up the hill to his home and gave him some antibiotics. "From then on we got to be good friends. He started to invite me to their meetings. I talked to him about conditions in the pueblo, particularly the role of women. Women were not even allowed to eat at the same table as men." The old chief listened, but he didn't say much.

At her going-away party Mary Aileen was the only woman invited to sit at the table with the men.

"What do you think I am, nonsexed?" she asked the chief.

"No," he answered. "You are our guest of honor. This is our culture."

Acahualulco proved the turning point. Colombia had opened her eyes to oppression; Mexico convinced her that the problems of poverty could not be solved by one nun with a stethoscope. For the first time she understood the frustration that had prompted Camilo Torres to join the guerrillas.

A sister had written to her about the revolution in Nicaragua. It was hard to believe, but even the bishops had supported the opposition to dictator Anastasio Somoza. Two Catholic priests were among the new leaders of the country.

She wrote to the government health organization to volunteer her services. "I heard the Sandinistas needed people and I wanted to be part of building a new society."

V

Mary Aileen and I drove through the streets of Managua, Nicaragua, in her beat-up Toyota, bought for a song from a friend of a friend. Her car's name was Harrison, she said, after Harrison's textbook of medical infirmities. Her Harrison had every infirmity known to cars.

Managua was a city of ruins, devastated by a 1972 earthquake that killed ten thousand people and destroyed three-quarters of the buildings. It was fifteen years later, and the streets were still lined with gutted structures, overgrown lots, and rows of makeshift wooden shacks with corrugated metal roofs. In sharp contrast stood brightly colored billboards and murals extolling the heroes of the Sandinista Revolution. The only two high-rises that survived the earthquake were the headquarters of the Bank of America and the Intercontinental Hotel, home to many journalists. The reconstruction of Managua was unlikely in the near future. Almost half of government monies funded the military fighting the Contras in the countryside.

Every month hundreds of North Americans arrived in Managua. Part-time volunteers and permanent expatriates came to see the fruits of the 1979 revolution firsthand. Brigades of volunteers—dubbed "the Sandalistas" by foreign journalists—traveled north to pick coffee on cooperatives. Organizations sent delegates into war zones. Of the more than eighty North American Catholic missionaries in Nicaragua, Mary Aileen was one of a dozen nuns living in Managua.

No signs identified the streets and dirt roads in the sprawling city, which looked more like a hodgepodge of shantytowns than a metropolis. Nicaraguans used landmarks to give directions, Mary Aileen said, even nonexistent ones demolished by the earthquake: Turn right where the Sears used to be; take a left where the old tree was.

Mary Aileen turned right at Casa Nazaret, a boarding-house for nuns. Most nuns who came here stayed for a few days, some for months. Like many temporary ar-rangements in Managua, hers was now in its second year. The narrow wooden building was hidden by a five-foot-high cement wall. To the north was an enclave of elegant homes barricaded by iron grilles; a few blocks south, shacks and vacant lots.

The makeshift hostel was partitioned into eight small bedrooms. The sisters shared an unfinished cement bath-room with an open shower and toilet. The kitchen sink, washboard, and stove were located outside.

"Everyone thinks I'm crazy to live here," she said as we toured the casa. "But I haven't been able to find an apartment I can afford." Compared with the more opulent convents I had seen, it was a fitting shelter for a woman who had taken a vow of poverty.

For the past year Mary Aileen had worked at a clinic in Managua for low-income families and at a maximum security prison outside the city. Her order sent her $3,500 a year to live on, allowing her to volunteer her services.

Her boxlike room contained a military cot, a small desk, a dresser, nightstand, and bookshelf. Photos of her niece and nephew and their crayon drawings were taped to the wall above the cot. Worn volumes of Virginia Woolf's *A Room of One's Own* and Carroll Smith-Rosenberg's *Disorderly Conduct* shared the bookshelf with medical texts. A two-inch crucifix leaned against the base of the lamp on her nightstand, the only clue that the room's occupant was a nun.

When we sat down to talk, I could tell Mary Aileen was having second thoughts about my visit. Her tone was neither hostile nor apologetic, but she was wondering who I was.

"Friends of mine think I should have checked you out more," she said. "They think you might be CIA."

That evening we joined several hundred Nicaraguans and foreigners in front of the U.S. Embassy to protest American aid to the Contras. Wounded veterans lined up in wheelchairs; a procession of mothers held white crosses inscribed with the names of their fallen sons. Orphaned children carried candles. At the embassy a brightly backlit American flag waved in the wind.

After fifteen years of living in the region Mary Aileen looked tired. Her face was pale, her forehead creased. In the words of her old friend Helen Girard, she was not the ebullient woman she used to be. ("In the old days Mary Aileen was so excited about things," Helen told me wistfully. "She still has the same earnestness. She talks with passion about Latin America. But the bubble has gone out of her, the zest for life. After so many years of struggling it's hard for her to keep buoyant.")

Mary Aileen watched most of the proceedings in silence, occasionally nodding in agreement. The message was always the same: *Patria libre*, a free homeland. After three years in Nicaragua she attended demonstrations and solidarity meetings almost as often as she once went to church.

"When I lived in other countries, I never supported

the government," she said. "I played devil's advocate because the government didn't care about the poor. Here we don't say we're with the government. The government is with *us*."

She waved to a sister in the crowd. For the first time she was surrounded by women who shared her political perspective. Maryknolls, Dominicans, Franciscans—they were her new community. These were the women she saw at demonstrations and meetings, the friends she joined for dinner or a quick beer.

"We don't all live together, but we're always there if a sister needs anything. We get together on different occasions. One weekend I'll spend with one sister, the next with another. My community used to be the nuns I lived with in a convent. Today it's my friends."

She spotted her closest friend, Sister of Saint Agnes Mary Hartman, the head of the National Commission for the Protection and Promotion of Human Rights, a government-sponsored organization responsible for investigating human-rights abuses.

Mary Hartman came to Nicaragua in 1962 to evangelize for the faith and was assigned to an upper-class boys' school. In 1970 she was transferred to a poor barrio, where she lived with a local family. The 1972 earthquake was a turning point. She watched Somoza funnel foreign-aid money meant for rebuilding Managua into the family coffers. When she joined a group of citizens for a peaceful demonstration to protest the lack of water and electricity in the barrio, she was hosed down by the National Guard. As the people began to organize, the repression increased. Before the insurrection the National Guard tortured and killed forty members of the barrio's youth club.

When the students in the barrio began joining the Sandinista opposition, Mary Hartman opened her home as a safe haven and offered her car for transportation. "They had everything ahead of them and they were willing to risk their lives," she told me. "It was a Christian testimony I couldn't forget."

Most of the native Nicaraguan nuns were more conservative politically and theologically, like their cardinal, Miguel Obando y Bravo, a staunch opponent of the Sandinistas. The nuns wore the habits of their orders and observed traditions North American sisters had long abandoned. School Sister of Saint Francis Luz Beatriz Arellano, a robust woman with luminous dark eyes, was an exception. After high school she joined a conservative Nicaraguan order. But she caught on early to the principles of liberation theology.

"In the mid-1970s I was expelled from Nicaragua because of my work with base communities. Somoza felt my work was subversive. It is difficult to fight when one's community doesn't encourage change. But every day more of my Nicaraguan sisters are becoming aware of the struggle."

Not all Mary Aileen's friends were nuns. Her community included lay missionaries and foreigners who had come to work for the revolution. Among them was a Costa Rican named Ana Quiros, a laid-back woman in her thirties who taught at a women's health organization. The fact that she enjoyed working and socializing with nuns—those sinister sisters she hated in Catholic school—still amused her.

"I'm a nonbeliever," she said. "I felt a lot of resistance to nuns when I came here. But I found out that progressive nuns like Mary Aileen understand the feelings of the people. They live in a humble way. Still, I make fun of them when we get together. I call them 'the nunnies.' Even though they don't wear habits, you can point to a woman like Mary Aileen and say, 'Oh, there's a nun.' "

"How can you tell?" I asked.

"They look different. They have short hair and glasses."

"You have short hair and glasses," I pointed out.

She laughed and glanced in the direction of the two Marys chatting in the distance.

"It's not something you can put your finger on, but I can always pick out a nun."

Four days a week Mary Aileen worked at a clinic in Managua, a modern white-brick building badly in need of a paint job. Her first patient on Monday morning was nineteen-year-old Maria, wide-eyed, round-faced, un-married, and pregnant with her third child. As Maria lay on the table, Mary Aileen gently touched the scabs on her legs. Looking closely at the cuts, she could make out the letters of a name: M-I-G-U-E-L.

"Did you do this to yourself, Maria?" Mary Aileen asked. The young woman nodded. "You're such a lovely young woman," Mary Aileen said, taking her hands. "Why would you do this to yourself?" Maria stared blankly and began to cry.

Mary Aileen cleaned Maria's cuts and sent her to see a social worker. But the memory of the wounds haunted her for days.

"It makes me so sad," she said. "Maria had literally carved a boy's name in her thigh. It's so obvious that she hates herself. I've seen so many women like Maria. They're so desperate for love, they give themselves freely to any man who wants them. We've got to teach women that their lives count for something."

For the past year Mary Aileen had taught women's health classes at the prison and at a community center in a nearby barrio. The courses were small, no more than twenty women at a time, to encourage discussion. "I work with women of all ages—those who haven't started their periods and those with five or six kids. I teach women about their bodies. If they don't know their bodies, they can't own them.

"I always start out by saying, 'If you had a house and somebody stole a radio, you would know it was missing.' But I've had literally hundreds of women say to me, 'Oh, yes, the doctor operated, but I don't know what he took out.'"

Many nuns and priests working in Central America believed the liberation of the poor had to come before the liberation of women. Feminism was considered a European and North American notion, a luxury of the privileged. Mary Aileen understood that mentality. Only recently had she identified with the goals of the women's movement, a cause she embraced with revolutionary fervor.

"I used to think feminists were draining energy from the larger class struggle," she said. "Not any more. Liberation won't mean a thing if we leave women like Maria behind."

On a balmy afternoon we drove to Granada, where Mary Aileen spent her first two years in the country, from 1983 to 1985. Located twenty-five miles south of Managua, Granada is a scenic colonial-style city on a lake. Mary Aileen had worked as an internist at a hospital built more than a century ago by the Sisters of Saint

Joseph. Once an elegant building with formidable columns and fountains, it was the oldest, most dilapidated hospital in the region.

Before the revolution the building was divided into two sections: private air-conditioned rooms for the wealthy and hot, dingy wards for the destitute. "Now it is a government-run hospital mostly for the poor," said Mary Aileen. "There is still a private hospital in Granada for those who can afford it, but the poor get just as good care."

As we walked through the dingy hallways, doctors and nurses greeted Mary Aileen with embraces. "Everybody in Granada wants attention from Mary Aileen," said Dr. Carlos Quiroz, a gastrointestinal surgeon. "She works with love first. When Mary Aileen came here, I helped her find a house. We became good friends. She is a feminist. Are you a feminist?" he asked. "Some feminists in the United States I can't understand," he said, shaking his head.

"Do you understand Mary Aileen?" I asked.

"He has to," Mary Aileen interrupted. "He has no choice. His wife is a feminist too. She's an epidemiologist at the regional office of the Ministry of Health. She makes more money than he does."

"This is true," said Carlos, smiling broadly. "But in the United States women have lost their love for children. They think women with children cannot be free. Women in Nicaragua are happy with children. They can be doctors, lawyers, and engineers. But part of their function is to procreate."

"Can a woman be happy without children?" I asked.

"No."

"Can Mary Aileen be happy?"

"I don't know," he said shyly. "Don't ask me that question. She is a religious."

We left Carlos and sat on a bench in the courtyard. "I like Carlos," she said. "He has a good heart."

Like Carlos, many Nicaraguans consider motherhood the most important role. Although every third or fourth Sandinista combatant was female, most women reverted to traditional roles when their men came home.

"On one level it makes sense to stress the *madre* role," said Mary Aileen. "Nicaragua is a country of children. Fifty percent of the population is under fifteen. But women shouldn't only be seen as mothers."

Although birth control was available in clinics, there had not been much emphasis on family planning. Some government leaders favored a high birth rate to replace the losses suffered during the insurrection. The burden of caring for children, however, fell primarily on the women, most of whom were unmarried. Mary Aileen had mixed feelings about family planning in Central America that had nothing to do with Pope John Paul II's condemnation of artificial methods of birth control.

"I think we should offer birth control to women," she said. "But the emphasis should not be on supplying it massively. That almost gives a sense that children are the problem and that they're not wanted. We've got to work with women so that they appreciate themselves and take care of their own bodies. Then we can give them the means to control reproduction. I have trouble with the methods of birth control available, especially tubal ligation. It's not that I'm against it. I've done tubals. But if we can put a man on the moon, we can certainly find a safe, reliable method of birth control that doesn't mutilate women's bodies."

Abortions are illegal in Nicaragua, although they are not difficult to obtain for those who can afford them. The abortion debate in Nicaragua began in earnest in 1985 at the Third Nicaraguan–North American Health Colloquium. A health team from a women's hospital presented a report stating that from March 1983 to June 1985 the hospital admitted 8,752 patients with complications due to induced abortions. The team argued that many doctors did not support legalizing abortion because they made a great deal of money performing illegal ones. The widely publicized report provoked public debate throughout the country.

"I don't think there should be any laws attached to abortion," said Mary Aileen. "It's not legislatable. Women have been having abortions throughout history. I wish everyone would be less judgmental about other people's decisions. I certainly don't want to be a judge."

I asked Mary Aileen if I could accompany her to a church service. She looked stricken.

"My God," she said, "you didn't expect me to go to Mass every day, did you?"

I assured her I didn't.

"Oh, good," she said, sounding relieved, "because I don't go to church regularly. I go to liturgies to celebrate something—life, an event, friendship, a closeness to people. I can't celebrate every day. Some days are terrible. I think that can be more depreciating of an event; when you make it so common, it loses its meaning. I find creative liturgies the most fulfilling. I've been to some women's liturgies in the United States I've really liked."

She didn't attend women's liturgies in Nicaragua. There weren't any. Even politically progressive nuns and priests tended to be conservative when it came to religion and ritual. There had been few efforts to change sexist language or to incorporate women into services.

"It's a war situation," she said. "People here have one aim: making it from one day to the next. The necessities of life have become so all-important, they haven't had the opportunities to read and think about these things. But the campesinos supply me with plenty spiritually—their love of the land, their appreciation of Mother Earth."

She dissociated herself from the leadership of the Nicaraguan church led by Cardinal Obando y Bravo. The mere mention of him made her stiffen. She blamed Obando and the majority of his bishops for failing to speak out against the Contras when the war started. "I have no difficulty condemning the cardinal or the pope for not using their influence to be a voice for the poor people they purport to defend."

Did she ever criticize the Sandinistas? I asked. "We bless them by day and curse them by night," she admitted. "The hardest part about living here is the mini-bureaucracies, the disorganization of a new government. But how can I criticize the Sandinistas when the Salvadoran government sends death squads to murder its own people? I don't feel I'm obligated to point out the defects and give them the same weight as the good things. In my heart I can't."

She dismissed claims of religious persecution levied against the Sandinistas. ("Just look around you. There's a church on every corner.") The fighting between the hierarchy and progressive clergy, she believed, had more to do with politics than religion. Obando's fear that a government with Marxist leanings threatened the survival of the institutional church was exacerbated by the participation of Cuban teachers in Nicaragua's national literacy campaign. Tension between conservative and progressive factions in the Church heightened when the pope asked the priests in government to resign during his 1983 Nicaraguan visit.

Mary Aileen's anger at church leaders had increased her skepticism about their teachings, particularly concerning the nature of God. "My impression of God didn't change much from first instruction until now. I thought that God was a he. He was just, but he demanded obedience. Now I think of a God with qualities we think of as feminine—compassion, sensitivity, love, nurturing. After so many years of conditioning, it takes a conscious effort to think of God as woman."

The "bride of Christ" imagery was no longer meaningful to her. The concept of marriage to God struck her as childish and false, a weak attempt to explain a more mystical relationship in human terms. She was still questioning the concept of the "white male" Trinity: the Father, the Son, the Holy Ghost. "I don't want to use this as a cop-out, but I don't go through the day thinking of God as Trinity. I haven't had the time to grapple with all the deep theological definitions in my life. I'm a doctor, not a teacher or a theologian. Teachers and theologians have to draw conclusions because they have to talk about doctrine.

"If I had the time, I'd love to spend six months studying women's issues within the context of organized religion. I am having a difficult time right now holding on to basic Christian beliefs. Many sisters are struggling with these questions. We have a common bond in searching for what women like ourselves are all about."

Her prayer life stemmed from this search. "If you ask many people what prayer is, they will act shocked. 'Everybody knows what prayer is,' they'll say. Well, I'm not sure everybody knows what prayer is, nor if I do myself. You're supposed to be talking to God. I do believe that prayer is contact with the divine. But I don't believe the answers come by saying a set of words that somebody else wrote. They're not my words and they're not me."

"Do you believe in an afterlife?"

"I'm not sure how to draw pictures of it. I just think that the energy or Spirit, or whatever you want to call it that holds us together, lives on. I think the spirit that united you with another spirit on earth is going to maintain those bonds. The Church has never made too many pronouncements on life after death because nobody knows what it's going to be like. I'm with the Church on that. If you've ever seen someone a few hours after they've died, you can almost see the energy flowing back to the earth."

Her feminist awareness had changed her perception of the Scriptures. "We used to read the Scriptures for fifteen minutes a day," she said. "Now I find it impossible to read the Old Testament with its definition of women and its lack of concern for human lives. I find it over and over again: 'We killed ten thousand.' I keep thinking every one of those ten thousand was a human being. In the New Testament there are many parts I can't read. Again, I find it devastating toward women, and I refuse to make all the jiggle-jaggle acceptable. I cannot accept Saint Paul's statements that women should be subservient, I don't care how you fix them up."

The vows of poverty, chastity, and obedience were still relevant to her, but not in the traditional sense. "I think the vow of poverty means to live respectfully of God's gifts in the universe. You don't eat too much. You don't have more clothes than you need. You don't take something if someone else is going to suffer. I think obedience comes from both the inside and the outside. Inside it comes from your own experiences because they are given only to you. Obedience is also listening to the people with whom you live and work. If the leadership of the congregation asks you to do something, you should make your decision with that in mind."

"What about chastity?"

"Chastity is the tough one. By chastity do you mean the sexual act or a long-term commitment? I don't think you can have a long-term commitment and be a nun. We wouldn't be free to do what we do. Being part of a community necessitates interaction with a group of people so you can't limit yourself to one person. That doesn't mean you can't have very good friends.

"For myself, I would have no part of a casual sexual relationship because of respect for another person. Perhaps a meaningful sexual relationship doesn't require a time commitment. I don't know. In my personal life the question doesn't have that much importance. Sure, I've felt sexual tension, and it doesn't get any easier when you get older. But I feel many kinds of tension. I don't give one more weight than the other."

When we got up to leave, she was still pondering the question. "The rules relating to chastity were always very strong," she said, "as if to be chaste were the end-all and be-all of religious life.

"How did chastity become so important?" she asked, looking quizzically as if I might have had the answer. "Why is being chaste any more important than being just?"

• • •

Three and a half years after arriving in Nicaragua, Mary Aileen decided to return home to Boston. Her parents were almost ninety. She had spent so little time with them, she wanted to make up for it during their final years.

Although Nicaragua had given Mary Aileen her first taste of community since the novitiate, life in a war zone had been one crisis after another. She had barely had time to grab a cup of coffee with Mary Hartman, let alone spend a Sunday afternoon with friends.

In Boston she could enjoy weekends with family and her extended family, the nuns and former nuns who had settled in the Northeast. Once again she depended on Rose, Bea, and Helen to show her the ropes. Only this time instead of learning to short-sheet beds, she was catching up on the dramatic changes in North American religious life.

Her friends prayed together often, not in a church but in their gardens and their homes. Mary Aileen was no theologian. She had never been good at articulating her spiritual feelings. She only knew that when she was among her circle of friends, she felt a strong sense of the divine.

When I visited her apartment in Boston, I was reminded of her room in Managua. The only furnishings were a bed, a desk, a chair. Where a crucifix might have hung, a lone poster was taped to the wall.

She had taken a job in a low-income health center that provided medical services for the poor. Care for the Third World hidden in the First. She also made house calls to the elderly, once again seeking out the sick behind closed doors. Loneliness, she said, was even more devastating than poverty. Some of her patients had not been outside in years.

Evenings were filled with Central American solidarity meetings. She planned rallies, spearheaded letter-writing campaigns, coordinated lobbying efforts. Her current work, she believed, had to take place outside the region. She had to convince the leaders of her own government to stop sabotaging their neighbors to the South, be it Nicaragua, Guatemala, or El Salvador.

"Have you gone on vacation since you returned?" I asked.

She looked surprised, as if she had somehow forgotten to take a day off. While younger sisters were emphasizing the importance of balancing work and recreation, Mary Aileen was still of the old guard. Other nuns had a mission; Mary Aileen *was* her mission. Her work was as much a part of her identity as her Boston accent.

"How are conditions in Nicaragua?"

"Terrible," she said, shaking her head. "The war just about destroyed that country." Mary Hartman had just written to say that people's morale was plummeting as fast as unemployment was skyrocketing. "Food staples are in desperately short supply. Hospitals lack the most basic antibiotics. Children are again dying of diseases they shouldn't be dying of."

Support for the Sandinistas had eroded rapidly as people became more desperate to end the Contra war. Mary Aileen was among the many who were stunned when the U.S.-backed opposition, led by newspaper publisher Violeta Barrios de Chamorro, won the national election. American supporters of the revolution left the country in droves.

Mary Aileen, however, refused to give in to despair.

Regardless of who holds power, she believes the revolution has been forever imprinted on the minds of the people.

"You can never turn back what the revolution has done for that tiny country," she said. "The average person has been deeply affected. Under Somoza the Nicaraguan campesinos didn't have a sense of their own importance. The revolution taught them their place in society. They have a right to education, to housing, to health care. They have a right to be heard. A campesino said to me, 'If they kill us off, the cockroaches will rise up in protest.'"

But the next revolution, she believes, will not be fought with guns and mortar. Women, she predicts, will lead the people in a nonviolent *evolution*.

"Women don't make war. We make peace. Societies will be transformed only when women lead the struggle with their unique powers: a sense of nurturing and justice. These are the qualities that make a woman a woman."

"But women have led their countries in wars," I say.

"Yes, of course that's true. But I just read a quote by Simone de Beauvoir that makes a lot of sense to me. She said, 'One is not born a woman, one becomes one.'"

Mary Aileen repeated the words to herself and smiled. "That's nice. I like that a lot. It doesn't make any difference how we begin. What matters is who we become."

CHAPTER 3

TAKE BACK THE CHURCH:
A FEMINIST DEFIES ROME

*Any God I ever felt in church I brought in with
me. And I think all the other folks did too. They
come to church to share God, not find God.*

ALICE WALKER

THE COLOR PURPLE

From her car window Donna Quinn watched a young
man pacing in front of the women's shelter as if waiting
for a delivery. She recognized him. He was the boyfriend of Cassandra and the father of her youngest
child. Donna knew why he was there. It was the first
of the month and Cassandra's public-aid check had
arrived.

Donna realized that his job prospects were even
worse than Cassandra's. Black teenagers had the highest
unemployment rate in Chicago. But where was he the
other twenty-nine days, he and the other men who
showed up religiously on the first of every month? He
was draining Cassandra of the funds she needed to find
an apartment. Donna worried Cassandra might become
pregnant again. She might contract AIDS.

For more than a year Donna had been teaching
classes in self-esteem, child care, and job training two
days a week at the Saint Martin de Porres House of
Hope. Located in Woodlawn, a poor neighborhood on
the South Side of Chicago, Saint Martin's is a transi-
tional shelter for homeless women and their children
funded entirely by private donations. Some 6,450

women and children have passed through the doors since it opened in 1983.

No sign identifies the two-story white-brick building. Some of the women, particularly those who have been physically abused, do not want their whereabouts known.

In the entryway Donna found Cassandra zipping the last of her children's jackets. Donna suspected that she would be embarrassed to see her. They had talked about Cassandra's effort to stop running to her boyfriend every time he called. But having a man in her life gave her status among the women at the shelter. Separated from family and friends, Cassandra found the loneliness almost unbearable at times. Cassandra counted the days till her boyfriend's visits.

Cassandra's four-year-old daughter reached out her hands; Donna scooped her into her arms. "You're going to need this jacket, sweetie," Donna said.

"I'm only going out for a few hours," Cassandra told her.

"Dress warm. Maybe I'll see you later."

Donna walked into the common room, where women gathered for meals, classes, and conversation, and into the dormitory containing forty cots and double-decker cribs. The second floor houses the two Missionary Sisters of the Poor who run the shelter. Sister Connie Driscoll, a former businesswoman and attorney known for her signature eye patch, founded the fifty-one-member noncanonical congregation in 1983 after she decided that canonical communities were too limiting for women.

Donna greeted the dozen or so women milling about and hugged a group of children playing with toys strewn on the floor.

"How's it going, LaTanya?" she asked a young mother. "Did you get the interview?"

"Yeah, I'm going on Thursday, Sister Donna. Can you help me go over it?"

"Sure."

The two women sat down at a table in the common room. In her lap LaTanya held her one-year-old daughter Dominique, a tiny replica of herself with colored beads laced through her hair. LaTanya had come a long way during her four-month stay at the shelter. When she had arrived with Dominique and her five-year-old son, she was straight out of detox. Nineteen years old, she was thin as a rail. Her kids were dressed in layers of unmatched sweaters, and she had little patience with them. The boy winced each time his mother raised her hand.

LaTanya had been eager to tell Donna about her life. At thirteen she was raped by an "uncle," one of her mother's boyfriends. When she learned she was pregnant, she had an abortion. She managed to finish eighth grade and had started high school. But by the end of her freshman year she was pregnant again. She was in love with the father and hoped to marry him. But he deserted her midway through the pregnancy.

She quit high school after the baby was born and stayed at home with her mother during the day. Frustrated and bored, she began going out at night with her girlfriends. Soon she was doing crack. She became pregnant again. The baby was born addicted. Mother and child enrolled in a detox program. They learned of the shelter.

Donna wasn't startled by the talk of drugs. And rape and incest, the unspoken taboos of polite society, were part of the daily conversation at the shelter.

It was the details of stories like LaTanya's that haunted Donna. She tried to imagine what it would be like to be afraid to ride the elevator in her own apartment building, to keep her clothing in a cardboard box, to sleep six people to a room. In crowded apartments none of the conventional boundaries applied. Children grew up watching their mothers having sex.

The reality of urban poverty was lost on some of Donna's friends. "Why don't the girls just use birth control?" she heard again and again. How could she explain how tough it could be for teenagers to use birth control when their lives were so out of control? Sex was rarely planned, and boyfriends often balked at using condoms. A young woman who didn't know where she was going to live from one week to the next had a hard time remembering to take birth control pills at the same time every day. The people who preached abstinence were the most naïve of all. How would women who had been deprived of the most basic love and attention "just say no" when offered affection?

The anti-abortion activists enraged Donna, particularly the bishops and priests in her own church who had threatened to dismiss her from the Dominican order after she had signed a *New York Times* advertisement calling for dialogue on abortion. How could these pompous men issue proclamations about women's bodies when they'd never bothered to talk to victims of incest and rape?

LaTanya had made remarkable progress at the shelter. She had stayed drug-free. Her five-year-old son was attending kindergarten. LaTanya had taken Donna's child-care class twice a week and was less prone to fly off the handle. She had particularly liked the class on how to massage a crying baby. Now, instead of hitting her children, she rubbed their backs to calm them.

In four months she had saved enough money for a security deposit and the first month's rent on an apartment not far from the shelter. She had made initial inquiries into a day-care center for Dominique. Working with a tutor, she had managed to earn her GED and was applying for jobs as a nurse's aid.

Donna knew that this was a critical point in LaTanya's life. If she failed, she would be back in a shelter in no time. For every LaTanya there were dozens of Cassandras who couldn't seem to break from the cycle of public aid and temporary housing.

"LaTanya, you've earned this," Donna said. "You're going to be great. Now, have you found someone here to take care of Dominique while you're out on Thursday?"

"Yes. Sister Terese said it was all right for the new girl, Tameka, to watch her."

"Great. So you're taking the El. You've got directions. You'll have your token. Don't forget the recommendation I wrote. Why don't we do some more role-playing?"

They spent the next half hour rehearsing answers to questions potential employers might ask. With a history lacking in traditional jobs, the trick was to stress life skills: the nurturing involved in raising two children, the discipline in earning a GED.

"Now, LaTanya, tell me what you're afraid of," Donna asked.

LaTanya nervously fingered her daughter's braids. "I'm afraid I'm going to fuck up again because I'm so nervous."

Donna put her hand on LaTanya's shoulder.

"You're not going to fuck up, honey. Just remember they'd be lucky to have such a fine woman as you on their staff."

LaTanya's friend Tameka walked in from the dormitory. "What are you guys doing?" she asked.

"Job stuff," LaTanya told her. "You're taking care of Dominique Thursday, right?"

"Calm down, girl," said Tameka. "I told you I would twice already." She turned to Donna. "She's so nervous about her kids. You got any kids?"

"She's a nun, stupid," said LaTanya.

"Oh, that's right," Tameka said shyly. "Well, do you want any kids?"

"I'll take this one," said Donna as she reached out to hug Dominique.

II

May 1943. The South Side of Chicago. It was time to crown the Blessed Virgin Mary, and Donna's first-grade class picked her for the honor. Her mother was delighted. For weeks Catherine "Kitty" Quinn stayed up late sewing the eyelet lace dress and long white veil. It was a chance to dress her daughter like the Madonna.

On Sunday morning Donna led her class in the procession. While her classmates sang,

O Mary, we crown thee with blossoms today
Queen of the Angels, Queen of the May

Donna placed the crown of flowers on the Blessed Virgin. She felt transported by the music and pageantry. It was as close as she could get to being a nun at the age of six.

In the 1940s the "Catlics" in Canaryville were loyal to two institutions: the Democratic party and the Catholic church. Activity centered around the parish of Saint Gabriel's, one of the largest in the country. Donna's parents were devoted to the Church, particularly her father, Bill, a member of the Saint Vincent de Paul Society and the chairperson of the annual dance to raise funds for the parish.

Politics came a close second in the Quinn household. Donna followed her father around to fundraisers, where he would introduce his daughters to all the Democratic candidates. On weekends he'd recruit the family to help with his latest campaign. Donna's brother stuffed envelopes. Her sister, Joyce, pasted them shut. Donna licked the stamps.

The Quinn girls attended parochial school taught by the Sisters of Mercy. Every morning Kitty pressed their uniforms and placed lace handkerchiefs neatly in their pockets. She worked a long time on their hair, curling it so it fell in ringlets like Shirley Temple's. She'd tell her daughters: "Now, if people ask if your hair is naturally curly, just say, 'It has a tendency to curl.' "

Pretty, well behaved, an A-student, Donna was a favorite among the Mercy sisters, and she, in turn, loved them. She helped the nuns pass out papers. After school she stayed late to clean the blackboards. Saint Gabriel's boasted the highest number of religious vocations of any parish in the country, so it was not unusual that both Donna and Joyce Quinn dreamed of becoming nuns. Their mother used to tell friends, "I think my little girls will become sisters someday. That's what they want to be."

As soon as she could read well enough, Donna absorbed every book she could find on the lives of the saints, from the "Little Flower" Thérèse of Lisieux, the nineteenth-century Carmelite whose romantic autobiography led many a young girl to the convent, to the fourteenth-century Dominican, Catherine of Siena.

By the age of seven Catherine of Siena had pledged herself to God. Eight years later she was devastated by the loss of her older sister, who died in childbirth. Catherine's parents wanted their surviving daughter to marry immediately, but she refused. To repel suitors, Catherine cut off her beautiful long hair and donned the Dominican habit of widows. During her early twenties she lived at home as a recluse, turning her room into a cloister. She practiced excessive penance, refusing to eat cooked food, thriving instead on the nourishment of prayer. Her confessor wrote that Catherine would fall into such a trance that her body would be lifted from the ground.

Donna was mesmerized by the stories of Catherine's devotion, but she had no intention of entering a cloistered order. She loved the outdoors. There were no public playgrounds in the neighborhood, so she played touch football in the streets with her brother and his friends. To her mother's dismay, she jumped from roof to roof in the alleys of Canaryville. Her favorite sport was baseball. One day when she was playing catcher, she got too close to the bat. The girl with the natural curls had broken her nose.

Her older brother was the first to choose a religious vocation. As soon as he turned fourteen, he enrolled in seminary. Donna was thrilled to have a brother studying to be a priest. But she prayed to God that he would remain the unassuming boy she loved. "I remember every night praying that God would make my brother just a pure, holy parish priest. I didn't want him to be a bishop or anything. Just a simple parish priest."

Every year the missionary priests used to come to her class to talk about life on the missions of Latin America and Africa.

"How many of you would like to be priests when you grow up?" a Maryknoll father asked the boys.

Donna Quinn raised her hand.

On December 18, 1948, Donna's neighbor took her and her sister to the Shrine of Saint Jude to pray for their mother. That morning Kitty had delivered her fourth child, stillborn. Donna knew her mother was not well, but no one would tell her just what was the matter. She knelt in her pew. "Please, God, please," she prayed over and over, "don't let anything happen to my mother."

When Donna returned home, her father called her into his study.

"I knew when I looked at his face," she said. " 'Mom died,' I said, and he nodded. Being Irish, I didn't cry. I just held it in. I felt a lot of anger toward God. I had to be angry at someone, and I couldn't be angry at my father. I guess I felt God had a hand in it."

When she returned to school, her teacher summoned her. "She asked me if I knew how to take care of things at home. And I answered, 'Oh, yes.' I always wanted people to think I was in charge. My father used to call me Miss Full Charge. I said, 'Oh, I know how to cook,' even though I only knew how to boil water. I said, 'And I know how to sew.' I told the nuns I could wash and iron collars and cuffs on our uniforms and that everything was going to be perfect."

Every Sunday the family visited Kitty Quinn's grave. "We grew up in the cemetery. My mother was always with us in a sense. One Sunday I asked God for a sign that she was in heaven. I said, 'If she is in heaven, there will be four roses on the altar at the church.' When I got there, there were four roses. It cleared up the matter in my heart. I could almost forgive God because I knew my mother was in heaven."

While other girls gave up their childhood dreams of a religious vocation, Donna remained firm. During her freshman year at Visitation High School, she decided she would enter the order of her teachers, the Dominican Sisters in Sinsinawa, Wisconsin.

"I never envisioned myself married," she said. "I didn't want to be a wife and mother. Becoming a secretary was a possibility, but it wasn't big enough for me. I was very impressed with the Sinsinawas who taught me. I liked their emphasis on the intellect. I liked the way they were in charge of themselves and in charge of the classroom. They were considered the best teachers, and I wanted to be the best."

She never doubted her vocation until her senior year. At a school dance she met a twenty-year-old young man named Phil. While she had dated sporadically, she had never been serious about anyone before.

"Phil was a real nice guy. He was Irish, very handsome with blond hair and bluish gray eyes. He was very kind. I liked his gentleness, his loving ways. We had a nice time together. We used to go dancing. I loved to dance."

Donna made it clear to him that she planned to enter a convent when she graduated from high school. In the beginning Phil said he understood; later he tried to dissuade her.

"He kept saying, 'Do you have to go? Do you have to go?' We went steady until the end. I wore his school ring and he wore mine. At dances we would hold each other real close until the chaperon separated us. We used to kiss in his car. It was so innocent, but I felt guilty. I thought, 'What am I doing?'

"I was very conflicted. I had planned to enter the convent since I was a little girl. It was my lifelong dream. I thought it was a great honor that God was calling me and it was up to me to respond. By the end of the summer I wasn't sure I wanted to go to the convent. I was in love with Phil, and I didn't know what the convent would hold. I was only eighteen—so young to be making such a major decision.

"But I had already bought the clothes, the flannel nightgowns, the crazy-looking shoes. I had sewed on all the name tags. After I had my trunk packed, my father said to my sister, 'Is she going or isn't she? What is this girl doing?' Finally I made a pact with myself. I decided to enter the convent, but I planned to come home after a month. I told Phil, 'It's okay. I'll only be gone a month, and then we can pick up where we left off.' "

She was due to leave on September 8th, but on the first of the month she received a phone call from the principal of her high school. Donna didn't have to report for another week because the Dominican mother general had died suddenly.

"I said, 'Oh, that's wonderful!' I felt like someone on death row who had gotten a reprieve. The first thing I did was call Phil. We went dancing that night. I spent the week just walking around the neighborhood. I felt like Emily in Thornton Wilder's *Our Town*. I tried to think about what Canaryville would be like on a normal day without me. I thought about everything I loved and was giving up: Phil, my family, my house, my backyard, the lot across the street. It was a very important week for me. It was my way of saying good-bye."

In the fall of 1955 Donna took the train to the Sinsinawa motherhouse with three other young women from Visitation High School. "We were dressed up in suits, hats with veils, and white gloves. Sitting across from us on the train was a group of tough-looking girls from Milwaukee. They were smoking cigarettes. They asked us where we were going, and we said we were going to college. They said they were taking a vacation." But when the train stopped at the station, both groups of girls got off.

"It turned out," said Donna, "we were all going to the same place."

During her first few weeks in the convent Donna tried in vain to stay in touch with life in Chicago. She sneaked outside and asked workmen if they knew how the White Sox were doing. During evening walks she strained to see the Illinois state line. She missed Phil, she missed her family.

She also missed the freedom of her high school days. Unlike some of her more obedient peers, she found no satisfaction in scrupulously following the rule of Saint Augustine, a rule that had been set forth in A.D. 413 for a convent once headed by his late sister:

Be regular in prayers at the appointed hours. . . . Chant nothing but what you find prescribed to be chanted. . . . Let your apparel be in no wise conspicuous. . . . When you go anywhere, walk

together; when you come to the place to which
you were going, stand together. . . . Though a
passing glance be directed toward any man, let
your eyes look fixedly at none.

The sisters were called to observe the rule "as lovers
of spiritual beauty, not as slaves under the law but as
those who have been set free by grace." Donna, however, bristled under the regimentation. She hated the enforced silence during the day. She hated not being able
to go outside when she wanted. Maybe it made sense
for medieval nuns to travel in pairs, but why should
modern women obey fifth-century rules?

Donna was not permitted to write to Phil, nor was
she allowed to read the letters he sent her daily. The
postulant mistress confiscated all mail from unrelated
members of the opposite sex. The lack of contact made
her crazy. But she told herself she could make it because
she would be home in a month.

By October, however, Donna was less eager to
leave. She wasn't sure how she would explain it to Phil.
She wasn't sure she understood the change herself. While
the rules still bothered her, she was getting used to the
routine of convent life. The prayerful atmosphere of the
convent appealed to her. She loved the Little Office of
the Blessed Virgin Mary and the pageantry surrounding
special occasions. The elaborate preparations for the feast
days the nuns celebrated evoked rich childhood memories.

One of the most festive days of the year was the
Feast of Our Lady of the Rosary. The sisters decorated
the altar with dozens of red roses. When Donna arrived
at the chapel the morning of October 7, the sweet scent
of flowers filled the air.

"The altar was so beautiful," she said. "Everywhere I looked, there were roses. I looked up at the crucifix and felt as if God were speaking to me. I wasn't levitated or anything, but it was an experience like none I'd ever had. From that moment on I knew I was meant to be a nun."

In the 1940s nuns were rarely permitted to complete their educations before they began working. Sisters had been attending college since the 1920s in order to meet state and regional certification requirements for teachers and nurses. It was not unusual, however, for sisters to spend twenty years studying for their degrees, fitting in classes at night, on Saturdays, and during the summer. The circumstances fostered an anti-intellectualism among overworked nuns, who dreaded reading assignments as much as their students did.

In 1941 a sister named Bertrande Meyers wrote a widely publicized book decrying the piecemeal education of nuns. "In the majority of cases, the experience seems to have destroyed rather than nurtured any love of learning," she wrote. It would be another decade before Pope Pius XII issued a discourse urging religious orders to wait until sisters were fully prepared both spiritually and intellectually before sending them to work. Superiors now had the support of Rome to resist bishops who wanted to assign young nuns to parochial schools before they were properly educated. In 1953 superiors established the Sister Formation Conference to develop college curricula specifically for nuns.

Donna's class became the second group of Sinsinawa sisters to earn their undergraduate degrees before beginning full-time work. During her postulancy she took college classes taught by nuns at the convent. She spent a cloistered novitiate year devoted to spiritual training and further study of the rule of the life and history of the Dominican order.

The order was founded in the early thirteenth century by Saint Dominic Guzman, then a young Spanish priest. Dominic recruited a group of laymen to defend the Church against the attacks of the Albigensian heretics, who taught that all earthly matter was evil and denied the death and resurrection of Christ. In 1206 he founded his first community of nuns, Albigensian converts, at the monastery of Notre Dame at Prouille in southern France. They were known as preacheresses, who, although cloistered, participated in this ministry through their prayers and instruction of young women. "To contemplate and to give others the fruits of contemplation" became the Dominican motto. Dominic did not found an order of friars until 1215.

A rivalry between the friars and the nuns developed early. By 1226 the men began expressing their opposition to Dominican convents. They thought their preaching might suffer if they had to spend time supervising their cloistered sisters. Consequently by the end of the thirteenth century only 140 Dominican convents were established, compared with almost 600 monasteries for men.

The Sinsinawa Dominicans' story begins in 1828, when an Italian Dominican missionary priest, Samuel Charles Mazzuchelli, traveled from Rome to the wilds of Wisconsin. After building the area's first permanent Catholic church and school, he founded a Dominican order of nuns in 1849 named after a hill the Indians called Sinsinawa. Despite pressure from his superior, he rejected the idea of a cloistered order in favor of an apostolic community dedicated to teaching.

By 1899 the order had grown to 389 professed sisters. When Donna arrived at "the Mound," the imposing limestone motherhouse on 140 acres, some 1,573 Sinsinawa Dominicans were teaching in two colleges and more than one hundred parish schools.

Donna completed her education at Edgewood College of the Sacred Heart in Madison, Wisconsin, graduating in 1960 with a B.A. in history and education, and eagerly anticipated her first full-time teaching assignment. Every year nuns waited until the fourth of August to receive notification of their placements. A mad scramble followed as they packed their belongings and headed for their new homes.

Donna's first assignment was in Omaha, Nebraska. Expecting a rural outpost, she was pleased to discover a city. When she asked her students how many lived on farms, not one raised her hand.

The school principal was a spirited Irish Catholic nun from the South Side of Chicago. She gave Donna permission to do as she pleased around the convent, and Donna reveled in the freedom. She could be a nun and learn to be a first-rate teacher without becoming an automaton. She would skip evening recreation with the nuns and shoot baskets in the school yard. She frequented the local library, where she checked out books on art, psychoanalysis, and philosophy. "I picked out titles that sounded the most outlandish to me, like *Freud on Broadway*. Then I'd check out a couple of books by Thomas Merton or Teresa of Ávila so no one would get suspicious."

When the weather permitted, she took a book up to the school roof. Nuns weren't supposed to think about their bodies, let alone expose them. Sunbathing was strictly verboten. But Donna loved the feel of the hot sun on her skin. "I'd roll up my nun's sleeves and take off my stockings. One day I fell asleep. I woke up and my face was so red, I looked like I was going to pop out of my nun cap. When I got back to the convent, the mother superior sent me to the hospital. The doctors were hysterical. They had never seen a nun with such a sunburn."

Raised on the theology of the Dominican Saint Thomas Aquinas, she began reading the work of the censured Jesuit priest, Pierre Teilhard de Chardin, who explored the relationship of human experience to the divine. Teilhard wrote of an evolutionary process in which distinctions of matter and Spirit were dissolving. He believed that the world was heading toward an "omega point" of love with Christ at the center. Donna loved this radical philosophy. It was closer to her own experience of God. Ever since she was a child, she felt God as a present, loving force, not the distant, judgmental figure portrayed in so many of the sermons she had heard. God was not just present in the chapel. God was manifest in all of nature. She felt most spiritual during her evening walks. The scent of burning leaves in the neighbors' yards was more uplifting than the incense that filled the chapel.

She continued to read about the fourteenth-century Dominican saint, Catherine of Siena. Donna was no longer impressed with the young girl who practiced austere penance, but with the woman who left her self-imposed cloister to minister to the sick and the poor. Although Catherine wore the mantle of the Dominican widows, she never joined a religious order. She tended to those no one else would touch, victims of leprosy and the plague. In her late twenties Catherine emerged as a woman of uncommon temerity committed to saving souls and reforming the Church. As her reputation as a mystic spread, she was sought out by the hierarchy for her wisdom and influence. According to her confessor and biographer, Raymond of Capua, Catherine was unafraid to criticize the pope and his coterie. During an audience with Pope Gregory XI, she addressed the state of the Roman Curia:

> The honor of Almighty God compels me to speak bluntly. The truth is, that even before I left my native city I was ... conscious of the evil of odour of the sins committed in the Roman Curia.

It was said that Catherine helped convince Gregory to inaugurate church reform through his choice of prelates, and she influenced the papacy's return to Rome after a seventy-year residence in France. Donna was inspired by this bold Dominican woman. When she had been asked to pick a religious name, she had chosen the Gallic form of Catherine, to honor her mother and her favorite saint.

During the summer Donna studied for the first of her two master's degrees, one in history at the University of Illinois, the second in administration from the University of Wisconsin. The order, in an attempt to expose nuns to the modern world, had decided to send some sisters to secular universities. Donna's habit set her apart, but she made a point of mingling with the other students. She had never been comfortable with the enforced separation of religious and laity, the division between secular and sacred that placed nuns on a higher plane.

While Donna was at school, the nuns back home

were discussing the call for renewal mandated by the Second Vatican Council. In the summer of 1967 fifty-three delegates met at the Sinsinawa motherhouse. They approved a wide range of changes. Daily meditation became the personal responsibility of the sisters; the Chapter of Faults was to be replaced by a monthly assembly of sisters to evaluate their participation in community life. Sisters could send and receive letters. Proposals for modification of the habit would be considered, as would procedures for electing new superiors. For the first time sisters would receive a monthly sum for incidental expenses.

Some sisters were less interested in changes of routine and attire mandated by the Second Vatican Council than they were in the social implications. While college students were protesting and trying out new lifestyles, these progressive sisters attempted some political and social experiments of their own.

Many were influenced by the women and men who had heralded the beginning of radical Catholicism in the United States. In 1933 Dorothy Day, a convert, founded the Catholic Worker Movement and its urban settlement houses—combination soup kitchens, shelters, and places of worship. Known for her tireless work on behalf of the poor, she was also a suffragist and staunch pacifist. More than three decades later two priests made national headlines with their antiwar activities. In 1968 brothers Daniel and Philip Berrigan, along with a group of seven that included a former Maryknoll nun, broke into the Catonsville Selective Service office in Baltimore. They were arrested after covering draft cards with homemade napalm and setting them ablaze.

In a similar spirit, nuns took to the streets to protest segregation. In their habits and veils they were a startling sight amid jean-clad marchers. When state troopers moved in on a group of demonstrators in Mississippi with tear gas and dogs, fifty-two sisters joined hands and stood between the marchers and the police. In Chicago nuns marched with Dr. Martin Luther King, Jr., into a Catholic neighborhood. An angry white youth in a Jesuit letterman sweater threw a brick at the head of a sister. "And that's for you, nun," he shouted.

In 1967 the Sisters of Loretto were among the first nuns to publicly declare their opposition to the Vietnam War. Sister of Loretto Mary Luke Tobin, the former president of the Conference of Major Superiors of Women and one of fifteen women auditors at the Second Vatican Council, traveled to Vietnam on a fact-finding mission. In March 1969 Sister Joann Malone and eight others ransacked the Washington office of Dow Chemical Company to protest its production of napalm for the war. Twelve Anglican nuns caused a scene at Saint Patrick's Cathedral in New York. After taking communion, they laid down on the floor wrapped in sheets that said, "Another person dead in Indochina."

Donna was inspired by stories of nuns on the front lines, particularly the civil rights activists. Raised in a white Catholic ghetto, she was deeply ashamed of the racism she saw in many Catholic communities. She couldn't join her sisters down South—young nuns had to get permission from the superiors to travel to the next town, let alone another state. She vowed to fight discrimination on the local level.

When she was transferred to Dixon, Illinois, she and several other nuns joined an interracial committee to improve race relations in the neighborhood. She helped organize meetings between black ministers and white pastors. For the first time black pastors preached in white churches, white in black. It was a simple plan, but it brought people into contact who had never crossed paths.

Her own church forbade women to preach—despite the fact that the Dominicans were the order of preachers—but a local Baptist church invited her to speak to the congregation about racism. It was an exhilarating experience to be welcomed into a Protestant church, and a black church at that. She was moved by the gospel music and the warmth of the congregation. Taught to speak softly, she was not used to projecting her voice in front of a crowd. But the community's enthusiasm bolstered her confidence. As she talked of the injustice of segregation, the men and women cheered her on with chants of "Amen, Sister, Amen."

Donna loved community life in Dixon. She and eight other Dominicans lived in a two-story white frame house. It didn't feel institutional like the convents she had known. The nuns were more like members of a family than an order. Decisions were made by consensus, and creativity was encouraged. While the sisters continued to say the Little Office of the Blessed Virgin, they added their own prayers and poems.

Donna looked forward to evening recreation. The nuns would pick up their scapulars and play basketball in the school gym. On weekend evenings they'd sit in the living room, drinking "Red Robins," a mixture of 7Up and wine, and talking about the politics of the day.

The sisters' ministry extended beyond the classroom. They visited inmates at the local prison and patients at the mental hospital. They socialized with their neighbors. The *Dixon Evening Telegraph* ran a photograph of nine nuns in ankle-length white habits and black veils dining with black clerics to celebrate Abraham Lincoln's birthday. "Both religiously and socially the dinner is believed to have been a first in Dixon," the paper reported.

The Dominican community showed her the camaraderie and commitment that was possible in religious life. But the idyllic period was to come to an abrupt end. Donna received her transfer notice. She would be teaching in a small town in Wisconsin. She was distraught at the news, but despite the radical changes in religious life, nuns did not question their assignments.

Wisconsin was a startling change. The prioress was an authoritarian nun who set the tone for the community. It was back to the Rule of Saint Augustine. Schedules were rigid; prayer was formal; nuns and "seculars" didn't mix.

Donna had no intention, however, of returning to the cloister. She joined a community group fighting for fair housing. After school she made a point to socialize with laypeople in the parish. It didn't take long for the superior to view Donna as one of the new breed of nun responsible for the decline in discipline. When Donna didn't show up for prayers one evening, the superior was furious.

"Who gave you permission to skip the Office?" she asked.

"Pope John XXIII and Jesus Christ," Donna replied.

Accused of being rebellious and disobedient, Donna was ordered to meet with the mother general at the Sinsinawa motherhouse. The mother general was used to discord in the convent. Sisters throughout the country were resisting superiors and bishops, and many were leaving religious life altogether. In 1968, four hundred Sisters of the Immaculate Heart of Mary in Los Angeles requested dispensation from their vows after they defied their cardinal by refusing to retract any of their post–Vatican II reforms. The 102-member Glenmary Sisters in Cincinnati had received national attention in 1965 when fifty nuns left the order to work together as lay-women in protest of the archbishop's attempts to restrict their hours and contacts with "nonreligious."

The mother general gently persuaded Donna to make peace with her superior. In August, the mother general promised, she would be assigned to a school in Milwaukee.

Once at her new post Donna experimented with alternative teaching methods. Catholicism, she believed, should stress love rather than penance. The service of the Eucharist should emphasize the communal nature of church. She taught her students that the Eucharist was a celebratory meal where friends joined one another to break bread.

The pastor of the school was disturbed by her unorthodox style. He recruited one of the students to report to him each day after class about Sister Donna Quinn's lesson plan. Donna found out and was outraged that a priest would recruit a child to act as spy. When she tried to talk with him about her lesson plan, he lectured her on traditional theology. To talk about the Eucharist as a meal, he said, smacked of liberal Protestantism.

When she returned to school after Christmas vacation, wearing a modified habit, the priest was pushed to his limit. The majority of Sinsinawa Dominicans had opted to retain the traditional habit, and the rest had chosen one of three alternative styles sanctioned by the order. Donna, however, had her own made from a store-bought pattern: a stylish white knee-length dress with three-quarter sleeves. That Sunday the priest raised the issue of progressive nuns before the entire congregation.

"These sisters think they are part of a liberal movement in the Church because of Vatican II. In fact they are a disgrace to this parish."

Donna's transfer notice came as no surprise.

III

Donna knew there would be trouble when the first buses of black children arrived at the all-white elementary schools on the South Side of Chicago. It was the fall of 1974. She had come to the city just two months earlier to teach at a black high school. Now she had volunteered to escort children who were being bused to white neighborhoods.

When she arrived at the elementary school, a crowd of fifty white adults had assembled to taunt the children getting off the buses.

"Go home, niggers. Go back to where you belong."

Donna recoiled at the blatant expression of hatred. "I was disgusted by the violence I saw from people living in my city. The crowd was getting more agitated, and I was afraid for the children. They were terrified of the mob. Three of the escorts were nuns. Although we were not in habits, there were people in the crowd who recognized us.

"Soon they were shouting, 'Sisters go home.' One woman even went home and came back dressed in a homemade habit and veil. Waving a cigarette, she genuflected before us. Clearly the changes were too much for the woman. The city had betrayed her. Now she felt the Church was betraying her as well."

Chicago was a haven for the progressive wing of

the Catholic church, despite its conservative archbishop, John Cardinal Cody. As soon as Donna arrived, she became involved in civil rights activities. She was also interested in the burgeoning Catholic women's movement. Like many nuns, she had begun reading the feminist literature of the day, Betty Friedan's *The Feminine Mystique*, Mary Daly's *The Church and the Second Sex*. These books helped her articulate what she had been feeling for some time. The men she worked with in the civil rights movement didn't seem to have a place on their agenda for women's rights. Few seemed to care about the double bind faced by black and Hispanic women.

She was invited to a conference on social justice sponsored by the Association of Chicago Priests, a liberal group of clergy. At a panel discussion she heard local sisters talk about their ministries: from providing health care to the poor to organizing tenants in low-income housing. Impressed with their commitment, she approached Sister Marjorie Tuite, a well-known Chicago activist.

"I would like to join your women's group," Donna said.

"Then you'll have to start one," Sister Marge told her.

She explained to Donna that the only group in existence was the Archdiocesan Council of Catholic Women. Although the council had a quarter of a million members, it was relatively ineffectual. Surprisingly, no progressive local group had managed to get off the ground.

Of the several national nuns' groups committed to women's rights, most notable was the Leadership Conference of Women Religious. Established in 1956, the organization was made up of the heads of congregations who supported sisters' involvement in civil rights and petitioned for fair salaries for nuns. It supported Network, a Washington-based lobbying group of sisters working for peace and economic justice.

A grass-roots alternative for all sisters was the National Assembly of Women Religious, founded in 1968. More radical was the National Coalition of American Nuns (NCAN) formed in 1969. Although only 2 percent of nuns belonged to the group, its constituents were among the best organized and most vocal in the country. NCAN supported prison reform, the passage of the ERA, and the decriminalization of prostitution. Its members actively protested the Vietnam War.

Donna envisioned more than just a local group of progressive sisters. She wanted an organization that would include both nuns and laywomen. "I felt that we needed a unified Catholic voice. Most of all we needed each other."

In December 1974 Donna and two other sisters invited fifty women to meet downtown, and Chicago Catholic Women was born. The group was evenly divided between laywomen and nuns. Marge Tuite was there. So was Margaret Ellen Traxler, a School Sister of Notre Dame, and cofounder of NCAN.

At age fifty Margaret had been a nun for three decades and an activist for two. Decked in full habit, she had faced Alabama troopers in Selma. Ten years later, in pants and shirts, she traveled the world from Tehran to Guatemala City to study the conditions in which women lived. She was a short and stocky woman whose wavy gray hair framed a strong, square jaw, which a Chicago journalist said reminded him of the jaw of Pope John Paul II. Margaret Traxler would become a reassuring presence in Donna's life, a gentle but firm mother superior of sorts, who would coach her about the ins and outs of organizing in Chicago.

From the beginning CCW had a full agenda, thanks to Cardinal Cody. Three years earlier he had refused to meet with the Archdiocesan Sisters' Advisory Council. Later he halted all funding for the liaison group. He also ordered funding terminated for an organization of religious women providing food and clothing for the city's poor.

Donna learned that women were discriminated against on all levels of Cody's diocese. Although women comprised 70 percent of the ten thousand members of religious orders, the vicar for religious was male. Of the 150 parish councils in the archdiocese, fewer than 12 percent were chaired by women. Parish finance committees were exclusively male.

When Cody heard about the new women's group in Chicago, he sent a male representative to CCW's third meeting at the Holy Name Cathedral to find out how many nuns belonged to this burgeoning feminist organization.

"How many of you are sisters?" the representative asked the group.

Every woman in the room raised her hand.

"No, no," he said. "How many of you are lay-women?"

All hands were raised.

Donna was thrilled by the spontaneous display of solidarity. "We were *all* sisters and we weren't going to let him divide us."

In 1975 CCW decided to launch an attack against discrimination at local and national levels. The timing was right. The bishops had just called for grass-roots participation from all Catholics during the planning stages of a bicentennial Call to Action conference to formulate a social-justice policy for the American Catholic church. In Chicago only one of seventeen planners was a woman. Donna wrote the vicar general of the archdiocese requesting that at least one more woman be added to the group of planners. She received no reply.

Donna called the vicar. He said that no women would be added and that a Jesuit priest was representing nuns. Donna was outraged. How could a man represent a woman's point of view? The archdiocese was still a boys' club, oblivious to the changes inspired by Vatican II.

Chicago Catholic Women decided to give the bishops what they had asked for: real participation. The group would gather testimony from women of all ages and races about their experience in the Church and present it to the representative of the archdiocese at the public hearings preceding the conference. Donna wanted them to hear firsthand what women thought about issues such as ordination and job discrimination. She wanted them to know what it felt like for black women to listen to priests talk about a white male God, for nuns to learn that "grass-roots participation" did not include them.

The prospect of challenging the most powerful men in the Catholic church was a heady experience for Donna. "Those were fearful days. I was shy and I was scared. I had never taken on something of this magnitude. But Chicago was my home. This was my church, and I wanted it to be different."

In April 1975, 125 women met at a local high school to prepare their testimonies and make recommendations to the bishops. Donna found the degree of consensus remarkable. They advocated the elimination of sexist language and an end to the exclusive use of the male image of God in the cathechism and liturgy. They called for the appointment of a female associate vicar for religious, the formation of a committee of men and women religious to monitor the status of women, and educational programs to teach male clergy about women's issues. On a national level they called for ratification of the Equal Rights Amendment.

Chicago Catholic Women invited church officials to attend a public hearing to discuss the recommendations in the auditorium of the Holy Name Cathedral. Only one of the seventeen members of the Bicentennial committee agreed to attend, and the Archdiocesan Committee sent a letter to its members stating that the Chicago Catholic Women's meeting had nothing to do with the Bicentennial committee. The Reverend Monsignor closed the letter, "Regretting the annoyance that has been caused you."

Annoyance. Donna couldn't believe it. The archdiocese, it seemed to her, was dismissing the women as members of a fringe group, as charges who had misbehaved. If they couldn't move the bishops, then they would reach the public and the press.

On the evening of the hearing Donna set up eleven chairs on the stage to represent Cody, the bishop, members of the chancellory, and heads of diocesan committees. She taped their names in bold letters on the backs of the chairs. More than 150 women and men showed up to hear the testimony. Newspaper reporters and television crews rounded out the crowd.

For four and a half hours women read their prepared testimonies to the empty chairs.

"Why can't I be a deacon in my own church?" a

woman asked. "We were deacons in the time of Jesus. What's wrong with us now?"

Most newspaper accounts were sympathetic to the women's position. But *The New World*, the Chicago Archdiocese newspaper, chastised them for desiring to make decisions better left in the hands of the church fathers:

> Women are represented in all agencies; they have a voice. . . . Perhaps the problem . . . is that some groups want not a voice, an opportunity to present views, but rather to make the decisions. And that is not their prerogative. . . . [A]nger might be avoided if this were realized as one of the facts of life.

Donna was surprised by the unabashed pronouncement of male superiority. "How is this statement consistent with a Bicentennial theme of liberty and justice for all?" she wrote in the Sinsinawa Dominicans' newsletter.

The women hoped to fare better at the bishops' regional hearing in Saint Paul, Minnesota, on June 14. The bishops had agreed to let Donna present excerpts from the women's testimonies. If taking on Cody was frightening, the prospect of addressing a roomful of bishops was more daunting still.

"I was terrified because I was in unfamiliar territory. I had never spoken at a national meeting. These weren't the Chicago priests I was used to. I knew I was carrying sacred testimony. I didn't want to let the women down."

She felt good after speaking. Her voice hadn't faltered, and the bishops seemed to listen to her stories.

But her heart sank when she heard a familiar voice from the back of the auditorium.

"This group has not been approved by the cardinal," the vicar from Chicago shouted. "Their testimony is invalid."

The bishops denied the women delegate status at the upcoming national conference in Detroit.

"It's like the Charlie Brown cartoon," she told Margaret Traxler later. "You work up some trust, and they pull the football out from under you."

Margaret had anticipated the bishops' lack of support, and she worried that Donna was taking the move too personally. In no uncertain terms Margaret told Donna to keep her distance emotionally.

"You have to stop being so hurt," she said. "Either we get out of the Church or we thumb our noses at them. If the priests don't tow the line, they'll be chided by Rome. They're clerically castrated."

Donna took Margaret's blunt counsel to heart. The only way to save the priesthood, she concluded, was to bring women into the ranks. It was a radical position, guaranteed to infuriate the bishops even further. While virtually all Protestant churches admitted women to the ministry by 1970, the Catholic church remained firm in its refusal to ordain. In 1972 Pope Paul VI had even issued an apostolic letter excluding women from the priesthood and from lay ministries of acolyte and lector. But Chicago Catholic Women resolved to press for the principle that ministries be open to all women and men who felt called.

In December 1974 Donna and thirty other women had met to discuss whether the issue of women's ordination should be raised during 1975, designated by the United Nations as International Women's Year. The meeting led to the first women's ordination conference in the United States. Twelve hundred women gathered in Detroit; another five hundred had to be turned away due to lack of space. Donna could hardly believe the turnout. The bishops could no longer dismiss them as some fringe group. "It was the first time Catholic nuns and laywomen had gotten together nationally. It was sisterhood on a level that we had never experienced before."

Some women wanted no part of ordination until the role of priest was fundamentally redefined. They didn't want an authoritarian priesthood, in which one person was expected to perform all functions in the parish. They envisioned a Church in which power was shared and people would participate according to their talents. One person would preach, while another would minister to the sick and dying. Priests would not be rulers but servants of the people.

Another group of women didn't want to wait for a perfect priesthood. Women, they argued, should be ordained now.

Donna sympathized with both sides. "I was worried that if women got in, they would be coopted. We had examples of ordained women who wore the clerical collar without making any changes in the system. They became just like the men they worked with. At the same time it would be politically smart to get a foot in the door. I hoped that women would be strong enough to create a new priestly ministry from within."

Many progressive priests supported the women's efforts to expand their ministry. An organization of Dominican priests singled out Donna and gave her a three-thousand-dollar grant to continue her work at Chicago Catholic Women.

On February 20, 1977, the Association of Chicago

Priests gave her their annual award for her work toward women's ordination.

At the ceremony Donna made the rounds in the room, shaking hands with all the priests, just like her father used to do. She hugged her brother, Bill, and her sister, Joyce, who as usual had staked out seats in the front row. When it was time to receive her award, Donna walked to the podium and looked out on a sea of clerical collars.

"I thank all of you," she said, her voice booming. "And I thank God. I know she will give us energy and the spirit to continue."

In the fall of 1980 Margaret Traxler decided it was time for Donna Quinn to go national. She encouraged her to apply to the board of the National Coalition of American Nuns.

"You're the next generation," she told Donna. "It's your turn."

Donna was elected to a three-year term as president of NCAN, now eighteen hundred members strong. The group addressed the most controversial issues facing American sisters, from prison reform to prostitutes' rights. Donna now held two leadership positions: the directorships of CCW and NCAN. She had new clout on the national level.

She had left teaching to represent the Sinsinawa Dominicans as a full-time staff person at the 8th Day Center for Justice, a coalition of eight religious communities of women and men. During the day she lobbied for state regulations on day-care centers and the establishment of homeless shelters throughout Chicago. Like many of her sisters, she had moved out of the convent into an apartment.

Ordination was still high on the Catholic women's agenda. In 1976 the Vatican had issued a decree stating that women could not be ordained because there had to be "a natural resemblance" between the priest and Christ. "As representatives of the head of the Church, the bridegroom, the priest, must be male." Women supporting ordination dubbed the declaration "the penis decree."

On a more hopeful note, the second women's-ordination conference in Baltimore—"New Women, New Church, New Priestly Ministry"—had been even more successful than the first, drawing more than two thousand women. Theresa Kane, the president of the Sisters of Mercy of the Union and the Leadership Conference of Women Religious, had focused national attention on the issue when she was invited to speak to Pope John Paul II in Washington, D.C., on behalf of leaders of congregations. The pope listened impassively as she asked him "to be mindful of the intense suffering and pain which is part of the life of many women." She called on the Church to allow "the possibility of women being included in all ministries of our Church." Some nuns were quick to apologize for Kane's "rudeness." But members of CCW and NCAN were buoyed by her courage.

In May 1981 CCW and NCAN members decided to raise a ruckus of their own at the annual ordination ceremony of Chicago priests. Only family members were invited to attend the chapel service at Mundelein seminary, but Donna and fourteen of her friends hoped to crash the party.

On the morning of the ceremony the women arrived early. The plan was to sneak inside the seminary chapel when the ushers were not looking. But only Donna and

Barbara Ferraro, a Sister of Notre Dame, managed to squeeze past the ushers before the heavy doors closed behind them. They slipped into the back pew.

"We were filled with panic," said Donna. "All fifteen of us were supposed to disrupt the service after the fifteenth ordinate was called, and there were just two of us. We decided to go ahead with the plan for the sake of the others."

Cody turned to the first candidate. "Are you ready for ordination?" he asked.

"I am ready to be ordained," the young man replied.

"Are you ready to be ordained?" he asked candidate number two.

"I am ready."

Donna was relieved to see her thirteen friends walk through the chapel doors as the fourteenth name was called.

"Are you ready to be ordained?" Cody asked number fifteen.

"We are ready and willing to be ordained," the women shouted in unison.

Rows of people turned to face the women. "They bared their teeth at us," said Donna. "They looked at us like 'How could you disrupt our special day?' They saw the ceremony as a family affair, but we viewed it as a public event. Women were being barred from ordination, and we just couldn't look the other way. An elderly woman in the pew in front of us got so mad, she took her scarf and wrapped it around Barbara's wrist, twisting it until she shrieked in pain."

Determined not to let the women preempt him, Cody continued with the Mass until a messenger handed him a piece of paper.

Cody read the note. He looked shaken. "I am sorry

to inform you," he announced, "that the pope has just been shot in Rome."

A hush fell over the congregation as eyes darted toward the rear of the church. "People glared at us," said Donna, "as if we had pulled the trigger."

In 1982 NCAN became one of the first Catholic women's groups to advocate a woman's right to choose abortion. It was the most controversial issue in the Catholic women's movement, and the most divisive. Many nuns who had supported Donna's work for ordination drew the line at abortion. NCAN, they believed, had gone too far.

The group's position was in direct opposition to the National Conference of Catholic Bishops. The conference had endorsed the Hatch Amendment to overturn the U.S. Supreme Court decision legalizing abortion.

Abortion had been a crime in the Catholic church since the year 300, when formal ecclesiastical legislation punishing abortion was enacted in the West by the Council of Elvira. While canon law named abortion as a crime, moral law, according to church fathers, regarded it as a mortal sin: the indefensible destruction of human life. Anyone who procured an abortion automatically assumed the penalty of excommunication.

While many nuns and priests approached the question on a theoretical level, members of the National Coalition of American Nuns had firsthand experience working with women in crisis in schools, shelters, and prisons.

Donna felt that theological arguments about the moment of conception seemed hollow compared to personal accounts she had heard from pregnant women who had been the victims of psychological and physical abuse, incest, and rape. The issue transcended age, class, and color. She knew middle-class members of CCW who bore the physical scars of back-alley abortions—not to mention the emotional scars. "They walked around with the guilt heaped on them by men, primarily the men in my own Church. If these priests and bishops spent even a day at a battered women's shelter, I doubt they would be so cavalier about women's lives."

Whatever reservations Donna had about the morality of abortion, she knew that the decision to terminate a pregnancy was not an easy one. When people asked her why a celibate woman should take on issues of reproductive rights, Donna said that what touched her sisters touched her. Besides, she said, no woman is invulnerable to rape.

"We are not pro-abortion," she told the press. "But we say we know the pain of making that choice. So we feel it should be up to those closest to the decision—the woman, her mate, and her doctor—to make the choice. Simply put, we don't believe a woman's body should be legislated."

The grass-roots support for NCAN's pro-choice position was overwhelming. Hundreds of letters poured in. "Women wrote to tell us they were tormented by guilt after having abortions. They felt they could speak to women of the Church who understood their problems instead of condemning them."

NCAN's stance, however, drew fiery protest from pro-life groups. Joseph Scheidler, of the national Pro-Life Action League, said it is "deceitful, hypocritical and damaging to stay in an organization that preaches one thing when you are teaching what we used to call heresy."

Donna heard similar sentiments from less vehement critics. Why stay in the Church if you disagree with its teachings? Even some of her friends—former nuns among them—told her she was wasting her energy if she thought she could change the Church.

Donna didn't understand such a defeatist attitude. This was just as much her Church as the bishops'. She could believe in the teachings of Jesus while disagreeing with the interpretation of men who had so little experience working with women. She was beginning to feel as if she were one of the few nuns who didn't struggle with whether to stay in her order. Whatever the frustration, when she woke up in the morning, she didn't have to ask herself what it was all for. She was passionately committed to her cause.

She couldn't imagine not being a nun. Every time she read about a Sinsinawa Dominican protesting injustice in Africa or Latin America, she felt proud. She couldn't be every place at once, but she could count on her sisters to cover the bases. Her affiliation with the Dominicans gave her credibility, and her membership in NCAN and Chicago Catholic Women gave her strength. If she had to, she and her sisters could mobilize hundreds of women within a matter of days. She and Margaret had access to the major media throughout the country.

Indeed, the press loved Traxler and Quinn. The two women were an attractive team: salty veteran nun and idealistic young sister. Reporters knew they could count on them for quick analysis and pithy quotes. "How can these rich, white male legislators express such great concern for fetal life," Donna told *People*, "when they do not support child nutrition programs, aid to education, or a thousand other things which would support babies after they are born?" Donna and Margaret were a hit on national television. When they discussed abortion on the Phil Donahue show, the producers received 540 responses, more than two-thirds supportive of the nuns' position.

Donna knew that a few members of CCW resented her growing leadership role. No one should be singled out in the women's movement, they said. Donna disagreed. Communities had to recognize the strengths of their members. She was good with the press and she knew how to work a crowd. Sure, she enjoyed the notoriety. But she wasn't doing this for some ego trip. She was doing it for the cause. This was no time to start playing the self-effacing nun. Margaret backed her wholeheartedly, and Donna continued to speak out.

She believed that her "marginal status" as a nun gave her the freedom to talk frankly without fear of reprisals. "What can [the male clergy] do to us?" she asked a reporter from the *Chicago Sun-Times*. "We don't have much to lose. Unlike male members of the church hierarchy, we are without power. We can't even be deacons or preachers. Today I hear women saying they might consider an alternative Church. If men in the Church refuse to bring women into the decision-making processes these women will celebrate our own liturgy and bring church to each other."

In 1983 the move for an alternate Church led to the first "Women-Church" conference in Chicago, sponsored by the Women of the Church Coalition, which had represented Catholic groups throughout the country since 1977. More than eleven hundred women showed up to discuss their vision of a Church where women and men would have an equal voice.

"We as women can indeed speak as Church," feminist theologian Rosemary Radford Ruether told the group. "As Women-Church we claim the authentic mission of Christ, the true mission of Church, the real agenda of our Mother-Father God."

While the meeting would spur yet *another* working group to plan further gatherings—Women-Church Convergence—Donna knew that Women-Church was more than a new coalition.

"It wasn't some new organization, religion, or sect. It was a global movement of women committed to building a new nonpatriarchal Catholic church."

For some women the movement represented a complete break with the institutional Church. For Donna, Women-Church was a rejection of the patriarchal aspects of the Church. She could embrace a new tradition while continuing to work toward reforming the institutional Church. She could join with women reclaiming their biblical tradition and create new prayer services that celebrated the feminine aspects of God and the power of women in community.

The power of Women-Church defied easy analysis. "It was not something you could get a hold of," said Donna. "It had no headquarters, offices, or elected leaders. Its essence was intangible. Women-Church pervaded our spirits."

IV

On a Sunday afternoon I joined two dozen people who had gathered to break bread together: ten nuns, ten laywomen, and several children. The oldest woman was well into her seventies. The youngest girl was less than a year old. Her name was Grace.

Every week Chicago Catholic Women holds a liturgy in a member's home. Many of the women rarely attend Mass in a Catholic church. Disturbed by the lack of female participation in traditional liturgies and the sexist tone of the services, they prefer to celebrate among women. Their homes become their churches.

The services have a 1960s sensibility. Women wear jeans and T-shirts and Indian-print dresses. Folk songs are played on acoustic guitars. The homilies are filled with references to peace, love, and sharing. While the feminist poems speak of righteous anger, there is no cynicism here. The pervasive mood is one of hope.

Men are absent from the group. While Donna says she can envision a day when men and women can celebrate together, she does not believe that time has come. "Men ask, 'Why can't we join you?' " said Donna. "But right now we need to allow women the freedom to express themselves without being intimidated or influenced by men. If you have men in the group, it's amazing how they will end up dominating and controlling. I'm a firm believer that women need a time and space in history to separate, similar to that of the black movement. I'm a little wary of women who don't go through that stage."

Donna's roommate, Paula Basta, a thirty-year-old seminary student, nodded her head in agreement. "There's a beauty when you pray and it's all women's voices you hear," said Paula. "I find strength there I don't find in a regular parish church."

The women sat in a circle on the floor. Each held a yellow sheet of paper with the words to the celebration. A fresh loaf of bread, two glasses of wine, candles, and flowers sat on a coffee table at the west side of the room. At the south end another candle sat on an end table. On the dining room table to the north was a bowl of water.

Paula led the celebration. "Hail to the women and children of the East, who bring us power of air," she said solemnly. "Hail to each of us who has come through the door on the East, bringing us strength and energy."

The women read in unison, "Blow the staleness away, fill our lungs. Help us bring freshness into our lives. Let there be clear skies, clear minds for us to see our way. Let our words create a safe place. Blessed be."

Paula opened her bible and read a scriptural passage from the Gospel of John. She recounted the story of the women at the tomb who carried Jesus' message to the disciples. "What if the women had kept silent?" she asked rhetorically. "What would have happened to the Christians?"

To the accompaniment of a guitar, the women sang a song they all knew well—"The Rock Will Wear Away," by feminist songwriters Meg Christian and Holly Near.

Can we be like drops of water falling on the stone
Splashing, breaking, dispersing in air
Weaker than the stone by far
But beware that as time goes by
The rock will wear away
And the water comes again.

They meditated in silence for a minute and then prayed aloud. One by one they offered their petitions to God.

"I pray for peace in the Mideast."

"God hear our prayers," the women answered.

"I pray for the homeless to find shelter."

"I pray for Carol, who is considering joining our community."

"God hear our prayers. Come into our hearts, warm us," they said in unison. "Help us emerge from hibernation and insulation to greet each other. Let passion flow as we fight injustice. Let our emotions out from all their hiding places. Blessed be." The women stood and hugged one another.

Paula rose and spoke forcefully: "Like those women who have gone before us, we bring forth the symbols of earth's harvest, bread and wine. We bless the bread of the land, symbolizing the body and blood of all those who have given their lives for others. We break this bread as our bodies are daily broken by oppression. Let us give each other a piece of their bread, food for journey as we work against oppression saying: No more! Let us also pass the cup of wine to quench our thirst as we thirst for justice."

Donna tore off a piece of bread. She poured herself a glass of wine. "The bread is symbolic of our bodies, the wine of our blood," she said. One by one the women drank the wine and ate the bread.

According to the church hierarchy only an ordained priest can perform this sacred act. In keeping with this official teaching, some women call the breaking of bread a celebration. Donna calls it Eucharist.

"There are women who are fearful of proclaiming what they really believe it is," she said vehemently. "I really believe it's Eucharist. Jesus said, 'Share this bread and do this in remembrance of me.' Jesus is truly present here."

Donna and Paula live in Logan Square, a Polish and Hispanic neighborhood on the North Side of Chicago. Their two-bedroom apartment is homey and inviting, a far cry from the austere convents Donna has known. Located in a refurbished prewar building, the rooms have high ceilings, exposed oak molding, carved oak bookcases with leaded glass windows, and brass light fixtures. The windows are covered with antique lace. Most of the furnishings are Paula's: the maple tables, the oak rocker, the overstuffed couches and chairs. Potted plants line the window ledges.

The fifty-year-old nun and thirty-year-old seminarian met at a meeting of Chicago Catholic Women. Donna was living in an apartment on the southwest side of Chicago. Her rent was too high and she was looking for a new place to live. When she heard Paula needed a roommate, Donna asked if she could move in.

The two women are an odd pair. While Donna is a dreamer, Paula's a pragmatist. Donna gets lost in the middle of a joke; Paula is quick with the punch line. Donna enjoys their relationship. She doesn't mind playing Gracie Allen to Paula's George Burns.

"Paula is just terrific," Donna told me. "This year my community has asked each of us to write down the good things that have happened because of the person or people we have lived with. . . ."

"I think you should write that we cooked Thanksgiving dinner together and didn't kill each other," Paula interjected. "That's a good thing."

". . . I'm going to write," Donna continued unfazed, "that Paula has been very influential in my life as a younger woman coming up and speaking the truth."

Paula admits that living with a nun has posed some problems beyond cooking turkey dinner. "When my friends heard I was going to be living with a nun, they didn't know if they should visit me anymore. My family was a little put off. My mom always believed a nun was holier than a laywoman with kids. Basically I said that Donna kept the place clean and she didn't throw wild parties so she could live here. The human side of nuns is hard for people to accept. They're afraid to lose the myth. They don't know what to replace it with."

Paula wasn't overly impressed with Donna upon first meeting. "She seemed very nunny," said Paula. "She was very proper and soft-spoken. I'm used to working with loud, mouthy types. She had on polyester the day I met her. All the nuns I knew dressed in polyester. She fit the mold. Later we talked more and I saw that she was strong, outspoken, and compassionate. Her social circles are not confined. She has young and old friends. Now my closest friends treat Donna like an older sister.

"We talk about everything. She's quite liberal regarding sex. She doesn't understand why people get upset about homosexuality or married priests. She thinks the male celibate mind that oppresses us as women oppresses us as sexual beings.

"Donna ruffles a lot of feathers," Paula continued. "I think she says out loud what a lot of nuns think and are afraid to say publicly. I think most nuns play it safe. Donna is one in a million. I don't know how she got to be that way except that she cares deeply about what she's fighting for. For the benefit of future generations she will devote her life to working for the rights of women. She's an idealist. She really believes that someday soon women will be bishops, that there will be a woman pope in our lifetime. I'm the practical person. I say, 'Come on, Donna, get back down to earth. I'll never be ordained in the Catholic church.' And she looks me right in the eye and says, 'Oh, Paula, yes you will.' She really believes she's going to change the Church and the world."

Later that evening Donna, Paula, and I joined their friend Cindy, a photographer, for dinner at a Mexican restaurant. Cindy, who had been reading about feminist spirituality, brought up the subject of women mystics.

"Did you know that Catherine of Siena saw visions of Mary Magdalene when she prayed?" Cindy asked. "She was so ecstatic during prayer, her body left the ground. Donna, have you ever experienced ecstatic prayer?"

"You mean an out-of-body experience?" Donna asked.

"A heightened awareness of being really in tune with God, creation, and yourself."

Donna laughed. "Oh, no! Well, maybe in the shower."

"That's Donna's prayer time," said Paula dryly. "She prays when she's in the shower."

"I pray the most in the shower and in the car," Donna said. "When I'm alone, it's my time to dream and commune with the energy I feel. That's how I see God. God is an energy, a spirit who speaks to us. I hear God through people."

"God forbid you should tell her she has a phone call when she's in the shower," said Paula, shaking her head in mock disapproval.

"I love the water on my body," said Donna. "I think it's so soothing and relaxing."

"Wouldn't that have been considered sinfully sensual a few years back?" I asked.

"The mystics were sensual," Cindy said.

"Yeah," said Paula. "The mystics wrote about heightened feelings about God in a sensual way."

"Can you be celibate and sensual?" I asked Donna.

Donna considered for a moment. "I think we have to see our sexuality and spirituality as one thing," she said. "I think that in the future we won't have the same taboos against our bodies that we have today."

"Is celibacy still relevant?"

"I think that there will always be space for women who want to be celibate and be in community. To me celibacy is relevant in the sense of a commitment to the women's movement. I am consumed with that. In the future I don't think it will be called celibacy. It should be called commitment."

"Have you read the book *Lesbian Nuns: Breaking Silence*?" I asked Donna.

"Yes. I went to the reading of the book here in Chicago, and about seven hundred women showed up. I wanted to support them. The author was very pleased that I was there. You know, people have called us the lesbian abortion nuns. They think that's the lowest thing they can call us. It's crazy. I think that most people are basically bisexual. I could say I've loved men and I've loved women, but I haven't found it necessary to express that sexually at this point. All my life I've respected choices that people have made. I want people to have the freedom to choose to be who they are, who they are born to be. It's not sexual preference as much as orientation. Why try to make people over?"

"Do you ever regret not having children?"

"In my thirties I began to think about having children. Now I'm entering midlife, and it's a little sad when you realize that you'll never have children of your own.

I guess what gives me satisfaction is that I'm still trying to make a better life for the next generation."

Cindy asked Paula if she had ever considered becoming a nun. "Oh, sure," she replied. "I went to Catholic school for sixteen years, and a lot of my mentors were nuns. I liked what they valued, the simple lifestyle. I thought it would be a very attractive life at certain points. When I was twenty-two, I was working as a social worker at a psychiatric hospital. I was involved with a man I thought about marrying. But I couldn't imagine moving to the suburbs and having dinner every night with him and the children. I knew I would feel too isolated. At that point I wanted to share my experiences with people on a daily basis. I wanted to live in a communal setting."

"So why didn't you enter a convent?" I asked.

"Celibacy," she answered without hesitation. "I've been celibate at different times in my life. I never plan to fall in love, but I do, and I like the freedom to act on that. And I didn't like the whole idea of giving up my property. I was making money for the first time in my life as a professional. Authority and privacy were also issues for me. I like to live my life the way I want to."

Watching Donna's conflict with the church hierarchy has not altered Paula's views. "Why should I join a community that's under the pope when I don't agree with the pope? For Donna it's different. She has a history in community. She's been a Dominican for twenty-seven years, and you don't just throw that experience away. For me to enter a religious order today at age thirty would be another story."

"Does it hurt you that your community will lose women like Paula?" I asked Donna.

She nodded. "I think our only hope is to form broader communities where nuns live with women who are not members of religious orders. I think we will see communities of women and children. Those of us who have worked with laywomen know we have a common bond. They don't want to be nuns, but they want affiliation with community. We need each other. As women come more into our own—either through Women-Church or by changing sexist practices in the institutional Church—we will be recognized in ministerial roles. I'm not even sure there will be a need for a separate group of women known as nuns. Women helping women, that's where it's at. Young, old, rich, poor. I dream of the day when we will have a place to come together."

Paula explored the possibility of joining a noncanonical order of nuns who are not accountable to the church hierarchy. The most famous is Sisters for Christian Community. A sociologist and former canonical sister, Lillanna Kopp, founded the group in 1970 after she concluded that the hierarchical structure of canonical communities was antithetical to the liberating teachings of Christ. Today more than six hundred sisters, Catholic and non-Catholic, are part of this community. They live on every continent yet meet informally at regional gatherings, and at the yearly meeting of the community. There are no designated leaders. Each sister supports herself and pays taxes. She decides how long she wants to serve and whether she wants to live alone or in a small group. Instead of professing to remain poor, chaste, and obedient, she vows to serve, love, and listen.

"Donna introduced me to a couple of people from the Sisters for Christian Community in Chicago," said

Paula. "I went on a retreat with them, but it wasn't for me. I really felt no sense of what bonds them. Many have given up their other orders because of the restrictions. But they no longer live in community. In Donna's Dominican community they have a sense of how to bridge the contemporary and historical that is comforting to me. I know I sound contradictory. Donna and I both have such a love-hate relationship with the Church. On the one hand the ritual can be so oppressive. The language is awful. The priests are usually pompous and condescending. But the beauty of the Catholic service holds us in awe at times."

"It's really crazy. It's in our souls," said Donna.

"How did you end up in seminary?" I asked Paula.

"I wanted some sense of spiritual grounding. Through Chicago Catholic Women I learned that women could go to seminary, which was amazing to me. I decided to go to a Presbyterian school because I thought it would be less blatantly sexist than a Catholic institution."

"Do you think you will ever be ordained in the Catholic church?"

"Yes," said Donna.

"No," Paula answered. "Not unless there's a major emergency. Institutions do not change unless they have to. The picture is so bleak under Pope John Paul. It's almost masochistic for Catholic women to be in seminary." She hesitated for a moment. "In the back of my mind, though, I haven't completely given up hope. I think, 'Maybe when I'm fifty.' Who knows. If women are ever ordained, I'll be ready."

"Would you change denominations to be ordained?"

"No."

"Why not?"

"Because it's my Church, too, damn it, and they need to know I'm out there. They need to know that my voice is as valid as anybody else's." Donna smiled approvingly.

"Donna, if you were Paula's age, would you choose to become a nun?" I asked.

She thought a moment. "Sometimes I feel called to a priestly ministry," she said. "If I were younger, perhaps I'd study to be a priest."

V

The year 1984 was pivotal in Donna Quinn's ministry to reform her Church. Democratic presidential candidate Walter Mondale had made history when he chose a woman as his running mate. Donna could not have been happier. Geraldine Ferraro, she believed, was a woman of conviction who could prove that the presidency, like the priesthood, was no longer a male-only vocation.

New York archbishop John J. O'Connor did not share Donna's enthusiasm. On June 24, 1984, he asked his parishioners not to endorse the Mondale-Ferraro ticket. "I don't see how a Catholic in good conscience can vote for a candidate who explicitly supports abortion," he told his flock, referring to Ferraro. A Catholic, Ferraro said that while she did not believe in abortion, she would not use her political position to force her views on the subject.

Pro-choice Catholics were incensed by O'Connor's statement and similar pronouncements by Bernard F. Cardinal Law of Boston and other members of the U.S. hierarchy. A group called Catholics for Free Choice, representing some five thousand people, bought a $30,695 full-page ad in *The New York Times* on October 7 calling for dialogue on abortion. The text contained a series of controversial statements:

> Statements of recent popes and the Catholic hierarchy have condemned the direct termination of pre-natal life as morally wrong in all instances. There is the mistaken belief in American society that this is the only legitimate Catholic position. In fact a diversity of opinion regarding abortion exists among committed Catholics. . . . According to data complied by the National Opinion Research Center, only 11% of Catholics surveyed disapprove of abortion in all circumstances. These opinions have been formed by:
>
> • A recognition that there is no common and constant teaching on ensoulment in Church doctrine, nor has abortion always been treated as murder in canonical history. . . .
>
> • An awareness of the acceptance of abortion as a moral choice by official statements and respected theologians of other faith groups.

Ninety-seven nuns, priests, and laypeople signed their names to the ad. Donna Quinn, Margaret Traxler, and twenty-two other sisters were among them. "I was furious at O'Connor," said Donna. "I had been so happy when Ferraro was nominated, I cried. I knew it was an important moment in our history as women. How wonderful to have not only a woman but a Catholic woman, nominated as vice president! How dare O'Connor use his influence to work against her. It was another example of the Vatican trying to exert pressure on the political process. I was more than eager to sign the ad. But I had no idea there would be such repercussions."

A month after signing, Donna learned that her "marginal status" as a nun did not protect her from the wrath of the Vatican. While the bishops in Rome could not strip her of clerical power she did not have, they could kick her out of a community she had lived in for twenty-four years.

On December 18, 1984, Jean Jerome Cardinal Hamer, head of the Vatican's Congregation for Religious and Secular Institutes, commanded the heads of religious orders to get public retractions from members who had signed the ad. The Vatican charged that the signers were seriously lacking in religious submission. The superiors were told to threaten to dismiss the nuns and priests if they failed to retract.

Donna was stunned. "It amazed me that the Vatican would turn to such extreme measures. It was the first time I had been asked to show obedience to the pope rather than my community."

The priests and brothers retracted their names from the ad. The men have left "us very much alone," Margaret Traxler wrote in the CCW newsletter. "As oppression grows in the Church, the voice of priests becomes more silent."

All twenty-four nuns, however, refused to take back their statements. "We believe we have the right to speak out when we have a differing opinion," Donna told *Time* magazine, "and this is something European men do not understand."

The only way the signers could beat the Vatican, Donna believed, was to stick together. On December 19, she joined thirty-five nuns and lay signers in Washington to discuss Rome's threat. "We prayed," said Donna, "and we planned our strategy. The first step was to get input from canon lawyers about the dismissal process." The next was to issue a statement as challenging as the ad:

> We are appalled by the recent action of the Vatican against women who are members of religious orders. We believe that this Vatican action is a cause for scandal to Catholics everywhere. It seeks to stifle freedom of speech and public discussion in the Roman Catholic church and create the appearance of consensus where none exists. A consensus on any issue in the church cannot be imposed.

The group urged fellow Catholics to write to the Vatican stating their "belief in diversity, pluralism, and honest discussion of church issues."

Donna and Margaret received more than one thousand letters of support. A bishop told Margaret, "We're glad you're saying the things we can't say." But their approach struck some people as unnecessarily combative. The liberal weekly *National Catholic Reporter* said the ad was poorly worded. "The muddle has been costing Catholics in general, and U.S. women religious in particular, dearly and unnecessarily ever since." *N.C.R.* said the use of an ad in a major paper would by its very public nature harden, not soften, the position of the church hierarchy.

Donna disagreed. The ad was not meant to present a unified position on abortion, but to call for dialogue. Private invitations asking church leaders to participate in discussion had failed. A public request was the only recourse.

More vituperative critics, such as Joseph T. Gill, a writer for the ultra-right-wing paper *The Wanderer*, declared that Margaret Traxler through her "espousal of what the Church knows to be the absolute abomination of abortion" has become "excommunicated from the Catholic Church."

It was easy enough to dismiss extremists such as Gill. It was harder to ignore the criticism from within their own communities. The leaders of Margaret's order decided to hold a vote to decide whether she should be dismissed. Margaret was deeply distraught. She was used to such actions from the clergy, but not from her own sisters. Her supporters won, but she would never again feel the same about her community.

"I always thought they tolerated me and I found this was not true," she said. "The sisters who opposed us didn't understand the kind of world from which we spoke. I know people thought I was very strident, but when they got to know me, they saw I had no venom for anyone. I forgave all. I wanted to be reconciled with all. The poor women in this world had converted me to much more militancy. I did not intend, and neither did Donna, to show a blatant stridency. But sometimes, as Flannery O'Connor says, for those who are nearly deaf you have to shout. And for those who are nearly blind you have to draw large pictures. I got to the point where I didn't follow my religious order as clearly as God's call.

"Donna's community was different. The fact that they allowed her to stay in charge of CCW and NCAN showed they were saying, 'Follow your heart. Follow the Holy Spirit as you hear it.' "

In reality the response in Donna's own community was mixed. "There were sisters who said they didn't like it when I used the community name in a newspaper article," she said. "They thought I should have consulted with them. But few of the letters were nasty. Most of the sisters showed a real caring and loving concern. Some of the sisters said, 'I pray for you. I put this in the hands of God.' A lot of them wouldn't have signed the ad. But they have come through by saying to me, 'We think it is wrong that the Vatican has come down on you. You are important to us and we want you as a member of our community.' I would say there were about thirty Dominican women who would have put their bodies and souls on the line for me. They said, 'If you're dismissed, I'm dismissed.' My sister, Joyce, and my brother, Bill, also supported me from the start."

The repercussions for the signers continued. In Los Angeles, Catholic Social Services asked Catholic agencies not to send women to the House of Ruth, a battered women's shelter run by Sister Judy Vaughan. (Ironically the publicity surrounding the incident prompted more women to come to the shelter and increased donations.) In Nebraska a church women's group was denied use of a Catholic church to hear a lecture by Sister Marjorie Tuite. (Months later she died of cancer, an illness her friends believe was exacerbated by the stress.) In New York the archdiocese pressured a campus ministers' group to cancel a talk by Sister Jeannine Gramick. Margaret Traxler said that funding from six groups for her programs to help women in prison "dried up" after she signed the ad.

Donna and Margaret were determined not to let their critics intimidate them. On the afternoon of January 22 they celebrated the thirteenth anniversary of the Supreme Court's *Roe v. Wade* decision legalizing abortion, by picketing the offices of Joseph Scheidler's Pro-Life Action League. An anti-abortion activist, Scheidler had been arrested for harassing women at abortion clinics.

He taunted the women with his musical bullhorn as they passed.

"There's Donna Quinn, the pro-abortion nun," he announced to passersby. "She's out of the Catholic church."

On August 21, 1985, Donna decided to take her case to the top.

Wearing a white-and-blue-striped cotton dress—and a black armband—Donna walked up the steps of Chicago's Holy Name Cathedral. She smiled as she passed a group of three dozen protesters gathered outside. They carried the signs she had helped letter that morning: WOMEN WILL NOT DROWN IN THE HOLY SEE. I'M ALL POPED OUT. REPRODUCTIVE RIGHTS FOR ALL WOMEN. She waved to her friend's daughter, Katie, a towhaired seven-year-old, already a veteran of women's rallies. High above her head, Katie held Donna's favorite poster: WE WANT A CHURCH FOR OUR DAUGHTERS.

Inside, some one hundred priests and six hundred nuns filled the pews. Nuns in ankle-length wool habits and long black veils. Nuns in knee-length polyester habits and short white veils. Nuns in dresses. And nuns in pants. They had come to hear Jean Jerome Cardinal Hamer, the Belgian Dominican prefect of the Vatican's Congregation for Religious and Secular Institutes.

None of the twenty-four signers had ever met Hamer in person. Despite Paula's and Margaret's skepticism, Donna felt hopeful. She would no longer be one of the faceless nuns who had signed the ad. Hamer was a Dominican and she would talk to him as a fellow Dominican, just as Saint Catherine had approached Gregory XI. Donna would tell him about the victims of rape and incest she had met in shelters. She would talk to him about the pain of choosing to terminate a pregnancy. She would invite him to visit a shelter. She would ask for dialogue.

Donna took a seat in the back pew. She watched the cardinal as he walked to the altar. Dressed in full regalia, he was an imposing figure, a large, balding man who reminded her of Yul Brynner. This was as close as she had ever gotten to a representative of the Vatican. Hamer was the pope's right-hand man.

After his sermon the cardinal greeted the hundreds of nuns who had lined up to meet him. She strained to hear what Hamer was saying. He suggested to one sister that the pink suit she wore was too bright. Didn't she have something a bit more subdued?

When Donna's turn came, she walked slowly to the front of the room. As she reached Hamer, someone from the audience snapped a picture of the two of them. Startled by the flash, Hamer glared at the petite woman with curly brown hair who stood before him.

He recognized her immediately. "You, you," he stuttered, pointing at her. "You organized the demonstration out front." Surprised by his outburst, Donna stared dumbly at the cardinal. She had not organized the demonstration. Within a few seconds she regained her composure and began reciting the simple statement she had prepared. "I am a Dominican and I love my community," she told him.

"You are not a good Dominican," he replied. "If you love your community, you had better do something about that ad you signed." Murmurs went through the line of women behind Donna.

"Secondly," she continued, "I work with women and children who are victims of rape and incest."

"If you work with women and children," Hamer interrupted, "you had better work at getting your situation resolved."

"Will you dialogue with the signers?" Donna asked softly.

"I'll give you dialogue," he said angrily. "You come to Rome. You'll get dialogue."

Stunned, Donna turned and walked away. When she faltered, another sister held her by the arm. She couldn't believe it. He was a Dominican just like she was. And he hadn't heard a word she said.

"Well, what did you expect?" Paula asked her afterward.

"I don't know," said Donna. "I thought a personal approach would work. I really thought he would listen to me. Just this once I wanted it to be different. I always say I'm working for the next generation, but that's bullshit. I want to see some changes now.

"Is that too much to expect?" she asked Paula plaintively. "I want to see some change for myself."

On August 25, 1985, Hamer softened his stance, probably because of the public outcry on behalf of the signers. The Cardinal said that the nuns could have their cases "resolved" if they would "clarify" their positions and indicate adherence to the teachings of the Church on abortion and if they would not advocate abortion publicly. The Vatican, it seemed, just wanted the incident to go away.

The process of internal "dialogue" was shrouded in

mystery. Hamer would not correspond directly with the signers. Rather he wrote to the leaders of their communities. Some signers never even saw the letters that went back and forth on their behalf.

The sisters were called to meet with their superiors to come up with statements clarifying their positions. "I told our president that I was pro-choice," said Donna. "I told her that I had deep feelings on the subject of abortion and that I would not be silenced, nor would I stop my work. I would not sign any communication that went back to Rome, but I clarified my position to the president and thus to members of my religious community. The most I could say was that I did not promote abortion. I didn't go around saying that it's a great thing and everyone should try one."

In some cases sisters signed vaguely worded statements. In others superiors sent letters on behalf of the sisters to Rome. Most of the sisters' so-called clarifications seemed to appease Rome. On October 25, Hamer "resolved" the cases of four Sisters of Charity in New Jersey. Two unidentified nuns were also resolved. It was unclear to the signers, however, why these six nuns got Rome's stamp of approval.

But the women were not going to sit idly by while Hamer pondered the merits of their statements. They wanted to take a unified stand. On December 19, 1985, the signers met in Convent Station, New Jersey, with the leaders of their communities to discuss strategies. "It was beautiful because we pulled together," said Donna. "We made a clear pact that if one of us was dismissed, we would all be dismissed."

By late February nine nuns had been informed that their cases were closed. "My case is closed, but I'm not sure what that means," one nun commented.

Donna's and Margaret's cases were cleared soon afterward without much fanfare. They did not, however, view it as an occasion to celebrate. They had asked for dialogue and they were answered with an arbitrary decree from on high. "The bishops are not their own men," said Margaret bitterly. "They are minions of Rome. Naturally they are not going to enter the dialogue with any intelligent motive. They just have to repeat like robots what the line of Rome is." Besides, they did not consider the matter closed until all the nuns were cleared.

By late March only eleven signers had not been "cleared." Given the secrecy that had surrounded the correspondence between the religious orders and Rome, it was uncertain why the Vatican had not closed the cases of these eleven sisters. In her discussions with her superior, Donna had not backed down on her call for dialogue or on her pro-choice stance. Had the superiors of the "cleared" nuns simply done a better job of finessing their statements in letters to Rome? Was this merely a game of semantics?

The Vatican stunned the eleven sisters when it announced that it was sending a papal delegation to talk with them. Among those who saw the Vatican entourage were Donna's friend, Barbara Ferraro, and Patricia Hussey, both Sisters of Notre Dame de Namur, who ran Covenant House, a shelter for the homeless in Charleston, West Virginia. At the meeting they rejected the delegation's request that they sign a statement saying that they adhered to the Church's teaching. Like Donna, based on their experience with abused women, they maintained that abortion could be a moral choice.

The leadership of the Sisters of Notre Dame de Namur issued a press release criticizing the sisters' "nonnegotiable" position and proposed a "process of clarification" that included dialogue. But the sisters did not want to talk with their leadership until they knew they were going to be cleared by Rome, and they asked that the rest of the congregation be included in any discussions about abortion.

Later that month Hamer complicated the matter when he claimed that the Vatican had accepted public declarations of adherence to Catholic doctrine on abortion from twenty-two of the twenty-four nuns. Donna was furious. She and ten other sisters issued a statement asserting that Hamer had misrepresented their stand on abortion in an attempt to "pressure and isolate Barbara and Patricia." At first the Sisters of Notre Dame resisted Vatican pressure to force the nuns out of the order. By the following June, however, the order began the dismissal process.

Although the leaders of Catholics for Free Choice celebrated Barbara and Patricia as heroines, some sisters found their actions more divisive than courageous. Two nun signers, Margaret Traxler and Jeannine Gramick, wrote, in an NCAN newsletter, that Barbara and Patricia were following a male model of dissent by failing to dialogue with their community. Communication with one's congregation, they argued, was as essential to religious life as the toleration of dissent. The two sisters were stung by the criticism. They maintained that they *had* communicated their position, both to their leadership and to Rome.

By June 1988 the leaders of the Sisters of Notre Dame backed down. They sent the two sisters a letter calling their actions irresponsible to the community, but said the dismissal was halted. The sisters celebrated at a press conference in Washington.

"You can be publicly pro-choice and still remain a nun," they told the crowd.

The following month, however, Barbara and Patricia submitted their letters of resignation. The Vatican released them from their vows. Donna was distraught when she heard the news. "I felt a great sadness. I thought that we were all in this together, and now two of us were gone."

If she had it to do over again, Donna would have handled the process differently. She would have insisted on corresponding with Rome directly; she would have encouraged the religious communities to work more closely with the laity. But the important thing, she believed, was that the nuns had emerged victorious.

"The irony was that Rome was forced to do what it had asked us to do," she said. "They wanted us to retract our statements and we had refused. Now Rome had to retract its threat to dismiss us. We were still nuns and we would still advocate a woman's right to choose. The process had been far from perfect, but it was the first time that communities of religious women had stood up to Rome together. In solidarity we had won."

She came away from the experience more committed than ever to staying in religious life. "I really learned what *sister* meant when Sinsinawa Dominicans came out not only to show support but to put themselves on the line with me. I'll never forget their loyalty. Whatever happens to nuns, this kind of sisterhood must survive."

VI

Two years later I returned to Chicago to see Donna's latest project, the fruit of twenty years of labor. "This is it," she said proudly as she parked her Toyota in front of a Victorian house next to a Methodist church on Chicago's North Side. "Welcome to the Susanna Wesley Women's Center."

The three-story building was painted a vibrant shade of blue, a cross between turquoise and teal. Some neighbors had complained that the touch of blue was an eyesore in a neighborhood partial to gray and beige. But to Donna it was a thing of beauty.

"This is just what we needed," said Donna as we toured room after room of the sprawling house. "A real place to meet, a place to strategize, to counsel women, to hold coffeehouses. Every week we hold liturgies in the downstairs living room to celebrate our lives together. People are looking for community in life. It's something that nuns have learned we can share with other women. At our coffeehouse on Saturday a young woman said that this was the first place she could ever come out and say she was a lesbian. If nothing else, we have provided a safe place where women can come and tell their stories. This is what Women-Church is all about."

Chicago Catholic Women rents the house for a nominal fee from the Methodist church. It is named after the eighteenth-century English lay preacher Susanna Wesley, the mother of the founder of Methodism, John Wesley. "She would lead up to two hundred friends in prayer in her kitchen," Donna told me. "The men wanted her to go to the church, but Susanna said, 'If you can't pray in your own home, where can you pray?'" CCW shares the house with several other women's organizations, including a Catholic group that works for gay and lesbian rights and another that represents women and children with AIDS.

Donna showed me her new office, a replica of her

old one, but embellished with a few more photographs and posters. Only the light-up Vatican was missing. A pope in the window no longer made her laugh.

She handed me the newsletter describing a new activity, the Eldercare Project. After visiting a senior citizen center located a block from the Saint Martin de Porres House of Hope, Donna had an idea: Why not bring together the young women at the shelter and the seniors from the center?

"I thought, Wouldn't it be great if the poor young and the poor old helped each other? A new kind of community. Young women with strong arms and legs could do the cleaning, cooking, shopping, and laundry for the seniors. And the seniors could give the young women the wisdom that only comes with age. Many of the seniors had been single mothers growing up in the inner city. Some had been prostitutes. I thought they'd have a lot to teach the young ones."

Donna received a grant to pay six young women to work at the center two days a week in two-month cycles. (Mothers pay other women at the shelter five dollars to care for their children during the day.) The program includes an eight-hour training session for the young women on the needs of the elderly, from nutrition to sex. At the end of each eight-week cycle the women assess their new job skills. If they are interested in applying for positions as aides for the elderly, they write résumés and submit job applications.

"We also have a party at the end of each session," said Donna. "One time we went to a soul-food restaurant. The last group I took to the Sinsinawa Dominican motherhouse for a weekend. These women are so street smart that within a few hours they had checked out every place on the grounds. They read each gravestone at the cemetery and asked me questions about the nuns' lives. They talked to everyone, including the kitchen staff. By the end of the weekend I was anxious to get home. But they wanted to stay. They said they loved the peace and quiet."

Later that afternoon we drove to the Saint Martin de Porres House of Hope. Donna walked around the shelter announcing her arrival.

"There's Donna," a woman told her friend. "Talk to her if you want to work."

A petite woman wearing a plastic shower cap approached Donna. "You want to work?" Donna asked.

"Yeah," she replied shyly. "I'm pregnant, but only two months."

"We've never had a pregnant woman in the program. Do you feel well enough to clean?" Donna thought for a moment. "I guess most women clean when they're pregnant. Tell Sister Connie you'd like to sign up for the next training session."

Six women gathered in the dining room with their mops and buckets. We walked a block to the seniors' home, a twelve-story housing project built in the mid-sixties. Inside, the halls were dark and dingy, filled with the scent of ammonia. Several women and men sat in the lounge watching television and playing cards.

"Hi, Zelda," a woman in a wheelchair called out.

"Hi, Mrs. Jones. I'll be visiting this afternoon."

The young women signed in at the front desk and walked down the hall to Bertha Noble's room.

"Come in, come in, darlings!" she greeted them.

At ninety-five Bertha Noble is the matron of the seniors' home. In her floral housecoat she holds court in a chair by the window. Her room is warm and bright, filled with photographs of nieces and nephews at assorted stages in their lives. Religious plaques decorate the walls.

"Put your coats on the bed," she instructed. One by one the women came over and kissed her smooth, unlined face.

"Hi, Miss Bertha, I missed you," said Zelda.

The women dispersed with their buckets. Bertha motioned for Donna and me to sit down beside her.

"You know, I love this project, baby," Bertha said. "I love these people. I was an LPN for twenty-two years. Before that I was a maid. I'd scrub your floors. I'd do anything. I've been through many hardships. I've been barefoot in the wintertime. But I never gave up.

"I remember when Donna told me the girls were going to come here and clean. I said it would mean the world to me that the girls come here. I'm in a wheelchair. I have a bad heart. The doctor don't want me to deal with the stove. He thinks I'll fall into the flame.

"I talk to the girls when I can. I say I'm their momma. Sometimes they may go in the wrong direction. I tell them to obey the rules and regulations at the shelter. I say, 'Remember, they took you and your children off the street and they didn't have to.' "

Bertha looked up and saw one of the young women, Carla, standing in the doorway.

"Hi, Miss Bertha," said Carla weakly. "May I come in?"

"Baby, you can always come in. You're new, aren't you? Come in and sit down. Want a Coke?"

"Can I have a cigarette?" Carla asked.

"Sure, darling."

"We started cleaning that nasty apartment," said Carla, grimacing. "We just ran into the biggest roach. I have a weak stomach. I think I picked the wrong job."

"Listen, baby, I used to have a weak stomach too," Bertha interjected.

"It's just a mess," Carla continued. "Garbage. Dead rats. Someone could have stopped this mess before it started. You know what I'm saying?"

"Now, listen, sweetie," said Bertha. "That's what could have happened. But it's not what happened. You just have to face it. That's life. Someday I'll tell you about my life."

Donna nodded approvingly.

"But it hurts my heart," said Carla, pointing to her chest.

"Don't let it hurt," said Bertha. "You ask God to give you strength."

"I know," said Carla. "If you let it get to you even one day, you fall into that trap."

"Now you're talking," said Bertha, slapping the arm of her chair for emphasis. "Look, honey, you remember, you're always welcome here. I love you and I want you to love me."

"I think I do already, Miss Bertha," said Carla. She leaned over to hug her new mentor.

Bertha turned to Donna. "Sister Donna, she loves me, and you know how I like that."

Donna smiled broadly and walked over to the bed to grab her coat. "I've got to run to a meeting, Miss

Bertha. Next week I'll bring you pictures from the party. I have some great ones of you singing." She hugged her tightly.

"Good-bye, Sister Donna," said Bertha, kissing her on the cheek. "God bless you, darling."

"God bless you, darling," said Donna. And she walked away beaming, like a priest just blessed by her bishop.

CHAPTER 4

HOUSE OF THE SPIRIT:

A CONTEMPLATIVE FINDS

HER VOICE

We have made a space to house our spirit, to give form to our dreams.

JUDY CHICAGO

Catherine O'Reilly celebrated with friends and family at her last going-away party. After attending Ohio State and teaching first grade for five years, she decided at twenty-six to change the course of her life. In a few days she would be trading in her blue jeans for the brown habit of the cloister.

It was 1968, and the rules of enclosure were strict. Once Catherine entered the convent, she could never leave except to go to the hospital, vote, or attend an occasional religious meeting. The only contact with her father and stepmother would be fingertips touching through a metal grille separating the nuns from the rest of the world.

Despite the party decorations the guests' attempts at good wishes sounded more like condolences. "You've always been so happy," a cousin told her. "I guess with your temperament you could be happy anywhere." But as the drinks flowed, the comments become less guarded, until a young man lashed out at the guest of honor. "What in God's name made you decide to do this?" he shouted, grabbing her by the shoulders. "You've had a good education; you're a fine teacher. You're throwing your life away. You might as well be dead."

"I was so devastated, I left the room and cried," Sister Catherine recalled sixteen years later. "So many people don't understand the contemplative life because there are no tangible results. Some people think we're here because we're escaping from life or are incapable of loving men. Others think we're holy women who spend all our time kneeling in prayer. They don't understand us either."

Catherine is one of some two thousand Roman Catholic contemplative nuns in the United States who devote their lives to the search for God through prayer. It is not a self-centered meditation. She believes that her union with God contributes to the salvation of all people and that her prayers for humanity touch the lives of the suffering everywhere. In an earlier century she might have been respected as a religious woman with a rare calling. Today she is often viewed as a rebel in a secular society that values action over contemplation. Her way of life sets her apart in a world where even many Catholics dismiss the cloister as an archaic institution and the nuns inside as weak women with an unhealthy attraction to solitude.

The time-worn image of contemplative nuns as escapists, spurned lovers, or naïve waifs has little basis in reality today. It takes more than a botched love affair to lure women in their twenties and thirties to the cloister. For many, choosing to leave behind family and friends and the possibility of marriage, children, and worldly careers is a long, difficult, and frequently painful decision. And opting to stay in the cloister after all romantic notions about life have been stripped away is tougher still.

Some women elect to enter highly traditional orders as "brides of Christ," to live behind grilles, to walk barefoot and practice penances, such as self-flagellation, that date back to the Middle Ages. A few seek greater solitude in hermitages. But most of those who choose the life today gravitate toward orders whose broad interpretation of the guidelines set out by the Second Vatican Council have freed members of the hair shirt habits and total silence of the past.

The majority of the 198 cloisters in the United States are offshoots of convents founded in Europe during the Middle Ages. The largest and best-known order—about eight hundred sisters in sixty-five convents—is the Discalced (shoeless) Carmelites, founded in Spain in 1562 and brought to the United States in 1790. There are at least a dozen other major American cloistered orders, including the Poor Clares, the Sacramentines, the Passionists, the Cistercians, the Redemptoristines, and branches of the Dominicans—the Visitation Nuns and the Benedictines. While other religions also have cloistered communities, their numbers are far fewer.

Until the 1960s nuns left the convent only in emergencies. Local doctors and dentists made house calls. Extern sisters, not part of the cloister, greeted visitors, answered the telephone, deposited checks, and shopped for food. The only people allowed to see the cloistered sisters were their immediate families and priests.

All contemplatives wore heavy wool habits even in summer. Some wore sandals in the winter. Rules of silence were rarely broken outside the daily hour of recreation. The mother superior or prioress was the unquestioned leader of the community. The sisters had to ask permission for everything from taking a bar of soap to staying up an extra hour. Mortification was considered an essential part of the life. Common penances included frequent fasting, kneeling during meals, and praying for extended periods with arms outstretched in the shape of a crucifix.

After the Second Vatican Council decreed that excessive mortifications and "outdated customs be done away with," many communities like Catherine's decided it was time for a change.

Saint Thérèse of Lisieux, a nineteenth-century Carmelite, described contemplatives as the "heart of the Church." She believed that their prayers were a source of strength for all Catholics. One nun's silent communion with God had a ripple effect throughout the Church.

The prayers begin before dawn in Catherine's cloister. For centuries the routine has been structured around the Divine Office (the Liturgy of the Hours), recited in the early morning, mid and late afternoon, and evening to praise God and sanctify the day. Some sisters still get up in the middle of the night to pray. Most think their early awakening is penance enough.

When the chapel bells ring at five-thirty A.M., Catherine pulls her patchwork quilt over her head to catch a few more minutes of shut-eye. She sleeps on a hard bed made of a board laid across two sawhorses and a thin mattress. After Vatican II questioned the necessity of extreme austerity in religious life, the other nuns switched to thick innerspring mattresses. Catherine kept her old bed. She found it comfortable.

Her cell is sparsely furnished with an oak dresser, a

small mahogany desk, and a ladder-back chair. On one wall hangs a plain wooden cross; on another is a framed reproduction of *Starry Night* by Van Gogh, her favorite painter.

She crawls out of bed at five forty-five and shuffles down the hall to the bathroom, where she washes her face and puts in her contact lenses. She dresses quickly in a simple blouse and skirt, then goes downstairs to the kitchen for coffee, orange juice, and toast.

Silence is observed in the convent throughout the day, except during meals and the hour following dinner. In the old days cloistered nuns scribbled notes or used sign language rather than break the silence. Today the sisters speak softly when necessary.

At quarter after six Catherine joins her sisters in the choir, a small room opening onto an airy A-frame chapel with oak beams and skylights. On one wall of the chapel a local artist has painted a mural of Christ in the stations of the cross. A plain wooden cross hangs above the altar. Next to the pulpit are two large stone vases filled with flowers from the monastery garden. The sweet odor scents the air.

Until the mid-1960s a metal grille separated the choir from the public chapel. Behind the grille hung a heavy curtain that concealed the nuns from the local men and women who came to the chapel for Mass. The only hint of the sisters' presence was the sound of their soprano voices emanating from the choir. After Vatican II the nuns took down the grille. They anchored it in the ground behind the convent. There it serves as a trellis and a reminder of their past life.

Catherine takes her seat in one of the folding chairs arranged in a circle. The eight nuns under age fifty sit tall and erect. The older sisters lower their heads in prayer, their hands clasped in front of them. Many have rejected the round-shouldered posture and downward gaze they were taught in their first year. Still, it remains etched in their bones. Bowing their heads is as natural as breathing.

Promptly at half past six the sisters begin the morning portion of the Divine Office, composed of psalms, hymns, scriptural readings, and the writings of the saints. The nuns' voices blend in perfect harmony as they sing a hymn written by Sister Mary Ellen, a wiry blond-haired nun who accompanies them on her guitar.

At seven Father Mike, a lanky high school principal, begins Mass. The sisters picked Mike after interviewing half a dozen priests. His simple homily is filled with anecdotes about his teenage students. His wry sense of humor appeals to the nuns, who laugh out loud during his stories.

After the homily the mood turns solemn as the sisters recite the intercessory prayers contemplative nuns have uttered for hundreds of years on behalf of the suffering throughout the world. One at a time they rise and pray aloud.

"I pray for my sister-in-law, who is having surgery today," whispered Monica.

"God, hear our prayers," the chorus of nuns answered.

"I pray for Mrs. Peterson, who wrote to us about her troubled marriage," said Carlota.

"God, hear our prayers."

"I pray for peace in the Mideast," said Catherine.

"God, hear our prayers."

They sit in silence for a moment and then walk in procession into the chapel, forming a circle around the altar. The handful of men and women in the congregation come forward to receive communion. Afterward the sisters sing a Gregorian chant. They join hands and wish one another, "Peace."

As Catherine stands in the chapel, her usually animated face is calm; her body quiet.

"Catherine doesn't move a muscle when she prays," Sister Carlota, an impish Mexican nun, whispered. "When she sits outside, the chipmunks walk right up to her."

"I don't try to be Zen-like," Catherine told me later. "It's just my natural way to be."

The sisters devote at least one hour in the morning and evening to private contemplation. Sister Monica prays in the chapel. Sister Alice prays on her bicycle as she rides around the neighborhood. Catherine usually prays in her room, sitting or kneeling on her Mexican prayer rug. "We don't know exactly how prayer works," she said, "but it's an energy that affects all living things."

Her method is free-form. "I just sit quietly," she said. "Sometimes something Mike said in a homily or a line from the Scripture will come to mind, but I'm listening more than talking; I'm ready to receive. It would be hard for me to pray methodically like a Jesuit priest. They start out at one point in their meditation and try to reach another. I'm not drawn to that. I try to have more spontaneity in my prayer life.

"I used to feel a lack of abandonment to God when I prayed. I was never just 'being.' Now when I pray, I try to leave everything behind. Things still distract me. I was the community cook for six months, and recipes would keep popping into my mind. But eventually I learned not to become upset by distractions. I just think about whatever is bothering me for a moment and then I let it go.

"Prayer is almost like an undressing, a stripping of the known to go to the unknown. It's an invitation to surrender. When you make yourself that vulnerable, there is always growth.

"Sometimes I'm so happy during prayer, it's like an overflow. I can't even express my prayer in coherent words. Some people call it praying in tongues. I used to think, Am I making this up? Am I bringing this on? I felt better after I read a passage in Saint Teresa of Ávila's autobiography. She wrote about God, 'I wish I could be all tongues praising you.' It struck a chord in me.

"When I first came to the monastery, I always felt God's presence. It was like a relationship growing in love. Now I go through dry periods, when I come to my hour of prayer and wonder where God is. I feel nothing. One hour feels like one hundred. I used to get depressed and frustrated. I thought I could be doing something more useful than just sitting for an hour. But now I look at these times as a test of faith. I know my motive is pure, because I am giving love without expecting anything in return."

Saint John of the Cross, a sixteenth-century priest, wrote about "the dark night of the soul," when believers doubt the existence of God. For a contemplative nun doubt is particularly devastating. If prayer has no meaning, her life's work has been for naught.

While Catherine has counseled her sisters through agonizing periods of doubt, she has not yet experienced what she calls a complete test of nakedness. But she has known the frustration of not seeing tangible results from her prayer.

"Prayer can be very painful. A friend who is living as a hermit says that when you go deep inside of yourself, your prayer is touching the world and you can feel the world's pain. Sometimes I get so discouraged because I see no end to that pain. I pray and pray, and wars don't end. I think about the violence in the Mideast and I feel so helpless.

"I feel helpless when I pray for my father's health and he doesn't get better. I ask God, 'Why does my father have to suffer so much?' At his age he should be relaxing and enjoying life.

"I don't understand all the suffering. It's a complete mystery to me. Sometimes I get discouraged and feel that everything is going backward. But then I realize that my vision is just so narrow. God must have something better in mind."

The cloistered nun's career is contemplation. Her work is prayer. But praying for a living is hardly rewarding financially. So, like poets who moonlight, the sisters spend part of their day earning money for the community. Most sisters devote three hours in the morning and three in the evening to their jobs. "Everyone does as much as she can," said Catherine. "We don't try to push anyone to equalize the load."

Traditionally, contemplative nuns baked altar breads and sewed vestments, tasks that were conducive to contemplation but not particularly lucrative. They relied on subsidies from the Church and donations from local parishioners with a fondness for contemplative life. Today many contemplative communities run cottage industries. Catherine and her sisters operate a small printing service. Her best friend, Alice, balances the books.

• • •

The two friends are a study in contrasts. Catherine, a stocky five feet five inches, prefers simple, wash-and-wear hairdos. Alice, a lanky five feet ten, ties her waist-length brown hair in an elaborate French knot. While Catherine's rapid speech is punctuated by laughter, Alice speaks slowly, enunciating each syllable. She values the few hours a day she spends conversing and considers each word carefully, pausing between thoughts. Like all contemplative nuns, she is not afraid of silence.

"Do you ever indulge in small talk with Catherine?" I asked.

"Oh, sure," said Alice, before pausing to consider the question. "Well, I don't know. We talk about people a lot. Is that small talk? It doesn't seem small to me. Sometimes Catherine and I talk too much. When we're driving to go shopping, she'll be talking and I'll have to say, 'Catherine, I need quiet now.' And we'll drive the rest of the way in silence. We try to get away by our-selves at least once a month to get some perspective on the community. Every Christmas we go on a shopping expedition. We hit all the used-clothes shops and then we treat ourselves to lunch. It's a tradition I love."

Catherine walked in with a plate of fruit and home-made oatmeal cookies. Asked what first attracted her to Alice, she squinted her eyes and scrutinized her friend. "Your seriousness has always appealed to me," she said. "I'm more easygoing than Alice, but I have a serious side too. We have a common feel for the life. I can relax when I'm with her. It's refreshing not to have to weigh my words. And I always know she'll tell me what she thinks."

Catherine smiled broadly. "Alice is very blunt. She holds nothing back. But to know Alice is to see she is very sensitive. I love talking with her during lunch. We pack a picnic basket or stay inside and listen to classical music."

The two women often discuss their daily hour of spiritual reading and their changing perceptions of God. "I am thinking more in terms of feminine images and the motherly aspects of God," said Catherine. "In so many aspects of my own life I've seen God's warmth and tenderness. My experience has been very different from Alice's. Saint John of the Cross talks about experiencing God in lightness or darkness, knowing versus unknowing. I experience God more in lightness. I talk to God as I would a close friend. It's a very personal relationship. Alice experiences God more in absence, as a mystery."

Alice grimaced. "My God is not impersonal!" she said emphatically. "That has awful connotations. It's more that my concept of God is inadequate at this point in my life. I don't know God. So my prayer now is being aware of the moment. That's why in good weather I pray on a bicycle. It's my traveling hermitage. I ride around in a five-mile circle and I never get bored with the beauty around me—the freedom and the fresh air. My concept of Jesus has been inadequate too. He is beyond my imagination of a person."

Catherine was quiet for a moment. "Alice is helping me become more aware of the mystery of God," she said. "But I have mixed feelings. This experience of God does seem more impersonal to me. I don't *know* God. But I feel God's love. During my week-long retreat in the cabin behind the convent, I read Jeremiah 31: 'I loved you with an age-old love.' It's a ripe feeling of complete acceptance. It's my foundation. Love for God, his love for us, my love for others is all one energy and one power."

Alice nodded. "It's not just meditation. I believe that prayer is a real force in the world. Maybe someday we'll be able to measure it, but that's not the point. I think that no matter how or where a person is praying, it does some good. It's obvious in our lives with other people. If you're surrounded by loving people, that's a life-giving environment. If you're surrounded by hate-filled people, it's destructive."

"We had a Quaker minister visit us," said Catherine, "and he said he could feel something perceptible in the atmosphere that was coming from our prayer life. Theologian Thomas Berry talks about an interconnectedness between all living things. If I have a rift with Alice, it won't just affect us, but all Creation."

Do a nun's prayers carry more weight than anyone else's?

"Oh, no," Catherine answered quickly. "I think that any person can exude the same kind of power and energy if they are living the life they were meant to be living."

II

Catherine was born in Louisville, Kentucky, in 1941, the only child of Ted and Anne O'Reilly. They lived in a two-family brownstone in a Slavic working-class neighborhood until Catherine was nine years old and they moved to the suburbs. Catherine adored her father, a supervisor at a local department store, a large, boisterous man, fond of parties and practical jokes. Her mother, small and soft-spoken, was more contemplative, and she cultivated this quality in her young daughter.

"Mom and I used to take walks together to a pond about a mile away from our house. We'd sit by the edge of the water and try not to make a sound. 'Shhh, Catherine,' Mom would say. 'Just be still and listen to the frogs.' I liked to be still. When I was four years old, I used to bring my red rug outside and place it next to a large rock. I'd sit there for hours with my hands clasped. I never thought I was praying. I liked to go to a certain spot and just be."

The most devout person in the O'Reilly household was Catherine's maternal grandmother, who lived in an efficiency apartment upstairs. Every morning Catherine would sit on the front porch waiting for her grandmother to return from Mass.

"When I saw my grandmother turn the corner, I'd race down the street to meet her. She was tall and so thin, her dresses hung on her. Her arms had no flab you could pull. But she was strong, and she had a wisdom about her, a foresight. Even though she lived with us, she was very independent and cooked her own meals. Every now and then she'd ask me to have dinner with her and I'd be so proud. I'd sit up straight in my chair. She was from Czechoslovakia and spoke little English, so we rarely talked. But I loved to just sit with her."

Catherine's early religious education was typical of the children in her neighborhood. She attended catechism classes and recited evening prayers with her mother. On Sundays and religious holidays the entire family went to Mass.

Her earliest idea of God was a paternal power watching over her. "He was somebody taking care of me. I also thought of God as a judge who kept track of all my sins. That used to scare me. I remember going to confession once and telling the priest, 'I've committed every sin there is.' He asked me when I had last been to confession. 'A week ago,' I said."

At age five Catherine began attending a parochial school run by the Sisters of Notre Dame. "I loved my first-grade teacher, Sister Mary Julianne. She was quiet and gentle. She had us each pick a day of the week to go to Mass, and I would go come hell or high water. I didn't think about my relationship with God much, but I said I would go, so I went. I continued to enjoy school until the fourth grade. I was terrified of Sister Dominic. She used to tell me I would go to hell if I didn't go to Mass. My mother tried to assure me that that wasn't true, but I was really frightened. They didn't talk about God as love in those days."

When she turned thirteen, Catherine's parents enrolled her in a girls' high school run by Ursuline sisters. "I hated it," she said, grimacing. "All the nuns were so old, they could hardly hear. In Latin class we would conjugate verbs, and the sister would keep time with her ruler. She used to come around the room and collect money for the missions, and I would say I didn't have any, not even a penny."

During her sophomore year Catherine's parents allowed her to transfer to the local public high school. Although she was shy around her male classmates, she enjoyed her newfound freedom. She tried out for cheerleading and made the squad. But she did not give up religion completely. To please her parents, she joined a school sodality group and was elected prefect. "That meant I was supposed to be an exemplary Catholic. I did go to church regularly, but it was all pretty automatic. I didn't yet have a deep personal relationship with God."

The following year family tragedy dampened what little religious spark Catherine felt. A few months after the death of her grandmother, Catherine discovered that her mother was ill. "One day I came home from school with some friends and found my mom vacuuming," Catherine recalls. "All of a sudden Mom froze. She said, 'Now, don't get excited, Catherine, but I can't move. Call the doctor.' I was so scared, I started crying. They rushed her to the hospital, where they found out that she had cancer. It had spread to the spinal column.

"When Mom came home from the hospital, she seemed okay. But she started teaching me more about the house. We'd be washing curtains and she'd say, 'Now, pay attention to this, Catherine, because you never know if I'm going to be here or not.' I'd say, 'Where will you be?' And she'd say, 'I just might be pushing up daisies from underground.' We never talked about death directly. She was only forty-nine years old. Perhaps she always had hope."

Her mother survived for another year. "When she died, I went into my room and closed the door. At first I felt as if it were a dream. I thought that you read about these things happening to other people. I was angry at God. How could he let this happen? My relatives all wanted to embrace me, but nobody's love could take her place."

At seventeen Catherine left home for the first time to attend Ohio State University. "As soon as I arrived on campus, I loved it," she said. "It was like another world. The atmosphere felt so good to me, probably because of the trauma I had been through after my mother's death."

Her closest friend was a quiet education major named Louisa. "Louisa was cool and kept a lot inside. But she talked with me. We'd go for long drives and sing in the car. Louisa loved music and she introduced me to Bach. She was also the only person I wasn't embarrassed to discuss religion with. She was Methodist and was always defending her faith. But occasionally she'd go to Mass with me, and she began to feel drawn to Catholicism."

Catherine continued going to church every Sunday throughout college, and for a brief period attended religious classes. But she was motivated more by a sense of obligation than spiritual fervor. She gave up religious instruction when she pledged a sorority. Even during Lent, which is supposed to be a penitential time, she went to college bars and parties.

"We had lots of sorority parties and I dated, but no one I intended to marry. I started seeing one fellow more than the others, but I stopped when I realized I was leading him on. Marriage wasn't a preoccupation of mine. Louisa once said to me, 'Maybe we'll end up old maids.' But I said, 'Oh, we'll meet somebody. There are plenty of men out there.' "

During her junior year Catherine left the campus for six months to teach at a public elementary school. She was certain that she had found her vocation. "I discovered that I had a natural facility for teaching, and I loved it. The students had such a sense of wonder and enthusiasm for learning. They never thought I was trying to put something over on them. I liked teaching art class the most. In Catholic school art class was very methodical. We had patterns to follow. I wanted the kids to be freer to express themselves. I taught them about painters and styles of painting. I'd say, 'Today we're going to paint in the style of Marc Chagall.' And we'd talk about his life and the colors he loved."

Catherine's teaching supervisor, Jill, an assistant superintendent of the public schools, became a close friend and adviser. "Jill was about twenty years older than I and a good mentor at that point in my life. She was a good listener and very caring. Perhaps I needed a mother figure after my own mother's death.

"Jill happened to be Catholic. We never talked about religion, but one day she was going to the Sacrament of Reconciliation, the confession before Christmas, and she invited me to come along. I told the priest that I had always been happy, but I knew in the back of my mind that there was more to life than the fun and frivolity of the sorority. I had always thought of God as a judge, but the priest talked of God in a more loving way."

After Catherine returned to school, she went back to see the same priest during her Easter vacation. "He was very welcoming and never judgmental. He gave me some basic books to read about doctrine. I told him I knew there was something gnawing inside of me, but I didn't know what. I just thought I was questioning the meaning of life. But I had no thought of entering a convent. Ironically that year a relative sent me a calendar made by the Poor Clares. I hid it from my sorority sisters. I didn't want them to think I was crazy."

Following graduation Catherine returned home to live with her father and his new wife. She taught first grade at a local public school and spent the summers attending the master's program in education at Fordham University. "I lived in a dorm in New York City and loved it. I went to all the theaters and museums I had always wanted to see."

When she received her master's degree, Catherine rewarded herself with a vacation. With Jill and two other women she traveled through Europe. She liked Spain best, particularly Ávila, the birthplace of Saint Teresa, who founded the Carmelite order of nuns. While the others went ahead, Catherine spent the entire day exploring Saint Teresa's monastery.

"I had no idea how I was going to catch up with my friends, but I didn't want to leave."

France was the next stop on the trip. "I remember standing in the hotel room getting ready to go to the Paris Opera to see a ballet. I was very excited. Chagall had just done the ceiling of the opera house and I couldn't wait to see it. But as I was getting dressed, my mood changed. I had my stocking halfway up my knee when I stopped all of a sudden and sat down on the bed. I thought to myself, 'What am I doing? What is my life all about?' Jill called in to me to hurry up. But I couldn't move. I felt paralyzed. Something intangible had struck me like a thunderbolt.

"I calmed down and finished getting dressed. But that feeling continued to come over me at the oddest moments. I began to realize that going places and having fun was not what my life was about. I felt as if I had been doing things automatically and not reflecting about life, about God."

When Catherine returned from Europe, she began to think about the possibility of religious life. "Sometimes when I was praying in church, I thought about becoming a nun, but I felt I had too much to lose. I didn't want to give up traveling, my social life, my family, and my career. I was making a good salary and I had just bought a blue Mustang. I thought to myself, Christ gave up his life, and I can't even give up my car. But I was still very attached to things. Also, I was very attached to men. At Fordham I dated a man I really liked. I avoided getting serious because I was thinking about becoming a nun, but I still wasn't ready to rule out the possibility of marriage."

The feeling of uneasiness persisted. "It was like a gnawing that wouldn't go away. I think there's a hunger in everyone that no person, job, or money can satisfy. A yearning for God. I began to crave more time for prayer, reflection, and quiet. I tried to pray before bed, but I always fell asleep."

Catherine considered joining the Peace Corps so she could combine a life of service and prayer, but the organization lacked the spiritual dimension she desired. "I also thought about making private vows and continuing to teach, but I didn't think I'd have enough time for contemplation. Finally I decided to look into teaching orders. I met a sister from a progressive teaching community and I went there to talk with them. I liked the sisters because they were their own women, and I took an application when I left. But I never mailed it. I'm an intuitive person and it just didn't feel right."

She planned to look into other teaching orders but got sidetracked when she visited a monastery of nuns.

"Jill used to go to their chapel to pray, and one day she invited me to go with her. I felt at home there immediately. I found it so peaceful that I started going there by myself to pray. It didn't bother me that the nuns inside lived behind a grille. That was a given in those days. I just loved the solitude."

She was still repelled by the prospect of giving up her secular freedom, yet the tension between her daily activities and her desire to immerse herself in a religious life was becoming unbearable.

"I couldn't stand being in limbo anymore. I felt I had to make some decision about my life. I didn't think,

Oh, now I'm going to give my life for the world. It was more like a drawing I couldn't resist. I understood what the prophet Hosea meant when he said, 'I'm going to lure her and lead her in the desert and speak to her heart.' "

"Eventually I called the prioress at the monastery and arranged for an interview. I was late for the appointment, which is unusual for me. It wasn't easy for me to go there. I met the prioress in the visitors' parlor, a large room divided in half by a grille. She asked me if I'd mind if the sixteen other sisters joined us, and I said all right.

"The sisters had taken down the black curtain behind the grille so I could see their faces. They had modified their habits and were eager to know what I thought of them. But I wasn't interested in discussing external changes. I wanted to know how they were implementing the reforms of Vatican II internally. I wanted to know how they interpreted the contemplative life in modern times.

"They asked me many questions about my life, and I tried to be very honest with them. Some of the sisters still tease me about something I told them during the interview. I said, 'I'm a very proud person. I want to whittle away my pride.' That struck them as very funny. I was emotionally drained after the interview. But a few days later I called and told them I wanted to go on with the interviewing process."

The prioress asked Catherine to make an appointment with a psychologist who specialized in determining whether applicants for religious life were emotionally stable. "The psychologist asked me lots of questions about my background," said Catherine. "Fortunately he decided I was a balanced person. Unfortunately he sent the bill for the visit to my house and my parents saw it. They must have wondered what I was up to. I hadn't told them I was thinking about entering a cloister because I was afraid that my father would have a heart attack. I didn't want any of my friends or family to know anything until I made a decision."

Next the prioress arranged an interview for Catherine with a priest at the church where she had been baptized. "I was so excited. I thought it would be like going back to my roots. But the priest was awful. He played devil's advocate the whole time. He said, 'Don't you think you'd serve the world better by being a teacher? Think of the lives you'd affect. Don't you feel that entering a cloister would be a cop-out after all the education you've had?' I said I felt a deep calling to the life and that through prayer I'd reach even more people. He said, 'You're doing this out of selfishness. All you care about is your own relationship with God.' I said that wasn't true. I spent the whole time refuting him. By the end of the interview I felt like a wrung-out dishrag. He recommended me with his blessing.

"Although I was angry at the priest, he made me confront my own motivation and reservations. In the end my biggest fear about entering did not involve enclosure. I accepted the fact that I would have to give up travel and my career, and I just looked at the grille as part of the package. It was celibacy. I've never felt above wanting to be loved completely and exclusively by one person. It's a human longing. I told another priest before I entered that the hardest thing for me to give up would be my relationship with men. And he said, 'What kind of a gift to God would it be if it wasn't hard?'

"I'd like to say that I wanted to enter the cloister because I was seeking God, but I don't know. There are so many unconscious motives for entering. You realize after you've been here awhile that no one's motives are completely pure. But I felt a calling to this life that just wouldn't go away. I felt a need for solitude and time for reflection."

After the interviewing process was completed, it was up to the sisters to decide whether to accept Catherine.

"They work very slowly. They wanted to give both of us time to think. When I hadn't heard from them in several months, I signed a contract with the Louisville public schools for the next year. Then one day in July 1968 I was in my blue Mustang heading out the driveway for a vacation in New England, when my father came out to tell me that the prioress was on the telephone. I ran inside and grabbed the phone.

" 'Catherine,' the prioress said, 'we'd like you to come.' "

A few days later Catherine broke the news to her father. "I came home from Mass one morning and found my dad home alone. I said, 'Dad, what would you think if I told you I was entering a convent?' He said, 'You mean the teaching order across the street?' And I said, 'No, a monastery.' He was quiet for some time. It was hard for him, I could tell. Finally he said, 'If that's what you want, if that's what will make you happy, Catherine.' But he was very sad. In those days you could only see your immediate family once a month in the parlor room with the grille between you. I think it helped him to discuss the matter with the priest who was my spiritual director. But it took him a long while to get used to the idea."

Several of her friends thought she was joking when she talked about entering a cloister. "I told a group of them one night at a bar downtown. Some started laughing. It was my fault. They'd had a lot to drink and I'd caught them off guard. But later my close friends told me it wasn't such a surprise after all, considering my nature.

"Jill was ambivalent. She had introduced me to the monastery and felt somewhat responsible for my decision. She admitted to me that she had mixed feelings because she thought we wouldn't have the same kind of relationship, and she wanted me to teach at her school. Some of the parents of my first-grade students reacted very badly. I came home one day and found my father sitting on the couch looking white. A mother had called up and said, 'How can you let your daughter do such a terrible, terrible thing?'

"But I think my mother would have been happy for me. And my grandmother too. I think she would have been proud. The one person who really understood the depth of my vocation was my best friend from college, Louisa."

III

Contemplative nuns were once revered as women of uncommon devotion and mystical power. Among the best known were Saint Clare of Assisi, mother of the Poor Clares, and Saint Teresa of Ávila, founder of the Discalced Carmelites. As with the stories of most saints, it is difficult to separate fact from fiction; their visions are the stuff of legend.

Born in 1194, Clare of Assisi grew into a woman "of a beautiful countenance." Her parents wanted her to marry a rich suitor who would secure the family's reputation. But Clare was less interested in potential husbands than in a preacher named Francis, who had left a wealthy family for an itinerant life of poverty and prayer. She conversed with Francis for a year before deciding to abandon her family and follow him. In 1212 she moved into the church of San Damiano. Her sister joined her; other young women of Assisi followed.

Like Francis, she called on her followers to imitate Christ, depending on divine providence for their needs:

> This is that sublimity of the highest poverty, which had made you, my dearest sisters, heirs and queens of the kingdom of heaven: poor in goods but exalted in virtue.

Although the sisters brought in some income from spinning and making altar linen, they relied primarily on alms collected by the friars.

In 1215 the Fourth Lateran Council required all new religious movements to adopt an established rule. Instead of choosing a conventional one, Clare asked Pope Innocent III to grant her community "the Privilege of Poverty." No one had ever desired the right to possess nothing; Innocent obliged this young woman's strange request. Two years later, however, the cardinal-archbishop of Ostia took it upon himself to write a rule for Clare's "Poor Ladies," which allowed them to own property. Without consulting the sisters, he declared the community part of the Benedictine family. Clare rejected this new rule, composing her own modeled on the one Saint Francis provided his friars.

Although it is likely that Clare would have preferred to follow Francis and his friars on their journeys, it was the nun's lot to remain in the cloister. Mystics, however, were not confined by the four walls of the convent, and like many women before her, Clare made a name for herself through her visions. She was credited with saving Assisi from the wrath of the Holy Roman emperor, Frederick II, through the power of her prayers.

A witness for Clare's canonization recounted the story: After Frederick II was excommunicated in 1240, he brought Saracen troops to Assisi and allowed them to run wild throughout the city. The men climbed the walls of the Poor Ladies' monastery and invaded their cloister. Clare asked her sisters to bring her the Blessed Sacrament in a small box; she prostrated herself before it and prayed: "Lord, look upon thy poor servants, for I cannot guard them."

"I will always defend thee," a voice cried out.

"Lord, be pleased also to defend this city," she pleaded.

"The city will suffer many dangers," the voice told her, "but will be defended." The troops departed without harming the nuns.

While Clare was known as a generous abbess who treated her nuns equally and looked after their needs, she was notorious for neglecting her own. Although she discouraged her sisters from extreme asceticism, she fasted four days a week and slept every night on the cold floor. She suffered a particular illness for twenty-seven years before taking to her bed in 1253. Just two days before her death she learned that her rule had finally been approved. According to her sisters, she kissed a copy of her rule and died peacefully, leaving fifty Poor Ladies behind.

Saint Teresa's story begins three centuries later. Devastated by the death of her mother in childbirth, a thirteen-year-old Teresa prayed to the Virgin Mary. "I went in my distress to an image of our Lady and with many tears besought her to be a mother to me." A beautiful young woman, fond of adornments, she was so popular with men that her father forbade them from coming into the house. After her sister married, Teresa was sent to an Augustinian convent to protect her honor. She disliked the excessive penances, but she thought convent life would be preferable to marriage to a man she might not love.

At twenty-one she left her father's home permanently to join the Carmelite Convent of the Incarnation in Ávila, Spain. The women's order was already a century old. While the Carmelite friars ascribe their origin to Elijah, who is said to have founded a community of hermits on Mount Carmel, the first women didn't become affiliated with the order until 1452.

The order grew rapidly, attracting daughters of the aristocracy, such as the duchess of Brittany, who founded her own monastery. Convents were established in France, Italy, and Spain, and the nuns were held in high esteem. By the time Teresa arrived at the convent of the Incarnation at Ávila, however, laxity had replaced discipline. The community had grown to 140 nuns who did not pool their wealth. The women with private incomes lived as comfortably as they had outside the convent, while poorer sisters lacked proper food and clothing. As many as fifty nuns left the enclosure on outings, and men were welcome inside the convent.

Initially Teresa fit right into the Convent of the Incarnation. Her father had provided her with a generous dowry and substantial income. While she enjoyed socializing with the nuns, she felt conflicted about her mission. "On the one hand, God was calling me," she wrote. "On the other, I was following the world."

Some of her biographers say that Teresa experienced

a sudden interior conversion, but it is more likely that her spiritual transformation was gradual. Inspired by the example of Saint Augustine and Saint Catherine of Siena, she began to reject worldly pleasures for a life devoted to prayer. She started seeing visions that continued and intensified as she matured. When she gossiped with the other nuns, she saw Christ watching her "with the eyes of the soul." One day she heard him say, "I will have you converse now not with men, but with angels." In her most famous vision she saw an angel pierce her heart with a burning arrow. Although some doubted the authenticity of her raptures—the Inquisition was beginning to explain trances as an example of sexual possession by the devil—her Jesuit and Franciscan confessors assured her that God was indeed speaking to her.

After she had a particularly vivid vision of being "plunged right into hell," Teresa could no longer tolerate the laxity in the convent. She felt impelled to start a new foundation dedicated to the primitive rule followed by the hermits on Mount Carmel. Despite local opposition, she purchased a small house in Ávila in 1562 and received permission to open the convent of San Jose with four postulants. The nuns were known as the Discalced Carmelites, which referred to the fact that her new order wore sandals, rather than the shoes favored by Calced Carmelite nuns. Inspired by Saint Francis's commitment to a life of poverty, Teresa forbade the nuns from accepting any income from home. Manual labor and alms provided them with the minimal funds needed for their austere life.

Teresa believed that nuns should live as members of a family, no more than twenty-one to a convent. "All the sisters must be equals," she wrote. "[The sister] who is from nobler lineage should be the one to speak least about her father." To prevent the cliquishness she had observed at the Convent of the Incarnation, she prohibited sisters from cultivating "particular friendships" and warned them that excessive love between nuns was more dangerous than too little love. No nun was exempt from the menial chores she thought conducive to contemplation. The Lord, she believed, dwelled among the pots and pans.

The Carmelites' day was to be an uninterrupted communion with Christ. Teresa did not advocate a formal method of prayer, but called on her nuns to enjoy frequent and friendly conversations with Christ. At the request of her spiritual advisers, she recorded her ideas about prayer in several books. In her most famous, *The Interior Castle*, she described seven states of prayer culminating with the soul's transformation from a sinful creature into the bride of the spiritual marriage. This mystical marriage was more than a metaphor; Teresa saw Christ as her spouse. She once had a vision in which he gave her his right hand and said, "Behold this nail, which is a sign that from this day you will be my spouse."

Teresa wrote in a colloquial style considered suitable for women. Her tone was deliberately self-deprecating; she presented women as ignorant, weak, and timid, probably to pacify potential critics who questioned a woman's right to engage in theological discourse. Some theologians doubted that a woman was *capable* of such discourse. "[Her works] exceed the capacity of women," an Inquisition prosecutor concluded. Teresa's supporters, however, echoed the sentiments of the early church fathers when they described her as a "virile woman" with a "manly soul."

During the last two decades of her life Teresa spent much of her time traveling. She founded sixteen more monasteries, and in 1567 received papal approval for a new constitution. It was primarily a spiritual declaration that outlined her view of the religious path nuns should follow. While she insisted her nuns be strictly cloistered, her constitution did not specify a great many rules and regulations.

In 1581 an assembly of Carmelite priests produced a revised constitution for the Discalced convents, a more legalistic document that called for a precise schedule of prayer and meditation. The nuns were required to wear wool habits and undergarments of exact specifications. Complete power resided in the mother superior. They could speak to outsiders only through metal grates. Teresa objected to aspects of the new constitution—she believed in discipline, not rigidity—but she died in 1582 before she could stop its implementation. In less than two decades her family of nuns had become an institution.

Sister Marie remembers vividly the year Catherine entered the cloister: 1968. A stocky woman with soft white hair, Sister Marie was responsible for guiding the community during the tumultuous period following Vatican II. For many years she was the community prioress, the unquestioned leader of the convent. The nuns knelt before her to ask for permission for a bar of soap. Every evening they kissed her scapular. She speaks with cool authority still.

"Catherine was one of the new breed of sisters. It was something to get used to. She had already established a career and had led an independent life. She was idealistic and a little intolerant. Idealism sometimes fosters intolerance until a sister gets more experience and realizes her own limitations.

"It must have been a confusing time for Catherine and the young ones. We were in limbo until we internalized our new values. I remember thinking that we had liberalized so many of the rules. But the young nuns still thought we were strict. I had lived here for almost twenty years; I accepted the way of life. It took some time before we realized that there are no absolutes except God.

"Before Vatican II many of the laws and customs militated against who we were as women, or perhaps it was our own interpretation of the laws. The way we interpreted silence and the way we related to our families was antihuman.

"We were not allowed to see grandmothers, aunts, uncles, or cousins unless they were accompanied by a member of our immediate family. I remember one time a grandmother came to see a young sister. But I would not let her in. She had come such a long way, but I believed that this was the rule and we had to follow it. I still feel guilty to this day.

"The rules of enclosure were also ridiculous. I remember our extern sister fell and hurt herself, and we could not go outside the enclosure to help her. We were so scrupulous, we would not cross the threshold. Fortunately a doctor came by to visit the chapel and found her."

She shook her head and sighed. "There are so many things that come back to haunt me. But I guess the sisters who lived the life back then weren't all crazy. Despite the rigidity, many strong, holy women emerged. At a certain point they were just able to break out of the mold."

In the late 1960s Marie led the post–Vatican II renewal in the cloister. She consulted all the sisters about their feelings concerning change and had them fill out detailed questionnaires. She spoke to priests from the local seminary, psychologists, and theologians. She invited a canonist to visit the community to discuss the laws of enclosure.

The early changes included modification of the habit. "We had these woolen habits that were so penitential— how they itched! So we had to deal with making new habits and wearing slips, brassieres, and girdles and stockings." They changed the Chapter of Faults into a weekly discussion group. And they decided that they would no longer kneel when addressing the prioress. "They stopped calling me mother," Marie recalled. "That sort of thing grew repugnant to me as my consciousness grew."

In 1967 Marie left the cloister for the first time to attend a workshop for contemplative women. "It was led by a sister who saw a dire need for us to have the freedom to determine the direction of our lives. We had some very exciting discussions about renewal. And later we went to Woodstock."

On August 17, 1969, in Woodstock, Maryland, 135 nuns from fifty-seven communities met, all wearing habits and veils. It was the first time in the United States that contemplative nuns had come out of their cloisters en masse to address their common concerns.

The youngest sister was twenty-one, the oldest, seventy-one. The group included forty-three superiors and former superiors and eighteen directors of novices. The theme of the conference was renewal. For two weeks the nuns discussed every aspect of contemplative life: their mission, vows, prayer life, personal development, community relationships, finances, and interactions with the outside world.

They addressed the concerns they considered critical in the aftermath of Vatican II: the isolation of enclosure and its effects. Had the artificial isolation cut them off from reality? What was "the psychic devastation" wrought by a mishandling of sexuality, detachment, and penance?

Among their more controversial recommendations was a call to sisters to "reappraise the concept of withdrawal from the world" and "affirm that the traditional forms of enclosure are detrimental to the human and Christian development of our sisters." They called upon nuns to reach out "to the wider human community." They also recommended experimentation with new forms of community governance.

This initial meeting led to the formation of the Association of Contemplative Sisters (ACS), an organization that would not receive the approval of Rome. Sisters were invited to join individually, and four hundred did over the next ten years, often over the objections of their fellow sisters.

The group met twice a year (but soon switched to every other year) and addressed the agenda put forth in their first meeting. Task forces were formed to discuss everything from the habit to peace and justice issues. Living in a cloister, they believed, did not mean living in an ivory tower. They could write to their senators as easily as other nuns.

Conservative nuns were understandably incensed. Sisters who believed in strict enclosure could hardly endorse such meetings. Even moderates were critical. They did not want to join an organization that was not under the auspices of the Vatican. A good many feared that meetings with several orders would lead to a melding of traditions and would take away from the character of each.

Catherine was among the early enthusiasts. She went to her first meeting in 1973 and embraced wholeheartedly the idea of an association committed to renewal. "ACS showed us what would happen when women bonded together. It made us trust our own lived experience. We were no longer afraid of self-government."

Soon her involvement in ACS required traveling to other convents for meetings. She loved the stimulation that came from associating with new sisters. She even managed to spend some time with Louisa, who was beginning to express interest in the convent. Her thoughts on prayer and community helped Catherine to reaffirm the fundamental values of contemplative life.

"Traveling broadened my horizons," said Catherine. "A danger of life in a cloistered community is that little things can start to seem so big. Talking with women from outside my community helped me to see what really mattered in this life. There were bigger issues than whether to use bread or wafers at Mass."

But she recognized a potential occupational hazard. "Our lifestyle is not geared to meeting a lot. Traveling became a struggle for me because I loved it so much. I began to question my motives when I left the convent. Why was I out? Was I traveling for a good reason or just to have fun? What was it doing to my prayer life? It's a delicate balance: being versus doing. And we all have to find the right balance for ourselves."

While the changes prompted by Vatican II freed nuns from antiquated customs and regulations, the new conservative hierarchy has attempted to turn back the clock.

In 1983 the Vatican issued a revised code of canon law that included a section on religious life. The Vatican stated that nuns were required to "wear the habit of the institute made according to the norm of proper law as a sign of their consecration" and to live in "their own religious house and not be absent without the permission of the superior."

Conflicts between the Vatican's and sisters' interpretation of religious life have become particularly divisive when orders have revised their constitutions and submitted them for approval to the Vatican's Sacred Congregation for Religious and Secular Institutes (CRIS). In many cases CRIS has questioned the more progressive tenets of constitutions proposed by contemplative orders and asked for revisions, particularly regarding rules of enclosure, silence, and dress.

Progressive sisters such as Catherine have protested Vatican attempts to regulate their lives. Catherine and Alice have spent hours discussing the potential ramifications for their community of a revised constitution. If the document does not reflect their vision of the life, how closely will they have to adhere to its tenets? Will their actions be scrutinized? Will communities retain their autonomy? They had worked years to form a community that nurtured their spirits. They were not going to return to a way of life that hindered their growth.

Catherine says she will do whatever it takes to protect her community, but she will not follow regulations that are not true to the life. "No one can force me to wear the old habit or remain inside the cloister. If I had to, I would consider leaving the order. It would be terribly difficult, a last resort. I guess at this point it's in God's hands."

•   •   •

Catherine believes that a woman's suitability for contemplative life is also in the hands of God.

Two years after she entered the cloister, her closest friend, Louisa, decided that she, too, felt drawn to contemplation. She wrote to Catherine's community expressing her interest, but the prioress did not think it would be a good idea for two close friends to live in the same monastery. "I was very disappointed at the time," said Catherine. "I wanted Louisa to come here. But now I am grateful that we joined different communities."

After exploring several monasteries, Louisa entered a neighboring community, against the strong objections of her devout Methodist relatives, who had viewed her conversion to Catholicism as a betrayal. Although she had visited the monastery several times and had completed a three-month trial live-in, she had a difficult time adjusting to contemplative life, and she wrote Catherine long letters about her unhappiness.

"Louisa was a very sensitive person," said Catherine. "Little things bothered her a lot. If somebody looked at her cross-eyed, she'd brood about it all day. She particularly hated the other nuns' taste in music. She wanted the community to sing Bach, but they liked low-brow popular songs. I'd write and tell her to take things more lightly. But you can't say that to someone who doesn't experience it internally. I worried about her intensity. Our life allows a lot of time for reflection. There are very few distractions. You can't have a temperament that's too ponderous. If you dwell on every little thing a sister says, you'll go crazy."

A year after entering, Louisa decided to leave the monastery. Within a few weeks, however, she regretted her decision and asked the community if she could return. The prioress told her to wait a year to be sure she was committed.

The following fall, Louisa returned to the convent with new determination, and she seemed to find the routine easier. The sisters chose her to be novice mistress, the nun responsible for teaching new entrants about contemplative life, and she was later elected assistant to the prioress. But the psychological strain of confinement proved too great.

"One afternoon I got a call from Louisa's prioress. She asked me if I was sitting down, and I said yes. Then she told me that Louisa had had a nervous breakdown and was recovering in a local psychiatric hospital. I was stunned."

Catherine wrote to Louisa immediately and telephoned her at the hospital the following week. "I wanted to assure her of my support. I didn't ask her to explain. I just listened. She was clearly very embarrassed. She said, 'I can go home tomorrow if I want to, but I think I'll stay and rest.' She liked her psychiatrist, but she thought that therapy was mundane. When the doctor asked her what she thought brought on the breakdown, she said she had no idea. In retrospect I think that her conversion to Catholicism was traumatic for her. She had always been a devout Methodist. It's hard to speculate, though. I never understood Louisa completely."

A few weeks later Louisa returned to the convent. Although her doctor recommended therapy on an outpatient basis, she refused to continue treatment. "She began to talk about her breakdown in religious terms," said Catherine. "She called it a spiritual breakthrough—disintegration before integration. It really disturbed me. She never owned up to the experience."

The prioress continued to call Catherine to discuss Louisa's health.

"She said that the community hoped that Louisa would decide on her own to leave the convent. To Louisa, leaving signified failure. But she no longer felt like she belonged. Eventually she decided to rent an apartment ten minutes away from the convent to give herself some time to think. She came to visit me here for a few days, and we had some good talks, but she still wouldn't admit that she had emotional problems."

Two months later Louisa's emotional problems were superseded by physical ones. In 1982 she had a mastectomy after a lump in her breast was diagnosed as malignant. The following year—after being told by two local doctors that a piercing pain in her chest was psychosomatic—a specialist informed her that the cancer had spread. During Louisa's final days Catherine left the cloister to visit her at the hospital.

"I stayed with her all day and most of the night," said Catherine, her voice quivering. "On the fifth day I stepped out of the room for a moment, and she died. All alone. It was so like her. She did things in the twinkling of an eye. In college I'd be sitting on a bus waiting for her, and just before the driver closed the doors, she'd jump in. I still haven't accepted her death completely. Sometimes I want to sit down and write her a letter."

Catherine took a deep breath and folded her hands in her lap. "Louisa made me realize the grace of my vocation," she said softly. "It's not something you can bring on yourself, no matter how badly you want it or how hard you try. It's a complete gift from God."

IV

Monica knocked softly at the door of my room, "May I come in, dear?" she said. "I feel up to talking tonight."

We sat around a small table. Like a loving grandmother, she held my hand as we spoke, squeezing it when she wanted to stress a point.

Despite her attachment to the formal habit, I had heard that Monica was a bit of a maverick when she entered in 1925. Catherine told me that Monica took baths long before it was considered decent for nuns to immerse themselves in water. She considered it a silly restriction.

Monica found other rules just as objectionable.

"Years ago an ill sister had to get permission from the bishop to go to the hospital. A sister could die before the letter arrived. I don't know how such rigidity evolved. The early nuns were not so attached to rules and regulations. I didn't like many of the old penances either. During one particular penance we had to prostrate ourselves to show we were sinners while a sister walked over us. We couldn't talk except during recreation, so many of the sisters would run around with pads and pencils. That was nonsense. If I had to ask a question, I didn't feel that I was breaking the silence. I was ahead of my time."

When Monica learned of the plans for renewal following Vatican II, however, she was upset. "I trembled. It was so sudden and new for me. But as soon as I began praying, the shackles fell off. I put it in God's hands." Gradually she learned to accept and even embrace many of the changes, but she thinks the younger nuns have gone too far.

"I don't agree with many things the sisters believe.

I would like a more quiet life, without radio or TV. What bothers me is they talk more. There is more visiting. Visits used to be limited to a half hour with friends and an hour with parents once a month, unless they came from out of town. Now visits are unlimited, which makes it difficult on the community workload. And sisters are always coming and going, which I don't think makes them happy. I don't leave except to go to the doctor or visit the sick in the hospital.

"Last year Sister Catherine went to so many meetings of nuns. She takes this course and that. She has many friends—including priests and bishops. I always say she has a man in every port. I say it in a humorous way. She can take teasing.

"She likes to go out and go swimming with the younger group. They pray in the woods or by the lake. They're kindred spirits in a way. I do worry about them, but I don't fuss and argue. I give them the benefit of the doubt that they are doing everything in good faith. I pray that the Holy Spirit guides and inspires them. Some people don't think I feel this keenly, but I do. I put it in the hands of God."

For a moment she was lost in thought.

"Catherine is so lovable and kind," she said softly. "When I want something, she doesn't refuse me. She drives me to the doctor. And I try to help her.

"Catherine gets broken up a lot and cries, especially when her father is ill. I try to say something funny to cheer her. Sometimes I have to admonish her. When I think she's being too demanding, I tell her, 'Catherine, you're an only child and you're spoiled.' She says she knows.

"I like to discuss spiritual insights with her. One time she said I helped her more than a priest could. I'm living the life. A priest doesn't understand the life entirely.

"You know, dear," Monica said, looking at me intently, "I've been here almost sixty years and I've found so much joy and happiness. One of the greatest joys is a life of service. We're the spiritual dynamos. The power of prayer is like a dynamo. I pray for all people. I feel that through prayer and sacrifice I can reach all souls."

Before she left my suite, Monica squeezed my hand one last time. "You know, perhaps you could help me. Maybe you could talk to Catherine about wearing the habit. It's so beautiful, don't you think?"

I looked at the regal woman draped in the flowing brown garment. Indeed it was.

It is difficult for outsiders to imagine the prospect of relating to the same group of people in a confined space 365 days a year. Some sisters believe that God designs contemplative communities, bringing together seemingly disparate personalities into a harmonious whole. Others are not so sure.

In the old days the life was so structured that there wasn't much opportunity for disagreement. Stringent regulations governed codes of behavior, and a mother superior made sure the daughters obeyed. Today the rule of the life is subject to interpretation—in this case seventeen different versions.

"We have a community of all chiefs and no Indians," Catherine said wryly. Alice nodded in agreement.

The sisters govern by consensus. They meet weekly to discuss community matters: whether to use bread or wafers during the liturgy, whether to allow a writer into the convent. The meetings are usually congenial, but occasionally the discussions can be heated.

"It can be very tough," said Catherine, "because we live together very closely—eating, sleeping, playing, praying. It's like being married to seventeen people. I read an article by a Cistercian abbot that said that the new asceticism is living closely with people with whom we wouldn't have chosen to live. Honestly speaking, living in our community hasn't been a trial. Somebody can drive you crazy with her little idiosyncrasies. Maybe an obsession with perfectionism. But I feel we're a good working group. We're honest and we try to discover the truth together."

"How do you handle disagreements?"

"I try to be direct," Catherine said. "In the past if I took exception to something someone said at a community meeting, I'd bring it up after the meeting. Now I try to say what's on my mind during the meeting. I think it's better that way."

Sister Alice shook her head. "But you have to be sensitive about when you bring up issues. We all have our histories. Sometimes I don't want to conjure up something from someone's past, so I'm careful about what I say and when I say it."

"Are there people you will never click with?" I asked.

"I think that's a given," said Catherine, smiling, "but I'm growing in compassion."

"How do you express anger in a community?"

"You don't want to let it build up," said Alice. "Better to express it sooner than later. You don't want to let anyone get away with murder. That's not good for you or the other person. I think as a community we've really rethought this issue. When I entered, I thought I should be able to put up with anything without getting angry. I thought, What does it matter as long as I can look forward to life in the hereafter?"

"Today we have crying and anger in community," said Catherine. "It's healthy that it comes out. In a way it's an advantage to live so closely with people because you get to know them so well. When I was accepted for final profession, I really felt accepted because these people knew me so completely."

"Does confinement in a cloister ever get to you?" I asked.

"It can be tough because we have no outlets," said Catherine. "We don't go out to teach. Our life is always right here. Even small problems become magnified. If you had problems when you entered—issues you weren't even aware of—they will surface. When you spend so much time in prayer, particularly during retreats, you have a lot of time to confront your problems. There's no escaping them."

"I disagree," Alice interjected. "You can escape through your work or recreation. We have TV in the recreation room now. Sisters with problems have at times watched TV a lot in the evenings after the Office. I've heard of some contemplatives resorting to alcohol. We drink wine at meals, so it's possible. At one of our national meetings a sister got up and said, 'I'm from an alcoholic community,' because two of the sisters were alcoholics. She was open about it. It can happen."

"I guess we're a microcosm of the rest of the world," said Catherine.

Alice nodded. "I think silence helps us to cope with

enclosure. Even though the place is full, I experience a privacy in silence."

Catherine agreed. "We really respect one another's privacy."

"But sometimes we get sloppy about keeping silence, and I get upset," said Alice. "I went to the basement one evening after the Office, which is quiet time except in the recreation room. There were two sisters in the laundry room talking in a regular tone of voice. I said, 'I would be glad if when I came down here it was silent.' One sister laughed and said, 'Oh, you would, would you?' But I found their talking jarring. I don't want it to become an accepted thing. Every now and then we have a community meeting to talk about silence, and it's better for a while. We put up signs to remind ourselves."

"I know you're surrounded by people," I said, "but do you ever get lonely living in a cloister?"

"Oh, yes," said Catherine, nodding. "I am by nature a warm person, and sometimes I think about how nice it would be to have a hug from a man. But I don't think about it every day."

"What are your relationships with men like?"

"They're much deeper than in the past," said Catherine. "I'd never really loved a man before I came to the convent. Back then my relationships were more romantic and superficial. Today when I meet someone with the same values as I have, we really click on a deeper level. I've met many men—priests, men who come here for spiritual counseling. I experienced a very beautiful friendship with my spiritual director, who died last year. He was so intelligent, I felt such a camaraderie with him. I really loved him."

She paused a moment. "I still feel a natural attraction to men, which troubled me in the past. I felt I was being unfaithful to God. I talked to my spiritual director, who told me not to worry about it. He said, 'Tell me when you're in bed with someone and then begin to worry.' Today I realize that I'm a healthy, whole person and I will always feel those attractions. But I chose a celibate lifestyle so I will not follow through on them. In the old days we hardly shook hands. I have no qualms about giving someone a warm hug or a kiss, but I won't go farther.

"I have a sign in my room that says, 'Take God for your spouse and friend and walk with him constantly.' I wear a ring that's a sign of my commitment to God. I'm taken and I'm happy to wear this ring. Some nuns have talked about a third way, meaning sexual relationships between nuns and priests. I don't want to be condemning, but I think it's sad, because they are not grounded in who they are."

"Do you think masturbation is a sin?"

"In the past it was considered a mortal sin you would go to hell for," said Catherine, raising her eyebrows in mock disapproval. "I don't consider it a sin, but I'd wonder about myself if I were obsessed with it. Celibacy can be unhealthy if it's not the life you're meant to live. It can be an overwhelming problem that disturbs the rest of your life. I know from experience that you can go through a phase where celibacy can be a struggle, but if it goes on decade after decade, this life isn't for you."

Alice has had her own struggle with celibacy. Several years ago she asked for permission to leave the cloister for a year. She had fallen in love with Bill, an Irish priest who had come to the convent to direct a four-day retreat. They had spent many hours talking during his visit and had begun a correspondence that lasted for years. Bill made it clear that while he loved Alice, he was committed to his vows.

"I didn't leave the convent to marry Bill," Alice said. "I left to find out if I was meant to marry at all."

Alice returned to her hometown and lived with her mother. Bill was stationed in the United States for one year, and he and Alice visited one another several times. She also began seeing an old boyfriend who had recently divorced. "It may sound like a funny thing for a contemplative nun to be dating," she said, "but it was something I needed to do."

At the end of the year she realized that she could not marry her old boyfriend. She did not experience in their relationship the depth she felt with Bill. If she was not going to marry him, she realized that she would not marry at all.

Eventually Alice felt a yearning to return to the cloister and, while she had some regrets, she was convinced that the contemplative life was her vocation. The community had reservations about her decision to return, but it was up to Alice to decide.

"Today I feel differently about my life here. I've experienced myself as loved, and that has made a big difference in my life. I had known friendship from good, strong women, but I guess I needed a meaningful relationship with a man. Through both of these men a lot of issues got settled. I had always been on edge, always searching. Today there is something at rest in me."

Catherine supported Alice's decision to leave and her decision to come back.

"It was very sad for me when Alice left," she said.

"But I knew she had to go. Living a double life can be treacherous. There is nothing more painful. Nothing. But I've noticed a real change in Alice since she returned. She's a lot more centered. I think she's more at peace with herself."

Through a life of deep prayer the contemplative nun is supposed to experience dying and rebirth. I asked Catherine to tell me about an ancient monastic concept—the death of self.

"I think you first have to find yourself before you lose yourself. If you don't have solidity or that rootedness—if you don't feel good about yourself—you can't go through that dying. In the old days women would enter before they knew who they were, and the mistresses would start whittling away at their personalities. It was destructive. They would cut them down, and the novices couldn't take it.

"But once you have sound grounding and you feel good about yourself, you can take it. I have gotten a lot of affirmation in my life, from family, friends, teachers. Now I am ready for the dying part. I want to learn not to be so centered on myself. I want to rid myself of the qualities I don't often acknowledge—my pride, anger, my jealousy, my selfishness. I want to let go of my false self. I am ready to let my ego die. My entire life here is like a death."

A woman who wants to enter a monastery will not find this community advertised in a magazine. The sisters do not print much vocational material. They seem to believe that if a woman is meant to find them, God will guide her.

"We're happy to get new people because we want to promulgate the order," said Catherine, "but we're not recruiting. We believe the call to this life happens very deep in a person's heart."

In the old days teenagers were accepted into convents to be molded into proper young nuns. Today the community prefers that entrants have at least a year of college or work experience.

"We want women, not girls," she said. "And we're looking for people who can stand up for themselves. Our community is strong, and you have to be independent to live here. When people come for an interview and they seem passive, we note that. We pick up body language pretty quickly.

"In order to survive here, you have to be self-confident and have a good idea of who you are. The sisters aren't going to pamper you. If you're coming for a warm, snuggly community, forget it. It would be like a needy person coming into a marriage and thinking she was going to get all her affirmation from the relationship. To live a life like this takes a lot of self-motivation. Nobody will cram it down your throat. No one will tell you, 'Today you're going to read this or pray for so many hours.' We're not watchdogs for each other."

The number of new entrants does not bode well for the future of contemplative life. Between 1977 and 1979 only 288 women entered cloisters, while 267 left. No organization has compiled statistics for the last decade—contemplative nuns are frequently ignored in statistical studies of sisters—but it is clear the downward spiral is continuing.

"It's true we've had only three postulants during the past ten years," Catherine said. "But we've had transfer sisters from other orders. That's a new phenomenon, active nuns who feel drawn to the contemplative life."

I asked Catherine if she thought her community would survive.

"Whatever happens to our order, I believe the *life* will survive," she said. "There will always be men and women called to live a life of prayer in silence and solitude. I don't know if ten years from now we'll have large convents in cities. Maybe we'll have monasteries in the desert. I've recently begun thinking about starting a community in the desert of Arizona."

"Will you do it?" I asked.

Catherine smiled. "You never know. Perhaps I will follow the call."

CHAPTER 5

DAUGHTER OF PROPHECY:
AN ACTIVIST TAKES THE LEAD

Your daughters shall prophesy.
JOEL 3:1

Margarita Barrios jumped when she heard the knock at the door. Who could be coming by at eight o'clock in the morning? She peered through the curtains at the front window and saw three burly men standing on the porch. Please, God, make them go away, she prayed. But the knocking grew louder, more persistent. What should she do? Sister Darlene was at a retreat in Michigan. She would not be home for several days. She had promised Margarita that she would be safe.

"Immigration and Naturalization Service," a man shouted in Spanish. "Federal agents. Open the door." He began counting. "One, two, three . . ."

The words were eerily familiar to Margarita, a small, round, rosy-faced woman who looked considerably younger than her twenty-two years. Five years ago in San Salvador—September 1979—she heard pounding in the middle of the night on the front door of the small house she shared with her mother and four brothers and sisters. Seven men barged in carrying guns. They ordered the women to lie down on the floor while they searched the house. They were looking for young men whom they suspected of sympathizing with the guerillas. Her twenty-year-old brother, Miguel, came out of the back room and said he would go with the men if they left his sisters alone. His mother scrambled to her feet in a futile attempt to stop her son. But Miguel hugged her tightly and went out into the night.

Early the next morning the neighbors found Miguel's corpse, and the bodies of scores of other neighborhood boys, hacked to pieces in a ditch. Dozens of women had been raped. This is how Margarita first learned of the death squads. Margarita's mother never recovered completely. She would speak of Miguel as if he were out on an errand. But it was Margarita's younger brother, José, who took it the hardest. Margarita listened as he cried himself to sleep every night. He did not suffer long. Six months later he went for a walk and never returned. A neighbor found his mutilated body at the bottom of a hill.

In the fall of 1983 Margarita witnessed violence again. Now a wife and mother, she and her husband were walking down a crowded street with their two infant daughters when they saw a drunken guard brandishing a gun at a teenage boy. When Margarita's husband tried to intervene, the guard shot him. Holding her husband's limp body in her arms, Margarita became hysterical. "You're not going to get away with this," she screamed at the guard. "My friends will kill you."

Her husband survived, but the guard did not forget Margarita's threat. Every day he searched the neighborhood for her. Afraid to stay at home, she hid out with relatives during the day. It was too dangerous to visit her husband in the hospital, but she sneaked home to see her daughters late at night.

Eventually she ran out of places to hide. A man at the food store where she worked gave her four hundred dollars and told her to leave the country immediately. She had heard numerous stories of women raped and killed while trying to cross the border, but she had no choice. She left with a stranger who was heading for the United States that night. All she took with her were pictures of her daughters and the telephone number of a family friend who had moved to California.

It took sixteen days to travel through Guatemala and Mexico. She and the man walked for miles, rode crowded buses, swam across streams. He taught her Mexican slang so she would not be mistaken for a Salvadoran if questioned by security forces. When they arrived at Agua Prieta, a Mexican border town, the man deserted her. She paid what little money she had left to a "coyote," a person who smuggled refugees across the border. They sneaked into Texas through a hole in the fence, and Margarita looked for the first telephone she could find. She called the number she had written on a scrap of paper, but the woman who answered refused to accept the charges. When Margarita collapsed to the ground in tears, a woman offered to drive her to Phoenix.

God was good to her in Phoenix. She stayed with a family who took her to a center for refugees. There she heard about a North American nun named Sister Darlene Nicgorski, who had taught little children in Guatemala. Sister Darlene had left the country after the violence had escalated. Since returning from Central America she was helping Guatemalans and Salvadorans who had fled their homelands. Margarita called the sister, who told her she could stay at her house for a few days. She ended up staying for two months.

Sister Darlene was not like the nuns back home. She dressed in pants and blouses and didn't even wear a cross around her neck. Margarita thought Sister Darlene was very, very serious at first. She wondered if she ever laughed. But later Margarita saw that Sister Darlene was just shy. In time she became like a mother to her, or more like a sister. They cooked together and played card games after dinner. Sister Darlene tickled her when she was sad. At night when Margarita cried for her husband and children, Sister Darlene consoled her.

She encouraged Margarita to put up pictures from her country on a wall in the living room. She said it might make her feel less homesick. Margarita taped up photographs of her daughters, pictures of San Salvador she had cut out of a magazine, and a poster of the late Salvadoran archbishop Oscar Romero that Sister Darlene had given her as a gift. "Margarita's wall," Sister Darlene christened it.

Gradually Margarita began assisting Sister Darlene with her work in the sanctuary movement. Religious people were helping to transport refugees fleeing political oppression and to find them shelter in churches and temples throughout the country. Once settled, the refugees would talk to people about the torture and murder of civilians in Central America. Some people said it was against the law to help the Guatemalans and Salvadorans—illegal aliens, they called them—but Sister Darlene said she was obeying the law of God.

Margarita did not know much about politics. But she helped Sister Darlene make phone calls and file papers. Later Margarita told her story in churches in Phoenix. It was hard to talk about her family and the death squads. Sometimes people didn't believe her. They thought that she had left the people she loved so she could earn more money. But Sister Darlene said it was important to try to make people understand.

She did not apply for political asylum because Darlene explained to her that the chances were slim. Only a handful of the thousands of Salvadorans who submitted applications were granted asylum due to the political biases of the Reagan administration. So she remained an "illegal" like the scores of others who fled their homelands.

". . . Five, six, seven . . ." the Immigration men kept counting. Margarita knew it was no use hiding. If she ran out back, they would catch her. She walked to the front door and turned the latch.

Three men stood outside. One held a large camera, the kind television reporters used. He began filming as soon as he walked in the door. Margarita squinted as he focused the bright light on her.

"We have a warrant to search the house," said a heavily bearded man. "Who lives here?" Margarita walked into the kitchen and picked up a small white card lying on the table. She handed it to him.

"This illegal alien has just handed me the business card of Darlene Nicgorski," the man said, talking directly to the camera as if it were a person. "You sit in this chair while we look around," he ordered Margarita in Spanish. She sat down obediently and watched the men in silence. While she did not speak much English, she caught snatches of their conversation.

The bearded man led the one with the camera around the house. For several seconds he focused the camera on the wall she had decorated. What did they see? she wondered. He filmed a poster of President Ronald Reagan that Sister Darlene had taped to the bathroom door. He then read the poster's slogan to the camera, "Dump the Dinosaur in '84."

They did not stop to film Sister Darlene's simple

shrine: a table holding a painting of Our Lady of Guadalupe, a candle, and a Spanish Bible. This was Margarita's favorite spot. Every morning she and Sister Darlene knelt in front of the shrine and prayed for the people of El Salvador and Guatemala. In the evening they read the Bible.

When the men finished touring the house, they began rummaging through Sister Darlene's closets and drawers and flipping through her files. "I want to read the files off," the bearded man said. "A list of volunteers. A file for screening and process. A file for refugee communications. A file for Texas." The list went on and on. His face lit up when he flipped through the last folder. "We have found a file listed terrorism," he said, as if he had found a secret plan. Margarita knew that one well. She had helped Sister Darlene fill it with articles about the death squads in El Salvador.

II

Entering the School Sisters of Saint Francis in the aftermath of Vatican II was like starting college during the Vietnam War. The order had responded to the dictates of the Vatican Convocation more enthusiastically than most. The rule that governed every aspect of religious life was discarded with fish and Friday and the Latin Mass.

It was Darlene Nicgorski's second attempt in the convent. She hadn't thought much about becoming a nun while growing up in Milwaukee. She just assumed that she would finish college, marry her boyfriend, Joe, start a family, and teach kindergarten. But when Joe finally proposed, she turned him down.

"I tried to explain to him that the ordinary wasn't

for me," she said. "I asked him if he'd ever considered a more exciting, spiritual, dedicated kind of life. Had he ever thought about joining the Peace Corps? But he hadn't. When I decided to become a Maryknoll missionary, he couldn't fathom it at all."

The Maryknoll Sisters ran a rigorous formation program of intensive study and manual labor. The women weren't just training to become nuns, they were being groomed as missionaries to work in Third World countries. Darlene looked like a perfect candidate for the program. At five feet eight inches she was an imposing figure, built like an athlete, strong and solid. But her hearty exterior hid a sickly interior. Plagued by allergies since childhood, she was kept up nights by a hacking cough. After six months in the formation program, the prioress asked Darlene to leave due to ill health.

She didn't take the news well. Why had God called her to be a missionary if the word of a prioress could dash her hopes? "I was bitter and angry," she said. "I didn't know what to do with myself, so I went home and returned to school."

In 1963, at age twenty, Darlene enrolled in Alverno College in Milwaukee, run by the School Sisters of Saint Francis. At twenty-two, with a degree in early childhood education, she decided to give religious life another chance. While the School Sisters lacked the glamour she associated with the Maryknoll missionaries, she was impressed with the progressive sisters who taught her at Alverno.

The order had been founded almost a century earlier by refugees. In 1873 three nuns from Schwarzach, Germany, fled their homeland due to the conflict between the German imperial government and the Roman Catholic church. They were among 460,000 immigrants to arrive in the United States that year. The women moved from the home of one Catholic benefactor to the next until a priest invited them to Campbellsport, Wisconsin, where they founded the School Sisters of Saint Francis.

In 1875 the first School Sisters opened a boarding and day school in New Cassel, Wisconsin. Eventually they settled in Milwaukee on ten acres of land that had once housed a dance hall and bowling alley.

Postulants arrived from Europe and America, and the women were encouraged to follow their callings. In 1885 seventy-five nuns began working among the Indians in Montana and Wisconsin. Others taught poor black students in Illinois and Mississippi. In 1907 a group of School Sisters started a school in the Caroline Islands. When the Japanese invaded in 1914, however, the nuns were forced to close their facility. Suspected of hiding money, they were imprisoned in their convent and eventually banished from the islands. Thirteen years later another group of nuns traveled to China to teach at a high school in Tsingtao. This school fared no better. During World War II it was seized and five of the sisters interned.

Still, the order continued to grow at home and abroad. By 1965, the year Darlene arrived at the Romanesque motherhouse, some four thousand School Sisters on four continents worked as teachers, social workers, lawyers, activists—even artists in the tradition of the Immaculate Heart of Mary Sister Corita Kent, whose contemporary prints in brilliant colors freed nuns from working within the narrow confines of "religious" art.

Life with the School Sisters was a far cry from Maryknoll. Rather than imposing the old rule of Saint Francis, the leadership asked the sixty new postulants to write their *own* rule. In the spirit of the sixties, they adopted just one regulation: to love one another.

Conformity was out; self-expression in.

"It was the age of psychology," said Darlene. "We were tested to the hilt. During the first few months we met with psychologists and took an endless battery of standardized intelligence, communications, personality tests. Were we extroverts or introverts? What were our strong points?" But there were limits to candor. "One test had all the questions about sex blacked out."

Though she tested as an introvert, Darlene quickly emerged as a leader of the class. While shy upon first meeting, she became increasingly assertive as she got to know the other postulants. She had no use for the excessive humility that once characterized good nuns. When she thought someone was being treated unfairly, she responded quickly, often pounding her fist on a table to make a point.

Her allergies, once exacerbated by stress, were no longer debilitating. She loved being in an environment that was more like a boarding school than a traditional convent. While attending college she had lived at home and found it difficult to cultivate friendships with students she saw only in passing. Here she was surrounded by her peers. The women with whom she discussed theology during the day, she played volleyball with at night.

Many postulants became disenchanted with the lack of direction. They had entered a convent to find answers and they were continually faced with more questions. "The community became a total mess," said Darlene. "There was a sense of rejecting what had been without knowing what to replace it with. Finally there was a moratorium on profession of vows because everything was so uncertain. There was a feeling among the leaders that the order couldn't profess new sisters before finding its identity."

Overwhelmed by the confusion, forty women left the convent, twenty from Darlene's class. In response to the crisis, the community leaders decided to delay the novitiate year, traditionally devoted to teaching second-year entrants the rules of the order. They simply weren't sure what to teach prospective sisters about religious life.

Frustrated, Darlene and a couple of her peers came up with a proposal for a new formation program. They suggested that during the first year, postulants live with sisters outside the convent to learn about their lifestyle. The second year, novices would reside in or near the Milwaukee motherhouse, combining a program of work and study. The leadership liked the plan and instituted it immediately. Darlene's group would spend its second year teaching part-time and studying two days a week with the novice mistress.

Darlene moved to the elementary school across the street. She enjoyed teaching fourth-graders; dealing with the administrators was more taxing. The priest who headed the school was a spoiled man, used to being waited on hand and foot by a nun. Accustomed to subservient women, he had great difficulty adjusting to strong-willed sisters committed to more progressive teaching methods.

"It was a bad experience," said Darlene. "I was so young and so new that the tension didn't hit me as hard as it did the older sisters. At that point I was concentrating on just making it as a nun. But the conflicts between the priest and the sisters certainly affected me. I guess you could say it set a tone."

Eager to leave her first post, Darlene volunteered for

a teaching position at a Christian elementary school run by five School Sisters at Alverno College. It was modeled on the English primary school; the teachers worked as a team in an open classroom. Initially intimidated, Darlene soon warmed up to team teaching. She was impressed by the way the teachers played off one another's strengths, and she was grateful for their efforts to welcome her into the fold.

Freed of priestly interference, the sisters experimented with new methods of religious instruction. Instead of teaching the catechism in the classroom, they tutored parents in how to prepare their children at home. At school they opted for a less structured religious education based on experience.

"We would talk to the kids about what their experiences meant to them," said Darlene, "and from there we would talk about God. It was an ideal environment. There was such an emphasis on trying to build community among students, teachers, and parents. When I finally thought about moving on, another teacher told me, 'You'll be sorry you left; you may never find the same sense of community.' "

By the time Darlene was ready to take her final vows, her class had dwindled to less than a dozen nuns. In the old days the final-vows ceremony had been a grand occasion when scores of sisters in full regalia pledged their lives to God. Now it hardly seemed worth it for the few sisters to gather at the motherhouse. Nuns made their profession wherever they happened to be stationed.

Darlene had no intention of taking her vows by herself. This was the most important day in her life, and she wanted to share it with the women with whom she had entered religious life. She wrote to the superior requesting that all the remaining sisters in her class be invited home for the ceremony.

On the morning of August 14, 1974, hundreds of nuns, priests, friends, and relatives crowded into the cathedral-like chapel of the School Sisters of Saint Francis.

Darlene did not wear a habit as she walked down the aisle, nor did she kneel before the bishop when she reached the white marble altar. But she did imagine she felt much as the thousands of sisters who had come before her as she contemplated the magnitude of her decision.

She had asked to address the congregation, and she had practiced her talk at least a dozen times. But as she looked out on the crowd, she could feel her hands shaking.

"When I look at my own weaknesses and failures," she said, "I can do nothing. I am immobilized. I can say neither yes nor no. When I look at the world around me with all of its tensions and insecurities, when I think about Watergate, it becomes very difficult for me to make a decision that will last.

"Then in the quiet of my own heart, I see him face-to-face. He comes to me and reveals himself. He gives that powerfully gentle look of love that he must have given to Peter or John when he called them. They left all and followed. It is this experience of seeing him face-to-face that urges me to say yes."

She turned to her sisters.

"Now, together, let us proclaim our vows."

The ten women recited in unison:

"I wish to live this faith commitment in community as a woman vowed to God.

"I profess service to all the people of God. I will

belong to Christ in love in order to be more free to love. I will be poor so that I will be more free to give.

"I will obey the Spirit as he speaks in community that I may be more free to serve.

"I vow chastity, poverty, obedience, and I promise to service God by ministering to his people as a member of the Third Order of Saint Francis."

As she walked down the aisle, Darlene felt a sense of peace. There was nothing final about final vows, she realized. She was just beginning the process of becoming.

For twenty-five years the School Sisters had run a high school in Holly Springs, Mississippi. When they decided to start a day-care center for the children of teenage mothers struggling to stay in school, they needed someone of high caliber to train staff and develop a curriculum. They called on Darlene.

She packed her things immediately and moved to Mississippi. She settled into a mobile home with a social worker and friend from the novitiate, Sister Margaret Held.

Rural Mississippi was a startling sight. The town of seven thousand was mostly black, the leadership entirely white. The white section of town had paved roads and gutters, the black section, dirt. Most blacks were farmers or factory workers, many living below the poverty level. Darlene had seen urban ghettos, but she had never seen families living in one-room shacks without heat or running water, women making corn bread over open fires.

The transition was more difficult than she'd imagined. "I was the white outsider and I had a lot of my own fear and prejudice to deal with," she said. For the first time in four years she had to cope with the isolation of living outside the community. While she could talk with Margaret at night, she was on her own during the day.

Gradually she got her bearings. She convinced the staff to abandon traditional teaching methods and conventional discipline for the more creative approach used at Alverno. "We developed a theme program. One month we would focus on mammals, the next birds. Our books, field trips, and artwork would reflect the theme. We also started a lending library so that the children could take home books and toys. And we'd meet with the parents to discuss how they could continue the teaching at home."

Darlene was adamant about maintaining high standards for the center. "She expected excellence, and if she didn't get it, she could be intimidating," recalled Margaret. "She encouraged her staff to go to college part-time. And she insisted that parents get involved in the center. They had to sign an agreement stating that they would attend meetings and participate in their children's activities. If they didn't, they couldn't keep their kids in school. Darlene was tough, but her method worked. She defied every stereotype about low-income parents.

"She was delightful with the children. She'd invite kids to come over to our house and bake Christmas cookies. She felt real compassion for the forlorn kids. She was always saying she wanted to bring them home, toilet train them, and give them love."

Her work did not go unrecognized. The school became known throughout the country as one of the best day-care programs in the South. In two years it had grown from eighteen to ninety-six children and twenty-six staff members. But Darlene was beginning to feel restless. "I was burned out," she said. "I didn't want to become an institution. I'd seen that happen to a lot of nuns who stayed in one place."

Her missionary yearnings had begun to surface again, and she was eager to leave the country. She heard about a six-month program, Living Aware, that sent religious men and women all over the world. She applied for a spot the following summer.

On May 4, 1980, Darlene arrived at the motherhouse for an orientation session for Living Aware. She and another School Sister, Pat, were headed for Los Amates, Guatemala. Fifteen nuns and priests had gathered to discuss the challenge of moving to the Third World.

While she liked several of the women, some of the men in the group struck her as arrogant. The intensity of her anger toward "the male priest types," as she called them, surprised and frightened her.

"Orientation began this morning," she wrote in the journal she would keep for the next three years. "During a group discussion, a Capuchin priest commented that most of priests' difficulties came from their association with the institutional Church. Something about his manner really bothered me. It was the male priest again telling us what attitude to take. I reacted strongly. I told him that my greatest difficulties came from dealing with white male priests in the institutional Church. I got a little scared when I realized the anger with which my feelings were coming out. I wasn't sure if I had come on too strong."

Two weeks later Darlene met with a sister from Guatemala who was visiting the United States. Darlene talked of her fears about speaking a new language and learning a new culture; the sister assured her they were natural. They also discussed the political situation in Guatemala, about which Darlene knew little.

"The sister told me that lay leaders are in the most danger," she wrote in her journal. "Some have been killed. Others turn up missing. It seems that some of the leftists are responsible." Months later she would cross out the word *leftist*.

In reality the Guatemalan army and government-supported death squads were responsible for routine assassinations of church workers, union organizers, and farmers who had organized cooperatives. The repression had begun thirty years earlier in 1954, when the CIA engineered the coup that overthrew the government of Jacobo Arbenz. Under the military dictatorships that persisted, supported by U.S. economic and military aid, the terror reached catastrophic proportions. Tens of thousands were killed or "disappeared."

Although Darlene didn't know all the players, she heard continuing reports of the violence. A sister from the Living Aware program had called to inform her that the political situation in Guatemala was "rather tenuous and if she chose not to go at this point it would be okay." The sister added that Marietta, a sister in Guatemala, was not sure if she would "be back alive." Darlene was shaken by the warnings, but she was determined to proceed with her plans.

On June 20, 1980, she and Pat arrived in Guatemala City. They spent the night at the Congress of Latin America Religious House, where they met several North American nuns and priests. A Maryknoll father spoke to the group about the history of the Church in Guatemala. "He is wanted by the government," Darlene noted in her journal. "He shaved his beard and keeps changing his location."

Her fears subsided on her arrival in Los Amates, a village in the district of Izabal, about one hundred miles northeast of Guatemala City. She was taken with the beauty of the mountains and lowlands. She and Pat moved into a plain brick convent that housed three School Sisters from the states and eighteen Guatemalan women studying to be nuns. The sisters taught local women about preventing malnutrition and caring for their children.

She took to the Guatemalan sisters right away. She was delighted to find that she was warmly received when she attempted to speak Spanish, and to her surprise she found conversing in another language liberating. "Everyone has been so welcoming," she wrote. "I was very much at home. This morning I learned how to make tortillas. Consuela showed me how. She was very patient. I learned that gentleness and patience are the important qualities. The view here is *'muy bonita.'* There are flowers and bushes of many kinds. The mountains and lowlands make this a very beautiful country. The women here seem so free, it is beautiful. They laugh very delightedly."

Her upbeat mood continued for weeks. "I have not laughed so much since I don't know when. I am so glad I can laugh at myself. Before I came, I thought I would feel more uncomfortable. I am enjoying myself and learning much."

The poverty in Guatemala was not surprising after her experience in Mississippi. "In some ways Guatemala is more primitive than Mississippi," she wrote, "in others not." The majority of Guatemalan resources were controlled by the ruling elite. Some 2 percent of the population owned 80 percent of the country's farmland. The poor, especially the Indian population, worked only two to three months a year harvesting crops for export for two dollars or less a day. More than 50 percent of the population got less than half the calories they needed to sustain them. Hunger-related diseases killed half of the children under the age of five.

Darlene spent much of her day visiting local families, most of whom lived in tiny homes without plumbing. "In one home I saw a very thin old woman on a straw-mat bed. She had a diaper on. She is emotionally disturbed and has refused to eat for months. In another home I spoke to a young man who was in bed recovering from gunshot wounds. He had been shot five times."

In the face of such adversity, she was impressed by the spirituality of the people. The church services moved her deeply. In contrast to the orderly Masses she was used to at home, the services were full of life. There were children crying, people talking and laughing throughout the service. The mood awakened in her a new sense of spirituality. "At liturgy I feel especially touched, a feeling of peace, aliveness, wholeness, holiness, goodness about being here. It just seems so right! Oh, my Lord, I feel an overwhelming openness to you and your Spirit. I want to be open to what it is you want, where it is you are leading me. This is a time of grace, indeed a time of gratitude. Somehow it is as if all my life has been a preparation for this."

She was particularly impressed with the delegates of the word, the laymen who taught at the base communities. "They are such little men, so small and thin. So simple and so committed. They really work to teach the people to work toward their own liberation."

Three days a week Darlene went to Mass at the local church. She liked the priests in Los Amates, particularly Father Tulio Maruzzo, an Italian Franciscan who had lived in the region for twenty-two years. Unlike many North American priests she knew, he was an unassuming man who never pontificated. "There was nothing particularly extraordinary about Father Tulio. He didn't come off like he knew all the answers. He listened to the people and he lived with them."

In January 1981 the School Sisters of Saint Francis asked Darlene to start a preschool funded by the government and international charitable organizations. She began making arrangements for the school immediately, painting wooden crates in primary colors, and gathering bottle tops and boxes to use for arts and crafts classes. Within a few months forty-five children were enrolled.

Darlene felt relatively safe in her parish. But she heard stories about killings in the western part of the country from sisters who traveled through. In the district of Quiché, all the priests and religious had had to leave because their names appeared on government assassination lists. They had been helping Indians learn to read and obtain land, activities considered subversive by the government. Hundreds of Catholic church workers had already been killed in Guatemala: priests, sisters, and brothers murdered by government-directed paramilitary forces.

By late June reports of violence came from closer to home. A woman told the nuns that her husband had been murdered along with twenty others who were running for labor union posts. A sister returning to the convent announced that she had seen a man shot in the distance. Every evening Darlene recorded the events in her journal: "Repression, threats, missing persons, and

murders are becoming regular events as the poor's cry
for justice grows louder."

"I'll never forget the day," Darlene said, "Wednesday,
July first. I had gone to Father Tulio's Mass at the par-
ish. Afterward I had driven home with some sisters and
gone to bed early. At ten o'clock I was awakened by
shouting outside. I grabbed my robe and ran to the gate.
Then I heard the men screaming, 'They've killed Father
Tulio. They've killed Father Tulio.' He and his friend
Abdulio had been followed by a truck and motorcycle.
They'd both been shot in the head.

"There was no phone nearby, so a sister disguised
herself with a kerchief and drove forty-five minutes to
the town where the bishop lived. She telephoned Guatemala City to let them know what was happening.

"A few days later people we trusted came from
Guatemala City to warn us that if we didn't leave, we
would be killed next. A few of us were on death lists."
Several Guatemalan sisters left immediately. Darlene and
the other North Americans stayed long enough to attend
Father Tulio's funeral.

"The people carried his casket through the street in
a procession. It was an open casket with a glass covering. I had never seen someone who had been killed before. It was very scary. We didn't know who in the
group was watching us.

"We had to make all sorts of decisions quickly. I felt
completely confused and lost. What did God want me
to do? I came here to start this program and now it was
gone. I felt so helpless. In the beginning we thought that
some of us would go and some would stay. It wasn't
long before we realized that everybody had to go.

"We decided to close the children's school and leave as soon as possible. We were advised to destroy all the records and photographs of the children. I took them out into the yard and burned them. We couldn't let anyone know we were going. We had to send the children home and take our money out of the bank.

"I could only take one suitcase when I left. I got a ride in a truck to the bus stop in the next village and took a bus to Guatemala City. Two of our Guatemalan sisters stayed three days longer. When they arrived in Guatemala City, they were in a terrified state. One of them was vomiting. Someone with a gun had been following them. I bought tranquilizers for the sisters at a local pharmacy.

"Finally we moved to a larger convent with the Sisters of Charity. They had worked for the government for a long time, and we thought that was the safest place for us. Even so, I planned an escape route out back just in case someone came for us. We knew we had to leave Guatemala, but we were afraid to go by bus. The Guatemalan sisters didn't have passports, so we had to wait there. I stayed for a month until we got the last Guatemalan sister out of Los Amates."

In mid-August Darlene and several Guatemalan School Sisters flew to the capital of Honduras to join the other sisters who had fled earlier. It was to be a temporary stop. They hoped to move on to Mexico, now home to thousands of Guatemalan refugees.

For three months Darlene lived with fifteen women in a four-bedroom house. "I wasn't scared. I was overwhelmed. I was responsible for fifteen young women who had never been out of the little area of the country in which they grew up. They were frightened in a big city and worried about their families back home. I taught them English and such basic survival skills as how to use a telephone."

Darlene wrote to the bishop in the state of Chiapas, Mexico, to ask if the Guatemalan sisters could find a safe haven in his country. In September the bishop offered Darlene sanctuary in his parish. Afraid to travel through Guatemala, she flew from Honduras to El Salvador to Mexico City to Chiapas. For nine months she lived in a local seminary near the Guatemalan border and visited the refugee camps, where 100,000 men, women, and children lived in subhuman conditions.

"Most were Kanjobal Indians, who had fled from a part of Guatemala where the killings had gone on for years. They had left with whatever they could carry on their backs. They lived in tents made of a couple of branches covered with pieces of plastic. They used the water from a river running through the camp.

"We found out when we arrived that there was a lot of suspicion of people who worked with the refugees. Still, we did everything from sorting medicine from international-aid groups to delivering food. We even managed to go to the camps with tape recorders and take testimonies from refugees about what they had fled. We sent the testimonies to various human-rights organizations in Mexico City.

"The refugees had confidence in us because we were the sisters who had worked in Guatemala. They called me *madrecita*, which means 'little mother.' Most of the men spoke Spanish. Some of the women didn't speak any if they hadn't been to school. They were very poor, simple, beautiful people. Many left behind their most valuable possession—their land. Mostly women told me horror stories. One melded into the next: A young In-

dian woman told me how her mother protested when
the militia came to take her fifteen-year-old brother for
army service. A soldier raped and killed her mother and
left her body in the street, where it stayed for days because people were afraid to take it away. Absolute horror stories. The army came and killed. The army came
and burned their crops and animals. There were some
stories about guerrillas, but most were about atrocities
the army was committing.

"The government would go after entire villages of
Indians, who were at the bottom of the totem pole socially and economically. The government thinks the Indians are sympathetic to the guerrillas and give them
food. So they burn their crops and force them to leave
the country.

"I certainly didn't know what a refugee was until I
got to the camps. I could say we were refugees too. But
I always felt a special privilege because I was a North
American. Even if I feared for my life, I somehow felt
they would think twice about killing an American."

Darlene knew she could not remain at the camps
indefinitely. But where could she go?

"I had a sense that everything I set out to do was
aborted. I started to set up a preschool and that was cut
short by the killing of the pastor. I started to work with
refugees and that, too, was cut short. I felt a real commitment to what was going on. I couldn't just leave it
and go back to teaching school. I thought, what does
God want now?"

III

Darlene arrived in the United States in October 1982
for a month's rest and fell ill. She thought it might be

parasites from the food in Chiapas. She had never been able to say no to refugees who offered her black beans. It turned out to be her gallbladder. Promising the surgeon she would not return to Central America for several months, Darlene moved to her parents' home in Phoenix to recuperate.

Like many returning missionaries, she had trouble readjusting to life in the United States. Simple things, like ordering a meal at a restaurant, the cost of which could feed a Central American family of four for a month, made her uneasy. The church services that once moved her struck her as sterile compared to the lively Masses in Izabal.

"I think we practice a religion of narcissism here. I feel differently now that I've experienced the faith of the Central Americans. It's where the vocations are, where the persecution is, where the martyrs are. The Church is part of their life. Going to church is not just something they do on Sunday morning."

As soon as she was ambulatory, she began looking into Central American aid groups. A local minister told her about the Valley Religious Task Force on Central America, a group of church workers that offered social services and legal aid to refugees. They helped raise money to post bond for those held in detention camps in the States. She was surprised to learn that there were thousands of exiles in Arizona. Against her doctor's wishes, she began speaking in churches and temples about the conditions she had witnessed.

Initially she was tentative in her remarks; it was difficult for her to stand up in front of an audience and talk about her experiences in Guatemala. Soon she was granting interviews to local journalists. Her affiliation with the School Sisters gave her a certain credibility. Nuns, it seemed, made good copy.

She left her parents' home and moved, along with two School Sisters, to a house in Phoenix owned by the Catholic church. Although the sisters were not involved in Latin American solidarity work, they were there to pray with in the morning and talk with in the evening.

As Darlene became active in the Valley Religious Task Force, she became frustrated by the failure of the Catholic church to respond to the needs of refugees. While Protestant groups were housing Central Americans and posting bond for those arrested, her own Church remained silent. "I had always believed that my Church cared about its people. I was beginning to feel like I had been duped."

Eager to shake the local hierarchy out of its complacency, Darlene helped organize a protest during Holy Week. She and several others staged a three-day fast on the steps of a Catholic church. Local dance and theater troupes performed, and television crews came to cover the event. Several priests talked to the participants about working with them, but the pastor responsible for Darlene's housing was outraged by the public display. He asked Darlene to leave church housing immediately. "I could hardly believe it," she said. "Here was some man outside my congregation telling me where I could and could not live."

Darlene packed her belongings and moved into an apartment with a nun from another order, once again feeling uprooted. She had moved three times in the past year alone. Every time she got close to someone, it seemed, she had to move on.

She didn't spend much time dwelling on her predicament. There was too much to do. She was invited to testify in federal immigration court, where she got a crash course in the legal system. She was shocked to find how few Guatemalans and Salvadorans who fled to the United States were granted refugee status. The courts wanted hard evidence of torture, death threats, fear of persecution. But how did one document harassment and fear?

An INS (Immigration and Naturalization Service) agent told a news reporter that he would deny political asylum to a family that had photographs of their murdered daughters' mutilated bodies. There was no written proof of why the girls were killed, the agent said. Darlene herself had not had time to document the reasons for her flight. Who stopped for written proof when they were running for their lives? And who would have provided it anyway—the National Guard?

Frustrated by the courts, Darlene had been looking for another way to help the refugees when she met Sister Mary Malherek. A Maryknoll nun, she worked with the Chicago Religious Task Force, a group that helped coordinate the underground railroad, arranging transportation for refugees from border towns to churches and temples throughout the United States. She had come to Phoenix to investigate rumors of Guatemalan Indians hiding out in the Chandler Desert and to look for refugee families to travel to churches in the north. Together she and Darlene drove to the desert towns.

They discovered five hundred refugees, mostly Kanjobal Indians from northwestern Guatemala. The conditions were deplorable: groups of fifteen men crammed into forty-six-dollar-a-week hotel rooms, dozens of people living in one-room ·shacks the same wretched way they had lived in the camps. While there were some families, most of the refugees were males between the ages of sixteen and forty who had left their families in Mexico and Guatemala. Darlene returned to the desert several times with food, clothing, and mattresses donated by local organizations.

When Mary Malherek returned to Illinois, the Chicago Religious Task Force on Central America asked Darlene if she would be willing to screen and counsel refugees in Arizona, coordinating her activities with a Tucson group of church workers who helped refugees cross the Mexican border. The Tucson contingent had heard about Darlene and was eager to work with her. The Reverend John Fife, the leader of the first publicly declared sanctuary church in the United States, called her "a marvelous gift from God dropped on Phoenix."

The sanctuary movement had begun two years earlier, in response to the mass exodus of Salvadoran refugees. An estimated twenty thousand civilians had been murdered or "disappeared" in El Salvador in 1980. On March 24 of that year Archbishop Oscar Arnulfo Romero, a leading advocate of peaceful reform, was murdered after giving a sermon imploring members of the army and the National Guard to stop killing their own brothers and sisters. He was one of sixteen Catholic religious leaders killed between 1977 and 1980. December 1980 brought reports of the rape and murder of four Maryknoll and Ursuline church workers by National Guardsmen. The killing of hundreds of Indians in the Guatemalan highlands had led to a similar flight of refugees into Mexico.

By 1980 the number of Salvadoran and Guatemalan

refugees entering Los Angeles alone had reached almost thirty thousand. As their flow increased, they began appearing in nonborder cities such as Tucson.

The refugees' plight made national headlines in July when thirteen Salvadoran refugees were found dead in the Sonoran Desert. They had been abandoned by their coyotes, guides they had paid handsomely to smuggle them across the border. When a group of Tucson church workers found out that the Immigration and Naturalization Service was planning to deport thirteen Salvadorans who had survived the trip without informing them of their rights, the church workers formed a task force to assist refugees. They raised $750,000 in cash and collateral for bonding Central Americans out of jail.

A year later in Tucson a retired Quaker rancher, Jim Corbett, had his first encounter with refugees. A friend of Corbett's had given a ride to a young Salvadoran traveling from Nogales to Tucson. They were stopped at a border patrol checkpoint, and the Salvadoran was arrested. When Corbett tried to post bond, he learned that the young man had been shipped to a detention center. As a Quaker Corbett believed he had to intervene. He and his wife, Pat, began harboring refugees and transporting them north, thus beginning a new "underground railroad."

Corbett asked the Southside Presbyterian Church in Tucson to assist in feeding and housing refugees who came into the area. On March 24, 1982, the Reverend John Fife and his congregation declared itself a public-witness sanctuary. Other churches across the country followed suit, offering individuals and families a place to live. In September the Chicago Religious Task Force on Central America agreed to help coordinate the growing movement of refugees north and place them in sanctuary congregations. By late 1982 the first thirty churches had publicly declared sanctuary, and many more supported the movement with money, food, and clothing. By 1983 almost every major Protestant denomination had endorsed the movement. Although the Catholic church hierarchy had not issued a statement, individual bishops lent their support.

The sanctuary workers believed that they were operating within the law. They maintained that the Refugee Act of 1980 granted safe haven to people with "a well-founded fear of persecution" at home. The Geneva Conventions of 1949 prohibited all signatory nations from returning refugees to a war zone.

During the early days of the movement sanctuary workers helped refugees process applications for political asylum. But they soon abandoned the practice. Of the 5,500 Salvadorans who requested asylum from 1980 to 1981, only two received it. The INS granted political asylum to less than 1 percent of Guatemalans who applied.

The United Nations High Commission for Refugees stated that all persons who left El Salvador after the outbreak of civil war in 1980 should be regarded as refugees. But the State Department disagreed. It maintained that most of the Central Americans came to the United States for economic reasons and faced no danger if deported.

Corbett and other sanctuary workers believed that the U.S. government did not want to acknowledge the presence of refugees because that would undercut its support for the Salvadoran government. Investigators from the United Nations High Commission concurred: "There appears to be a systematic practice designed to secure the return of Salvadorans, irrespective of the merits of their asylum cases."

Eventually sanctuary workers decided to circumvent INS policy altogether, transporting and harboring refugees without notifying the INS. They began clandestinely at first. Later they became increasingly public with their activities, appearing on national news programs and traveling with reporters.

Darlene was torn about the sanctuary movement. She wanted to return to Guatemala, but there were refugees right here. "I thought, Who could understand what these people were fleeing from? Who could they trust to tell their stories? I saw the sanctuary movement as a way of showing that it was time to stop sending missionaries to preach to the poor folk of Latin America. It was time for us to receive the prophets from the South."

The Task Force gave her a stipend to live on, and Darlene became a crucial link in the underground railroad. While the leadership of the School Sisters had given her permission to work with refugees, they hadn't fully understood the ramifications. As the sanctuary movement gained notoriety, they began asking Darlene questions: For what was she using the congregation's car? Could the order lose its tax-exempt status if a sister was involved in an activity that could be construed as illegal?

Darlene tried to explain her work within the context of larger issues, that as nuns they took vows in order to be more free and ought to be the ones most ready to take risks. Their mission statement called on sisters to refuse to "sit helplessly in front of misery, disease, ignorance, injustice and ugliness ... to move into [Christ's] risen life with hope in the future, knowing that He may require something of us tomorrow that He does not today." The possibility of losing tax-exempt status should not deter them from responding to refugees. Saint Francis had urged his followers to risk hunger and homelessness. The School Sisters had been *founded* by refugees.

For the first time she had a significant conflict with the leadership, and she was distraught. "I had always been affirmed and supported by the leadership in everything I had done. Here I was all alone in Arizona, which was my choice but difficult nonetheless, and I was bombarded with questions. It was ironic. My faith had led me from the convent to Guatemala, and when I came back, I felt like I no longer belonged."

Despite the questioning, Darlene continued her work. The Task Force began sending refugees to her home for a week of screening and orientation. Sanctuary wasn't a massive resettlement program. Only one out of two dozen people might be able to live in a church. Many families didn't want to be isolated from the Spanish community in congregations in the North and East. Some refugees had serious emotional or medical problems. Others were too shattered to tell their stories in front of congregations.

Sometimes the problem lay with the sanctuary churches, which amazed Darlene with their special requests. Some specified the nationality of the refugee they wanted; others requested children by age. One congregation asked her to send a nonsmoking vegetarian. Refugees were people, not pets, she reminded them. The point was to shelter people in need.

If some North Americans exasperated her, the Central Americans inspired her. On a Friday morning in July 1984 Darlene welcomed a young Salvadoran fam-

ily: Francisco Nieto-Nuñez, thirty-two; his twenty-
eight-year-old wife, Sandra; and their three children.
Darlene gave the children some crayons and paper from
her toy chest. She spent a few minutes sitting with them
on the floor while they colored, then joined Francisco
and Sandra on the couch.

She began by recording their history. She had already filled dozens of notebooks with stories of rape,
torture, killings, an oral history of the refugee experience.

Francisco told Darlene that he had studied medicine
for five years at the University of El Salvador until
government troops had closed the school. For two
years he worked as a paramedic for an ecumenical
church group while Sandra taught young children at a
church-run school. They knew their work was risky.
The government had accused the church workers of
helping the "subversives"; employees regularly van-
ished from their homes.

One night armed men burst into Sandra and Francisco's home. They were taken from their children,
including their two-month-old infant, and sent to
separate jails. After eight days the children were
brought to an orphanage and declared abandoned. Fortunately relatives tracked them down and brought them
home.

Sandra was held for seventeen days until the International Red Cross arranged for her release. Francisco
was tortured for twenty-seven days with electric shock
and beatings. One afternoon the guards brought Francisco's infant son to the prison. While he watched, the
guards held the baby under water in a tub until Francisco signed a confession saying he was a subversive.

Eleven months passed. Francisco bribed his way out

of prison and left the country under the protection of the Red Cross. Sandra and the children joined him in Mexico.

Darlene listened intently. She was impressed by Francisco's quiet resolve. Passionate and articulate, Francisco and Sandra were the perfect candidates for sanctuary. They understood the complexities of the political situation in Latin America and they were committed to educating North Americans about what they had witnessed.

For several hours they discussed the political situation in El Salvador and how to communicate their experience in religious terms to North American congregations. They should not come on too strong, Darlene told them, or they would put off the more conservative members of the congregations. Francisco nodded. Yes, they understood. They would speak from the heart.

Darlene set up medical appointments the next day for each of them. They would be tested for communicable diseases and parasites. Long-term disabilities, frequently the result of torture, would be noted on medical records. She would try to set up an interview for them with the local press and maybe arrange a speaking engagement in a church. But she suspected Francisco and Sandra would not need much practice.

In the evening they attended a Bible-study meeting held in Spanish at the Alzona Lutheran church. Francisco and Sandra talked about how the Scriptures related to the refugee experience. They said they found comfort in the Book of Exodus: "You shall not oppress a stranger for you know the feelings of the stranger, having yourselves been strangers in the land of Egypt."

Darlene talked to Francisco and Sandra about problems they would face living in sanctuary: the feelings of isolation, the difficulty of living with people who mostly didn't speak Spanish, the lack of independence, the paternalistic attitude of some North Americans. Living in a church was nothing like living in your own home.

She was still coping with her own feelings of isolation. She felt a bond with Central Americans like Francisco and Sandra. Although she liked and admired the North Americans in the sanctuary movement, she couldn't open up as easily with them. She felt detached, like a perpetual newcomer among a group of old friends.

The refugees knew that she understood their suffering and were devoted to her. But some sanctuary workers were annoyed by the intensity of her commitment. Darlene was willing to work sixteen-hour days; others could not. Many had spouses and children to worry about. Several people refused to work with Darlene. They found her manner off-putting. And she was so consumed by the cause, it made them feel guilty. She seemed to forget that they weren't all nuns.

Nor was Darlene getting much support from the sanctuary workers in Tucson. Every week she traveled there to meet with the Reverend John Fife and members of the Tucson Ecumenical Council Task Force on Central America. The meetings were congenial, but Darlene sensed tension developing between the members of the Chicago Religious Task Force and the Tucson group.

Their differences were essentially political. The Chicago Task Force felt that only Central American refugees fleeing oppression in Guatemala and El Salvador should be given aid. Several members of the

Tucson group, including Jim Corbett, maintained that sanctuary workers had a biblical mandate to help refugees crossing the border, whether they were from Guatemala or Nicaragua.

Darlene agreed with the Chicago Task Force. She was not interested in helping only the refugees who fled, when thousands more were left behind. She believed that the sanctuary movement was nothing more than a Band-Aid unless it publicized the conditions in Central America that were forcing people to flee. Equating the plight of a Guatemalan fleeing the death squads with that of a Nicaraguan draft resister, she believed, was missing the point.

The disagreement came to the fore when the Chicago Task Force sent a letter to the Tucson contingent: Since the movement could only help a tiny percentage of refugees entering the United States, it should focus on those going into sanctuary churches. Incensed, Jim Corbett responded with a series of protest letters, which he sent to sanctuary churches and Quaker meetings throughout the country.

The disunity in the group exacerbated the rift Darlene felt with her own congregation. She desperately missed the camaraderie she had known in Guatemala and in the novitiate. A handful of close friends from the novitiate visited occasionally and wrote letters. But she sensed that the leadership was tolerating more than supporting her. She had entered the School Sisters for community and she had never felt more isolated from the women she thought of as her family.

Darlene talked to a friend about leaving the convent. Should she stay in a community that professed commitment to help the poor but turned its back at the first sign of conflict? She had devoted almost two decades to serving the School Sisters. Where were they when she needed them? For weeks she contemplated her decision.

Finally she concluded it was her turn to take the lead. "I could no longer look to the women I saw twenty years ago as visionaries and follow them. I had to be the one with vision. I had to be faithful to what God was calling me to do."

Early Sunday morning Darlene peered out the window. She saw three men in sports cars pull up her driveway. One drove a Trans Am. She didn't like the look of them. She knew one of the men, Jesus Cruz, a sixty-year-old who claimed to be a retired roofer. He had been working for the sanctuary movement for several months, transporting refugees and attending Bible-study meetings. He was a little overeager, too available. Now she was sure something was up. The other men looked like agents.

When Darlene questioned Cruz, he said the men were friends of the Reverend John Fife. They had volunteered to drive Francisco and Sandra and their children to a sanctuary church in New Jersey. Darlene considered calling the trip off. But the arrangements had been made. She told Francisco she didn't trust the men and that he shouldn't say anything during the trip.

When Francisco arrived in New Jersey, he asked a nun to call Darlene and confirm her suspicion. He didn't trust the men. They asked too many questions.

Six months later, in January 1985, Darlene found out that her hunch about Cruz had been correct. He had worked as a government informant since 1978, when he was arrested for transporting four hundred illegal aliens into Florida. During the previous nine months he had

been involved in an undercover investigation, infiltrat-
ing sanctuary meetings in churches in Arizona and Mexico. The man Darlene prayed with, the man who
professed to love Jesus Christ, had been wearing a body
bug to church.

IV

I awakened to the sound of guitar music coming from
the living room. It was eight A.M. Sunday in the two-
bedroom white-and-brown-brick cottage in Phoenix
Darlene shares with Judy Connolly, a School Sister of
Notre Dame. The living room was warm and cozy, a
cross between a 1960s dorm room and a family den.
Tapestries and posters from Guatemala decorated the
living room wall. The plaid couch and assorted chairs
were garage-sale bargains and hand-me-downs from
parents and friends.

Judy was dressed for work in a blue blazer, silk
blouse, pleated skirt. Darlene had on an embroidered
cotton shirt, jeans, and sneakers. She wore a simple gold
ring on her left hand, a sign of her consecration to God,
and tiny gold hoop earrings, a gift from a Guatemalan
friend.

They pray every morning they are together. Judy
plays guitar and sings in a lush alto voice. Darlene sings
along with gusto, struggling to stay on key. She opened
the Bible and read a passage from Kings. The two nuns
sat in silence for a moment contemplating the meaning.
Darlene rubbed her forehead.

"Anyone would think there were no females, that
everyone doing anything was male." She was silent
again.

The sisters finished their service with intercessory

prayers. For centuries nuns had believed that their meditations were the link between men and God. Now they were simply two women praying.

"I pray for Darlene, the defendants, and the refugees," said Judy.

"I pray for the men, women, and children in Guatemala and El Salvador," said Darlene.

Many progressive nuns have eliminated formal daily prayer from their lives, feeling the routine forced. But Darlene continues to find solace in the ritual.

"I got my first Bible after Vatican II," she told me. "Before that only priests were supposed to have Bibles, and they would interpret the messages for the rest of us. I think having our own Bibles has been one of the elements that's helped to subvert religious women. We pray with the Scriptures and reflect on what they mean for us today. The messages are pretty radical."

"Morning is my best time to pray. I read from the Scripture for twenty minutes. Sometimes I just sit in silence."

"How do you envision God?" I asked.

"I have visual images of God. Before I know what I'm feeling, I often have a visual image. When I'm angry, I have a vision of being in a tiny room with thousands of stacked dishes and breaking those dishes. When I'm still, I feel a special presence of God. It's like a beam of light that comes to me right here." She pointed to her heart. "It makes me feel peaceful and connected and confident.

"I think twenty years ago I looked at God as male. God the father. The wise man with the white hair. My image of God was probably a lot more formulated by what my religion teachers and priests said, more in line with an authority figure, I suppose. Over the years God went from being a calculator to being a very present, loving God—more of a female figure. Jesus is sister and brother. I feel God is faithful, but I don't think of God as a lover image. Nor do I think of an all-controlling, all-powerful, all-knowing kind of super image. There is a spirit and light of God that speaks for a wholeness, rightness, and integrity. And because we haven't achieved a just society doesn't mean God isn't real. I have been asked how I can explain violence if there is a God. I guess I turn the question around: How can you explain justice if there is no God?"

I glanced at a picture of Dorothy Day, the founder of the Catholic Worker Movement, hanging on the wall. "Do you look to her for inspiration?" I asked.

"I look to the two Dorothys," she said, folding her arms behind her head, "Dorothy Day and Dorothee Sölle, the German theologian. They've become more important to me this year after all that's happened. I met Dorothee Sölle. She's an academic, but she doesn't start out with abstract principles. She begins with her own experiences. It's like beginning in a base community in Latin America. Even a poor campesino can look at his experience in light of the gospel and reflect on it. It's not something reserved for people of higher levels of learning.

"I'd always admired Dorothy Day and her work with the Catholic Worker Movement, but I didn't know much about her life until I started reading. Did you know that she had an abortion? Did you know she was a socialist–Communist party kind of radical before she converted to Catholicism? She had a lot of trouble justifying to some of her socialist friends when she converted that she wasn't selling out the poor, because the Church is identified as an institution. Many people called her a saint when she died. That's pretty amazing considering the institutional Church stand on abortion."

I asked her how she felt about the vow of celibacy.

"I haven't read or talked much about celibacy. I think my ideas are still evolving. I'm not sure the vow doesn't come out of a paternalistic, male-oriented Church. When I think about the future of religious life, I'm not so sure that celibacy has to be an element. Maybe there need to be more creative communities within the Church for singles and couples. I think there will always be a place for people who choose celibacy, but I hope we develop many more role models for community. I think the specifics of lifestyle—whether you have sex, whether you're heterosexual or homosexual—aren't as critical as what I see at this point in my life: community and service. I think you need community to maintain your vision: a commitment to the poor and oppressed. A community keeps you challenged. As a School Sister I am challenged by other people's ministries and the wider world vision of an international community. I like the faithfulness of sisters in community prayer. All of this impacts my life differently than a family might have. I don't think I'd be at the point I am without the challenge of a community."

"What did the community teach you about dealing with celibacy?" I asked.

"We never talked about it," she said, smiling. "I think it was supposed to be imbued in you by the Holy Spirit."

"I've heard a lot of talk about 'sexual celibates.' What does this mean?"

"It means that sexuality is broader than genitalia. Your sexuality, your fullness as a woman, and knowing who you are is deeper and broader than how you relate to another person physically—an appreciation of your own sexuality rather than a negation of it. To be a celibate, you don't have to negate that you are a woman. This is who you are; this is how you respond, and this is how you feel physically, which may be different from someone else."

"Do you ever regret not having had children?"

"That's one of the hardest things to deal with," she said. "It wasn't something I thought about much when I entered. When I was thirty and working with a lot of small children, kids were always crawling all over me. My nieces and nephews were small at the time. The choice to be celibate came to the forefront. But I think the bigger issue is aloneness, not having one person in my life."

"When do you feel lonely?"

"At points of extreme pressure the loneliness comes out more and more. In one sense you'd think that stress and crisis could keep you so preoccupied with responding to the immediate crisis that you wouldn't have time for other feelings. But for me the stress causes my feelings to overflow and it becomes real difficult to deal with them. The other difficult thing is always having to say good-bye. You develop close relationships, and ultimately you have to leave. It can lead you to avoid risking any kind of involvement because it's so painful to leave, or it can make you feel freer to become involved with more people."

"How do you cope with the loneliness?"

"I guess I've learned that some sense of balance or stability keeps me feeling more in control. And the terribly insecure feeling brings me back to God. Prayer opens me up and helps me deal with things."

"What would you do if you fell in love tomorrow?"

"I'd deal with that tomorrow." Darlene grinned. "Most of the men I've wondered about have already made some kind of commitment. I've had lots of occasions to be alone with some married men I respect a great deal. But I've been superconscious that they have wives and families, and I would never want to interfere with that. I certainly would say I could fall in love: I move in a lot of different circles. But I think there are signals you give when you are available."

"Would you ever leave the congregation?"

She leaned back in her chair. "There were points in the past where it would have been devastating to leave. I wouldn't have been sure where my life was. Now I have a sense of rootedness and commitment to my God. If I left, my sense of who I am would not be shattered. I think we ought to get to a point where if a person gives a good twenty years of her life in service and then leaves, it shouldn't be looked at as a lesser commitment. Fifteen years ago I remember looking at a woman my age who was leaving and thinking, 'Why now?' Today I understand it. Religious life does not have to be forever. I'm not planning on leaving today. But you never know what tomorrow will bring."

V

The indictments came on January 14, 1985. Darlene was not alone. Sixteen church workers were charged with "conspiracy to smuggle illegal aliens," some sixty of whom had been arrested in coordinated raids. The indicted group included three Catholic nuns, two priests, and a Protestant minister. Federal agents and paid informants, such as Jesus Cruz, had routinely worn body bugs to church services and Bible-study classes for many months. They had taped nearly one hundred hours of conversation.

The agents who had searched Darlene's apartment had confiscated dozens of files, photographs, her passport, and a notebook from a class she had taken on liberation theology. (Later she would learn that the agents had circled the words *poor* and *oppressed* whenever they appeared in her notebook. In the margins they wrote, "Marxist ideology.") Margarita, the young Salvadoran woman staying in her home, was under arrest.

The crackdown on the sanctuary movement did not come as a surprise to Darlene. Although the government had not gone after a single employer, two sanctuary workers had been arrested the previous year for transporting refugees. She was startled, however, by the scale of the investigation. Why go to such extremes to capture nuns and priests who had publicized their actions?

The public responded swiftly to the news of the indictments. Religious organizations and individuals contributed more than a million dollars to help pay for their legal defense. Darlene appreciated the moral support, but she was uncomfortable with the huge sums being spent to keep the defendants out of jail. She would have preferred to use counsel provided by the court. But others insisted that high-profile lawyers would help publicize the case and thus the plight of the refugees.

John Fife was the first to retain a lawyer, Robert J. Hirsh, one of the top criminal attorneys in the Southwest. Together they helped assemble a legal team that included James J. Brosnahan, a senior partner at a major San Francisco firm; A. Bates Butler III, a former federal prosecutor from Tucson; Ellen Yaroshefsky, a staff attorney for the Center for Constitutional Rights in New York; and several veteran activists.

A couple of the lawyers asked Darlene to wear religious garb to the trial: "The jury would really respond well if you wore a habit."

"Forget it," she replied. She did not own a habit; she wasn't going to rent one.

She fired the first lawyer assigned to her. Too arrogant and macho. And he didn't know a thing about Central America. She was impressed by attorney Michael Altman, a professor of criminal and immigration law at Arizona State University who had advised the school's Catholic center on the legal implications of providing sanctuary. Altman agreed to represent her. He had been counsel to one of the two other nuns indicted, but the government had dropped charges against the sisters because one was in ill health and the other was caring for her. Darlene was suddenly the only nun in the case.

Three defendants pleaded guilty to reduced charges, leaving six women and five men to stand trial. The government referred to them as co-conspirators, even though some of the defendants had never met. The press dubbed them the Tucson Eleven.

It was certainly a diverse group:

• Jim Corbett, fifty-two, wiry, gray-haired, a Quaker, once a philosophy professor and later a rancher. The father of the sanctuary movement, he had smuggled hundreds of refugees across the border.

• The Reverend John Fife, forty-five, long and lanky, favored jeans and cowboy boots over clerical garb. The pastor of Southside Presbyterian Church, he was the main spokesperson for the movement.

• Wendy LeWin, at twenty-six the youngest defendant, a former waitress, swimming teacher, heavy-equipment operator. A self-declared "nonbeliever," she worked with refugees in Phoenix.

• Phillip Willis-Conger, twenty-eight, the son of Methodist missionaries and director of the Tuscon Ecumenical Council's refugee task force. He met his wife, Ellen Willis-Conger, while transporting refugees.

• Margaret Hutchinson, thirty, Methodist, graduate student in Mid-Eastern studies. She set up a border ministry for Mexicans and Central Americans.

• Father Ramon Dagoberto Quiñones, forty-nine, a parish priest in Nogales, Sonora, Mexico, who ministered to jailed refugees. As a Mexican native he did not have to be tried in the United States, but chose to stand by his friends.

• Maria del Socorro Pardo de Aguilar, fifty-eight, a widow from Nogales who visited refugees in Mexican prisons. Her situation was the same as that of Quiñones.

• Nena MacDonald, thirty-eight, Quaker, a registered nurse and volunteer for a refugee task force.

• Father Anthony Clark, thirty-seven, a parish priest, chaplain at a juvenile detention center, and director of a boys' home in Nogales, Arizona, on the U.S. side of the border.

• Mary Kay Espinoza, thirty-one, director of religious education at Clark's church.

The pretrial hearings began in May 1985 and wound into June. The defense sought to have the charges dismissed on the grounds that the defendants' First, Fourth, and Fourteenth Amendment rights against illegal search and seizure had been violated by the use of wired informants in churches and other tactics. Judge Earl H. Carroll criticized the government's methods but denied the motion. He also denied the defense's motion to dismiss charges on the grounds that prosecution of sanctuary workers violated international law and freedom of religion.

The government fared far better. Judge Carroll granted several prosecution motions and ruled that the defense could present no evidence or testimony about the conditions or dangers to civilians in any foreign country or the defendants' religious beliefs or motivation. He also forbade the defense from arguing that the actions of sanctuary workers were necessary to save the lives of refugees.

Later Carroll would rule that the defense could not argue that Central Americans helped by the defendants were legally refugees or that international law compelled humanitarian aid. Further he found that a 1967 United Nations protocol, which prohibits the deportation of people who have fled their homeland for fear of persecution, did not give aliens any rights enforceable in U.S. courts. More important, he granted the government's motion to bar the defendants from arguing that they had a "good faith" belief that their aid to Central Americans was legal. The strongest lines of defense were blocked.

Michael Altman was beside himself. Despite the judge's pro-government reputation, he was shocked, especially when Carroll took intent out of the case. By proving lack of intent to break the law, Altman thought he could win. Now the strategy changed to putting the government up to its proof: Make the prosecution prove that the defendants knowingly supported aliens, whom they knew to have entered illegally, and that they knowingly transported them in furtherance of illegal ends.

The defense lawyers charged Carroll with bias against the defendants and asked that he be removed from the case. A chief judge denied the request.

The prosecutor also surprised the defense with an eleventh-hour maneuver. He announced he would use only one of the ninety-one tape recordings made by the government, and would rely instead on the testimony of paid informant Jesus Cruz and immigration agent John Nixon. The defense had spent hundreds of hours pouring over transcripts of the tapes—all wasted. It was not a fortuitous start.

Darlene approached the impending trial with trepidation. If she could not use religion as a defense or describe conditions in Guatemala, how could she justify her actions on behalf of refugees? The defense lawyers were reduced to grabbing at technicalities and discrediting the character of the government's main witness.

She worried, too, about the refugees who would be called to testify. Many were unsure what to do. If they refused, they would be jailed during the course of the proceedings. If they complied, they would be testifying against their friends.

Growing discord among the defendants disturbed her. She continued to stress that sanctuary was a movement to publicize conditions in Central America, while Jim Corbett and John Fife downplayed the political dimension. She was also concerned that the female defendants were in danger of being overpowered by the men and that the lawyers were exerting too much control.

Unlike some of the lawyers, her greatest concern was not emerging as a victor with a nonguilty verdict. Even if she went to prison, it would be less brutal than

everyday life in Guatemala or El Salvador, let alone the
life of a political prisoner there.

It wasn't enough to blow holes in the government's
case. She needed to find a way to talk about the refugees,
not just to help one family but the thousands who would
never make it across the border.

Darlene made a plea for unity in a letter to the defendants. She felt isolated and lonely. If she were going
to spend the next several months with these people, she
wanted a sense of community.

> To my beloved friends who must face Judge
> Carroll's bench: I am not ashamed to say that I
> need you, that we defendants all need each other.
> Above all the protection of the integrity of what
> we have been trying to do, and the welfare of
> those whom we are trying to help, demand that
> we consult together, plan together, often in the
> closest communion of mind and prayer and soul.

The response to the letter was lukewarm. Most of
the lawyers and defendants ignored it. Although they
did not tell her directly, several of the defendants felt
her urgings inappropriate. A couple thought it revealed
an embarrassing neediness. They weren't all nuns. They
had families at home.

But Darlene was not alone for long. The School Sisters, who had since passed a resolution supporting Darlene and the sanctuary movement, sent Sister Anne
Taveirne to stay with her for the duration of the trial.
Anne would prepare summaries of the trial proceedings
for the School Sisters and coordinate communications
with the motherhouse. She would be Darlene's main ad-

vocate and source of support. "To me she was a god-send," said Darlene.

On Friday, November 15, 1985, in downtown Tucson, Darlene and Anne walked into the federal courthouse, which was packed with reporters who had staked out places in the eighty-four-seat courtroom hours earlier. Nervous and self-conscious, Darlene walked briskly to the front. The defendants and their attorneys were to sit around three L-shaped tables. Darlene took her place behind her lawyer, Michael Altman. Uncomfortable in her new blue-striped jacket and pants, she sat stiffly in the hard wooden seat.

The prosecutor was Special Assistant U.S. Attorney Don Reno, grandson of a Methodist minister. In 1968 Reno had joined his father's law firm in Central Illinois and had successfully defended a drugstore owner charged with selling sexually explicit materials. For the next several years he represented clients such as theater owners who presented pornographic films like *Deep Throat*. He appeared before the U.S. Supreme Court in 1977 to appeal the conviction of a client for selling obscene material. He lost. In the late 1970s he left his practice to devote himself to business interests, including partnerships in restaurants and nightclubs. In 1983 he passed the Arizona bar exam, and a year later he received a special appointment from the Department of Justice to prosecute alien smuggling cases.

Darlene watched Donald Reno walk to the podium to make his opening statement. He was short and balding with the rigid bearing of a military man.

Over the course of four hours he constructed his conspiracy argument. He described the case as one of "simple alien smuggling." He said the highly regimented sanctuary movement resembled a drug-smuggling operation consisting of three levels. The first level—chief executive officer—consisted of the Reverend John Fife, Jim Corbett, Darlene Nicgorski, and Phil Willis-Conger.

The second tier, Reno said, was made up of smugglers and transporters. At this level Wendy LeWin, he charged, took orders directly from Darlene Nicgorski.

The "Nogalas Connection"—Father Quiñones, Doña Socorro Aguilar, Mary Kay Espinoza, and Father Clark—made up the third tier.

Darlene searched the faces of the twelve jurors for a hint of their reactions. Were they amazed, amused? Convinced? Could they possibly believe that three priests, a minister, a nun, and six layworkers modeled themselves after a drug cartel? Did they really believe she was at the helm? CEO, she thought wryly. Well, that certainly was a first. After twenty years in religious life she had finally earned a promotion.

Days later Darlene's lawyer rose to present his opening argument:

> When Mr. Reno referred to my client, a Catholic nun, he called her a CEO, he called her a travel agent, he called her a general. Well, one thing is sure, you won't hear any witness in this case refer to her that way. They will call her Sister Darlene, sometimes Darlene. . . . The most important thing is that she is a Roman Catholic nun. That dominates her entire life. It is her life.

Despite the judge's rulings, Michael Altman managed to say quite a bit about conditions in Central America. He referred to a young Guatemalan man having his ears cut off by soldiers and to people fleeing political conflict in the country. He told the jury that when Darlene was helping the poor in Guatemala, her pastor had been assassinated.

Reno objected strenuously to Altman's comments. He complained that Michael Altman had violated Judge Carroll's ban. Carroll admonished the attorney for his reference to the pastor and the mutilation, but the point had been made, Darlene thought. The jury had heard.

Altman continued his opening remarks: "The evidence in this case will not show that Sister Darlene committed any crime. The evidence will show that she deserves a humanitarian award, an American heroine who will be recorded in history."

The judge interrupted: "Mr. Altman, that's argument. That is not proper in an opening statement."

Altman smiled. "It is my concluding comment, Your Honor."

Darlene's anger frightened her at times. The degree of hostility she felt—toward Judge Carroll, the legal system, and even toward some of the defendants—overwhelmed her. How was she supposed to respond to this anger—as a woman, as a Christian, as a nun? To her diary she confided her frustration:

I pray that my own anger does not come from any evil sources within, but that it can be used only in a very positive way. I know that I feel very, very angry. My subconscious thoughts are violent—breaking of boards, sticking knives. I feel a great anxiety and restlessness, and oppression. There is a natural oppression, I think, in a situation like this, having to face the great limitations of the courtroom, the bias of the judge, the whole legal system. The added oppression is that, even in our own group, people are not respected, treated individually. There is no sense of group process. How can we stand firm?

Two months passed, and the trial dragged on. Darlene sat in the courtroom silently watching. The lack of involvement was grinding. She was beginning to think it would never be over.

Jesus Cruz took the witness stand. He testified for weeks on end. Cross-examining, the defense lawyers elicited details about oppressive conditions in Central America and the sanctuary workers' motives. They hoped this would elicit the jury's sympathy.

Michael Altman's turn came to cross-examine Cruz. Over Reno's objections he asked Cruz about conversations overheard at church meetings in Phoenix.

"Do you recall people discussing disappearances in El Salvador?"

Cruz answered, "At times they said that, yes, sir."

"Do you also recall them talking about people disappearing in Guatemala?"

"Yes, they spoke of trying to locate family members."

Michael indicated Darlene. "Do you remember among the words she used how she described the white phosphorus that the Salvadoran army was throwing on people in El Salvador?"

"I already said that she talked of many things, sir."

"Do you remember the words that she used: 'Five-hundred-pound bombs'?"

"She spoke of many things, sir."

"Do you remember her saying this: 'We hear you. What you are saying matters very much to us. We call upon our people to share your sorrow, protest our government's part in your pain, and try to get the killing stopped'?"

"Part of that she did say, yes, sir."

Only when Altman asked Cruz about another refugee statement—"A lot of us are disappearing, many are dying horribly"—did Judge Carroll sustain Reno's objection.

Darlene was amazed and delighted that Altman had managed to speak so freely. It was the first time so much graphic information had entered as evidence, and it gave her some hope.

During the weeks of testimony that followed, the defense attorneys' cross-examination revealed that Jesus Cruz had become an agent of the INS only after the head of the Arizona Farm Workers Union threatened to turn him in for illegally transporting Mexicans from Arizona to Florida. Rather than face a possible prison term or deportation to Mexico, Cruz agreed to cooperate with the INS.

The defense attorney produced evidence in court showing that Cruz continued smuggling aliens even while he was working for the INS, that he had also purchased guns for undocumented workers on many occasions, that he helped smuggle the guns into Mexico, where it was a crime to possess them.

During questioning, Cruz was caught lying outright. He testified that he had not seen José René Argueta, a material witness in the case, after the sanctuary investigation ended. He said the INS had paid him only for the sanctuary investigation. INS Agent James Rayburn was present in the courtroom when Cruz denied involvement with Argueta, but said nothing to contradict him.

Later Reno stated in court that Cruz and Argueta had participated together in another paid undercover investigation. He said that Cruz had the mistaken impression that he was not allowed to reveal any details of his undercover work. Reno further allowed that Cruz had falsely attributed statements to defendant Phil Willis-Conger.

Defense attorneys asked Judge Carroll to strike Cruz's testimony, as it was tainted. The judge chastised Agent Rayburn for failing to disclose Jesus Cruz's false statements, but refused to disallow any of the testimony.

Darlene was not surprised. Judge Carroll had yelled at her attorney more for chewing gum in the courtroom than at the government for telling lies.

VI

I sat with a dozen reporters in the press area. Some were there to catch a few days of the proceedings, most were in town for the duration. The press was clearly rooting for the defendants. "I think when these folks get together, their halos must knock," a correspondent from *Newsweek* told me. A writer for a leading daily asked to be reassigned because he could no longer report objectively.

Darlene looked bored in her seat. She wrote letters and journal entries, occasionally glancing at the proceedings to sketch a portrait of one of the players. Next to her, Tony Clark periodically dozed.

The defense attorneys argued with Judge Carroll,

out of the presence of the jury, about his orders barring testimony about the violent conditions in Central America. The day before, the first refugee witness, Alejandro Rodriguez, a former industrial technician, production manager, and labor organizer, had taken the stand. He had made several attempts to tell about the chain of events that brought him to the United States. Prosecutor Reno interrupted with a steady stream of objections. Carroll sustained them.

The judge ruled that the refugees could only use the most general terms in describing conditions that prompted them to leave their homelands. They could use such terms as "political persecution," "fear" and "concern for one's safety," but he warned them against using more graphic language. Sometimes the witnesses or attorneys managed to say the word *kill* before Carroll sustained an objection, sometimes he ruled it stricken from the record. They could not say "death," but could say "people who feared they wouldn't remain alive."

Altman protested strenuously to what he regarded as an arbitrary and unjust ruling. "We submit that this witness is entitled to tell the jury everything about what was said, what happened, what was within his personal experience. To take away from this witness his story is to deny the defendants an opportunity for a fair trial. You rob us of the opportunity of showing the jury what the truth is. One cannot rub out of a conversation words here and words there and expect the jury to understand what is the truth. I implore you to reconsider this issue and to allow all the evidence to get to the jury."

Judge Carroll cleaned his glasses, glanced at the clock, and shook his head vigorously. In the end he dismissed the defense lawyers' arguments, refusing to alter his position at all: "We are not going to get into individual details about what was allegedly happening to any of these people and their families. We are not going to get into ears, eyes, or those other things or the torture. That isn't relevant."

The judge announced the afternoon recess. The reporters moved in. Most sought out John Fife. With his cowboy boots, Western twang, and easy, self-assured manner, he was a hard man to ignore. A veteran preacher, he was also an accomplished raconteur, a skill Darlene had been too shy to master. During the breaks he would banter with reporters, coming up with pithy comments that continually made page one of the dailies. Darlene's unyielding seriousness and biblical references were off-putting to some of the journalists.

I approached Darlene. She showed me her latest sketch of Judge Carroll.

"Not bad for an amateur, don't you think?" she asked, smiling. I agreed, and we went outside to talk.

I asked her how she felt about Judge Carroll's behavior in the courtroom.

She grimaced. "Anyone who has observed the proceedings can feel his hostility and bias against us. At a defendants' meeting we discussed at what point we want to take symbolic action to show our disgust. Do we want to hold hands in protest or turn our back on the judge? Most of us agreed we should not act as rudely as the judge. So we've decided that we will just express our feelings facially. Carroll doesn't have the right to control our feelings."

"Why do you think the government went after you?" I asked.

"I think it's because we were so outspoken in our criticism of U.S. immigration policy and U.S. foreign policy. When we moved the refugees out of the Southwest, the government knew it had a real problem on its hands. We put these refugees in churches in the Midwest, the North, and the East, and they told their stories of the terror. People in the churches got to know the refugees as brothers and sisters. They were no longer aliens, terrorists, or Communists. That's when the government probably figured it had to put someone on trial to silence the dissent and keep the reality about Central America from the North American people. I sometimes think they would have left us alone if we had helped refugees quietly."

"Why this particular group of sanctuary workers?"

"I think they wanted to go after the leadership of the movement. Corbett is certainly looked at as one of the founders and the guru. John Fife and I were looked at as the speakers. And they were smart enough to go after a Wendy LeWin so that it wouldn't look like they were selectively prosecuting. I think they thought if they went after us, they would intimidate people from getting involved."

"Have they succeeded?"

"No, I think more people are becoming involved. More than three hundred churches across the country are now involved. Twenty cities and eleven universities have endorsed sanctuary."

How supportive had the church leaders been? Archbishop Rembert Weakland of Milwaukee was an outspoken supporter. What about the rest?

Darlene sighed. "Very little attention to the trial has been paid by the hierarchy of the Catholic church, despite the fact that five of the defendants are Catholic. We've gotten public statements from the Protestant hierarchy but not the bishops. There has been no response from Rome. The rumor is that they are not supportive. What I do now is based on my own faith, knowledge, and experience. I'm not going to depend on their support. If it comes, good; if not ..." She shrugged.

"One thing that keeps me going is the prophetic role of women in the Church. The prophet comes from the people. She is not elected or appointed by somebody above. The prophet is always coming into conflict with the institution, the status quo. The prophetic role of women has not always been emphasized, but if you read Church history, it's there."

I mentioned that I noticed that the prosecutor did not call her "Sister Darlene."

"That's very true," she nodded. "At one point he referred to me as a woman between the ages of thirty and thirty-five who 'claims to be a nun.' He's trying to discredit me. He is trying to imply that I am not a real nun, I guess because I'm not a teacher or a nurse. He wants to suggest that I'm a revolutionary or a Communist."

"Well?"

She laughed brightly. "I'll quote the famous archbishop from Brazil, Dom Hélder Câmara; 'If I give a man a fish, if I give a man food, I'm often called a saint. If I ask why someone is hungry, I'm called a Communist.' "

Sister Anne Taveirne was protective of Darlene, and suspicious of me. Darlene was under enough pressure, her cool demeanor seemed to suggest, don't subject her to any more.

Every morning Anne took her seat in the courtroom audience. Most days she was joined by another School

Sister of Saint Francis who had come to Tucson to support Darlene. The entire order had issued a statement backing the sanctuary movement. Not all the sisters agreed with Darlene's political position, but when she was in trouble, loyalty prevailed.

The other defendants and lawyers couldn't help noticing Darlene's fan club. "It flips us out how much they love and support her," said Nancy Postero, lawyer for Mary Kay Espinoza. "It seems only fair since their entire life is built on consensus. Their structure gives them strength. How wonderful to have all those sisters—a big built-in family."

During a recess I managed to get a few minutes with Anne. She was tall and graceful, with wavy brown hair and finely chiseled features. She wore a brightly colored embroidered blouse from Mexico.

I asked her how she decided to come to Tucson, to stand by Darlene.

"When I heard about the indictment, I wanted to support her. The community wasn't gung-ho yet, but I wanted to organize a prayer service at the motherhouse. I did, and two hundred people came. All of us came up to Darlene and said, 'We support you.' It was really beautiful. The people who would have opposed her didn't understand the issue well enough yet to know to resist. A lot of the older nuns went along simply because the leadership of the community said it was okay. Later Darlene asked me if I wanted to help out during the trial. I said yes. I came to the trial for two weeks and we got along well."

"How do you help her?"

"I do whatever I can. I try to be a personal support for Darlene. My feeling is she has enough to worry about. The trial is her life now. Darlene gets so wrapped up in what she's doing, she forgets to eat and go to bed. It would be very serious if she got sick. She could be severed from the trial and would have to be tried alone. She wouldn't have the resources and the lawyers. I make sure she has time to relax. There are times when she gets twenty calls a night, and I have to say she's not home."

I asked her how she would describe Darlene. She considered a moment. "Darlene can project an image and share what she's thinking about a situation, but to know her real personality is more difficult. She doesn't jump right out with personal feelings. Immediate emotion is difficult for her. But then again, it often surprises me when she shares with people things I'd be hesitant about sharing. I think she has a real belief and trust in people. I think that trust brings out the best in them. She wants them to understand what is happening.

"Darlene draws her strength from the refugees. I think it hurts her that all this energy is being put into the trial instead of working with refugees. But it's been real satisfying for her to share their story with others. She sees that as a mission.

"I feel proud to be in the same community as Darlene. I feel privileged to know someone who has personally experienced the struggle in Central America and worked with and loved refugees. She learned about liberation not just in theory but in reality. One of my values is to learn the way of God through other people. When a person in community does something, she brings us all into her ministry. Darlene has reached out to us. Some people would have thought of the trial as private hell. Darlene has called on us to come with her in justice."

•   •   •

It was the end of January 1986. Francisco Nieto-Nuñez took the stand. Michael Altman was worried about Francisco's testimony. He might be overconfident and turn the jury off with his arrogance. Worse, his testimony could help the prosecutor establish that Darlene was guilty of transporting refugees. Darlene wasn't worried, however. If anyone could tell the jury about the plight of the political refugee, Francisco could.

She watched intently. Francisco looked calm as he took the stand, unintimidated by the prosecutor's gaze.

Francisco testified in Spanish; a court officer interpreted. He explained that he had been a medical intern in San Salvador when the university was shut down by government troops in 1980. He began practicing medicine at some refugee clinics set up by churches in El Salvador for people displaced because of "war activity." A murmur went through the courtroom at the mention of fighting. The trial had a bit of a game-show flavor. Every time a witness or defense lawyers managed to get in a sliver of information about conditions in Central America, the public reacted as if a point had been scored.

During Prosecutor Reno's direct examination, Francisco looked right at the jury as he spoke.

Reno said, "Mr. Nieto, who did you leave El Salvador with in July of 1984?"

"Well, I went from prison to Mexico City under protection of an international organization." Reno objected, sounding exasperated. "Your Honor, I ask that that response be stricken."

Judge Carroll concurred; motivations for leaving the region were again ruled inadmissible. Darlene smiled.

Reno had asked for a simple name, and Francisco had used the opportunity to say he'd been imprisoned. What more would he manage to say?

Another question was posed. Francisco answered. He and his family crossed the border to Mexico with one of the defendants and then drove to the Southside Presbyterian Church. Afterward he was taken to Sister Darlene's house. There he was picked up by Jesus Cruz and INS undercover agents John Nixon and Lee Morgan.

Reno asked Francisco if he had told Lee Morgan that Darlene made the travel arrangements.

Deadpan, Nieto-Nuñez replied, "During my trip with Mr. Morgan we spoke about my situation, what had happened to me in El Salvador, not the things here."

Reno seemed frustrated. "Your Honor, I ask that that response be stricken."

Darlene looked moved by Francisco's repeated attempts to avoid implicating her in the conspiracy. Of course she had made the arrangements, but Francisco was not going to reveal any more than he had to about her.

Reno repeated the question about travel arrangements several times, and each time Francisco avoided answering: "I really don't know, but you as Americans should know better than us how the underground railroad works."

At the evening recess Altman expressed grave disappointment in the testimony. "The jury knows you're the one who arranged transportation," he told Darlene as they left the courtroom. Altman felt that Reno had scored a critical point. The prosecutor, it seemed, was particularly eager to convict Darlene, whom he considered the most overtly political defendant because of her work with the Chicago Religious Task Force.

Darlene didn't care. The jurors had heard mention of war activity in El Salvador and the slim chances for refugees to get political asylum through legal means. "The lawyers look at testimony in terms of whether it implicated us in the conspiracy," she said as she left the courtroom to meet Francisco. "To me that wasn't important. I thought today was terrific!"

The trial dragged on for five months. The prosecution had rested its case at last, and the jurors were ready to begin hearing the other side of the story. The twelve defense lawyers had prepared a list of 150 possible witnesses, so the jurors were anticipating many more weeks in Judge Carroll's courtroom.

Carroll called the court to order, and attorney Robert Hirsh faced the bench. "Reverend Fife is going to rest, Your Honor," he said. The jurors turned to one another, visibly confused.

Attorney James Brosnahan stood up. "On behalf of Mrs. Socorro Aguilar, we rest."

One by one, each lawyer stood up and recited the same message. Reno sat rigid in his chair. Judge Carroll looked astonished, but remained silent until the last lawyer, William Walker, rose.

"Father Anthony Clark and the sanctuary defense rests," he said.

The startled judge turned to the jury. "Members of the jury, the defendants rested, and I have found out for the first time in your presence that the defendants have rested."

True, the decision had not been finalized until the

night before, although the attorneys and defendants had
met every evening for a week to discuss the strategy.
Most felt that their position had been presented through
the five months of cross-examination of the government's nineteen witnesses and that they had nothing to
gain by calling witnesses whose testimony would be re-
stricted.

Darlene was distraught by the decision. She had
desperately wanted the chance to speak out in court
after months of sitting silently by. But she lost the
vote.

Fortunately her friend Pat was coming to spend a
few days with her in Tucson. They had been novices in
the same class of School Sisters. It would be good to
have the company, someone new to talk to. Pat, too,
was an activist. She would understand Darlene's frustration during the trial.

On a Monday Pat arrived and met Darlene at the
sanctuary media office, where they spent the afternoon
helping Anne stuff some mailing envelopes. Afterward
they ate a picnic lunch outside, followed by a game of
racquetball at a nearby gym. Over dinner they talked
about the trial, their political views, their vocations. Pat
said she had not always been too sure of herself, but
now had a clearer idea where she was heading.

"I'm so frustrated trying to respond to this crazy
world," she said, "I'm becoming more contemplative."

That night Darlene lent Pat her car so she could
drive to the home of the sisters with whom she was
staying. They'd meet again at seven-thirty the following
morning in the cathedral near the courthouse for a prayer
service.

Tuesday morning Pat didn't show. By midmorning
Darlene was worried.

When the proceedings were over, Anne met Darlene in the witness room.

"Pat was in a car accident," she said. "She didn't survive."

For the next two days Darlene felt like a robot. She notified friends and relatives and helped arrange the funeral. At night she had vivid dreams of Pat. "I would see her in the smashed car and watch her spirit ascend from her body."

Pat's body was flown to the motherhouse in Milwaukee for the funeral. Seven hundred people came, including all but one of her remaining classmates, all eight of them. Eight from an original group of sixty.

Darlene requested that the jury's deliberations be postponed for two days following the funeral. She wanted a chance to mourn with her sisters. But most of the defendants said they didn't want to lose more time. After all, they said, Pat was a friend, not a member of her family.

Darlene was beside herself. " 'Not a member of the family.' It was just another example," she said, "of how people don't understand nuns."

She flew home Thursday for the first day of deliberations. The defendants and lawyers wore electronic beepers so they could be notified the minute the jury concluded.

At 2:12 P.M. on May 1st, the ninth day of deliberation, the buzzers went off. The jury had reached a verdict.

VII

"It was May Day," said Darlene, "and the Feast of Saint Joseph the Worker. When my beeper went off, I ran to the courtroom. Wendy LeWin's lawyer, Ellen Yaroshefsky, broke into tears, she was so nervous. I was concerned that Anne wouldn't be there.

"By the time I got to the courtroom, it was almost full. I'd say three-fourths of the people were press. The TV cameras were set up right outside the courtroom.

"The lawyers and defendants met in the back room and we said a prayer. Father Quiñones said it in Spanish. John Fife said it in English. Everyone was feeling hyper—up. There was a lot of anxiety in the air. Here the day had finally come. Reckoning day.

"We had tried earlier to decide what to do in the courtroom. We considered rising and holding hands in solidarity. Everybody liked that idea except Tony Clark. He said, 'I don't like this holding hands stuff.' We talked about singing songs. Fife wanted to sing, 'Gloria in Excelsis' if there were acquittals. I said, 'No, that's too churchy.'

"There was a serious mood before the jury came in. The judge said he did not want any outbursts or demonstrations, then he asked his bailiff to bring in the jury."

As the jurors filed in, Darlene tried to read their expressions. She saw blank faces.

Carroll addressed the group. "Members of the jury, I am advised that you have arrived at a verdict. Is that correct?"

"That is correct."

"The clerk will read the verdicts."

"*The United States of America* versus *Maria del Socorro Pardo de Aguilar,*" the clerk read. "We the jury in the above entitled and numbered case find the defendant guilty as charged to count one of the indictment."

Darlene stiffened in her seat. Count one was conspiracy. She could hardly believe it. If Doña Maria was found guilty, more convictions were coming.

"John Fife," the clerk continued. "Guilty as charged to count one."

He went down the list. Socorro Aguilar was guilty on two counts. Fife was guilty of three counts. Father Quiñones on two counts. Peggy Hutchinson, one. Tony Clark, one count. Wendy LeWin, one count. Phil Willis-Conger on three counts.

Darlene sat impassively as she listened for her name.

"Darlene Nicgorski. Guilty as charged to count one." Again and again, she heard the clerk, "Darlene Nicgorski guilty as charged . . . guilty as charged." In the end she was convicted on five counts, more than any of the others. If Carroll felt like it, he could sentence her to fifteen years.

She felt numb as Michael Altman escorted her into the witness room.

Socorro Aguilar's lawyer spoke first. "Brosnahan got all teared up," Darlene said. "He thanked the defendants for what we had taught him about integrity. Peggy said a few words: 'Nobody is going to leave this case the same as when they entered. We are not going to be put down by this.' I said that we had reached a critical moment: 'We have to continue to move the refugees north. This cannot stop the movement.'"

As they left the witness room, the defendants sang softly:

We shall overcome,
We shall overcome,
We shall overcome someday . . .

Hordes of supporters reached out their hands in sympathy; scores of newspaper reporters and a dozen television crews vied for interviews.

"Have you regretted anything you've done?" a reporter shouted.

"How can I regret being a Christian?" Father Quiñones responded.

They led a procession of supporters to the civic-center plaza two blocks away for a press conference. Darlene was to be the main speaker. Expecting some convictions, she had written her statement the day before.

The trial, she told the group, had not been about truth. "The jury was denied the facts and uninformed about its power to acquit," she said.

A reporter asked Hirsh what went wrong. "They had the wrong jury," he said.

When Mary Kay told the audience she thought the verdict was the will of God, Darlene grimaced. She did not think God had willed any of the convictions.

After the press conference Darlene raced home, packed a suitcase, and drove to the airport. There was no time to contemplate the verdict. She had a flight to catch to New York City. The following morning she was to appear on television.

I called Darlene at her hotel in midtown Manhattan. Her interview on a morning news program had been postponed. She had a couple of days before she was to appear on the Phil Donahue show.

She told me she had slept fitfully. She was uncomfortable in the expensive hotel room a public relations firm had booked for her. "I went downstairs to get a glass of juice and it cost two dollars," she told me in astonishment.

I offered her my apartment and promised her cheap orange juice. She accepted gratefully.

When she arrived at my home, she looked pale and frightened. "Will you be staying here?" she asked me.

"Would you rather be alone?"

"No," she said. "I don't want to be alone."

I suggested dinner and a movie to take her mind off the trial, but the comedy failed to distract her. Later that evening we sat down to talk.

"What now, Darlene?"

"I'm preparing for the worst," she said pensively. "It's kind of scary. I do have a sense that I've gotten through this and I hope I'll have the strength to continue. I'm worried about the lack of privacy. At a federal minimum-security prison I'll probably have more privacy. Fife said, 'Oh, they'll probably have racquetball.'" She smiled weakly.

"Maybe this sounds like a martyr, but there may be a whole lot of things to learn in jail. Maybe I think about jail the way I think about the trial. I've gotten some graces. There are so many things I've learned, like my talent for public speaking. I've become more of an extrovert. Sometimes I think I look forward to doing some of the physical work in jail, helping in the kitchen, cleaning, whatever it could be. I could have my own thoughts and not have them taken away from me. I know some people who have spent time in jail for antinuclear work. One fellow described jail as the new cloister."

"Are there ever moments when you feel you just can't cope anymore?" I asked.

She shook her head. "Yes," she said softly. "A lot of times it happens in the middle of the night. Nights are so vulnerable. I guess nights are vulnerable for everybody."

By the time I got up the next morning, Darlene had been awake for an hour. She had already made coffee and said her morning prayers. She looked rested, more relaxed.

"Do you know of any inexpensive shoe stores in the area?" she asked.

Her loafers had fallen apart; she held the skin of a shoe in one hand, the heal in the other.

"What do you consider inexpensive?" I asked.

"Five dollars," she announced. "I paid five dollars for these shoes and they lasted a year."

"You can't find shoes for five dollars," I mumbled. But we would give it a shot.

We walked to a strip in Greenwich Village that is known for its bargains. Darlene liked the neighborhood. "I love walking around here," she said. "There are so many different kinds of people, all ethnic groups." Every few blocks someone caught her fancy. She stared too long at a girl in black leather with spiked hair. "I don't know why people in New York are so concerned with their image." She shook her head. "Maybe it's a form of expression—the orange hair."

We walked in and out of shoe stores, scouring the sale racks. Darlene didn't like anything she saw. "Too cheap," she said. "Shoddy workmanship."

Not only did she want five-dollar shoes, she wanted them to last a year. I discouraged her from trying on a few pairs. "I don't think that would be good on TV," I said, rejecting a pair of sporty tie shoes. I could see her respect for me diminishing.

"Why don't you consider something with a little heel?" I asked.

"They have to be comfortable," she responded firmly. I was on shaky ground.

After fifteen minutes of this she was ready to go home. "I'll find a budget store tomorrow morning," she said.

"You might not have time!" I said, showing too much alarm at the prospect of Darlene wearing sneakers with her suit on national television. "Five more minutes," I pleaded.

To my surprise I spotted a pair of gray leather pumps in her size, and exactly five dollars. Just right for *Donahue,* I thought. Great color. Not too high, not too low. Perfect for a nun recently convicted of a felony.

On a sunny day in early July 1986 while thousands were celebrating the centennial of the Statue of Liberty, eight church workers were being sentenced for ministering to refugees.

Darlene walked slowly to the lectern in Judge Earl Carroll's courtroom. After seven months of silence, she finally had the chance to speak. She was nervous, but she was ready.

She even brought visual aids: a slide projector and a small screen. In a darkened courtroom she conducted a tour of a Salvadoran refugee camp in Honduras, the camps in Chiapas, Mexico, and a detention center in California.

Afterward she turned to face the bench.

"I am glad to finally have this opportunity to address the court. After many long months of listening to legal arguments I'm eager to address what I consider the heart of the case.

"I made my vows as a Catholic sister some twenty years ago here in the United States. It was not until five years ago today, however, that I understood, for the first time, the cost of that commitment. Having walked with our Guatemalan sisters, lived those weeks of fear, terror, and hope with them, I came a little closer to experiencing what horror repressive military dictatorships exert upon their citizens. I experienced in my own flesh a little bit of what it means to be persecuted, to flee in order to save one's life.

"Judge Carroll, having seen 'official' reports of what happened and having been there and knowing what happened, I know whom to believe. Who would you believe, Judge, if you had seen what I had seen and heard what I had heard? I ask you, Judge, what do the missionaries, the campesinos, the religious have to gain by lying or distorting the truth?

"The conditions I have seen and heard in which our brothers and sisters from Central America are forced to survive, both there and here, call out to me and all persons of faith and decency. Archbishop Oscar Romero, one of the clearest prophets and martyrs of Central America, had no doubt whatsoever what the answer must be. There is no room for neutrality where life and death are involved. He was well aware that abstaining from the struggle constitutes aiding and abetting the criminal act. My faith has brought me to the realization that we are either at the service of life or we are accomplices of death of the Central Americans.

"Six years ago Archbishop Romero was brutally assassinated while saying Mass. Because of his death more people in the United States became aware of the tragedies of that tiny country of El Salvador. After the rape and murder of the four North American church women, more people began to question our involvements in El Salvador. Now some of us who are clearly identified with the Church have faced a long trial, and after your interpretation of the law we have been convicted. That, too, has raised the awareness of more people to the plight of the refugees in the United States and this government's complicity in maintaining the situation in Central America through the sending of arms and advisers.

"But nothing has changed for the Central Americans.

"Judge Carroll, after prayer, reflection, fasting, and discernment I urge you to treat me no differently than the INS treats them. I do not believe I have done anything to warrant a sentence, but neither have the Central Americans who remain detained in camps here in the United States.

"My attorney advises me that these are the days in which courts look favorably upon alternative sentencing. I offer to work in the refugee camps in Mexico or any other country if you cannot allow me to continue ministry to Central American refugees in the United States. I offer to work with Central American refugees in or around any of the detention camps where the INS treats Central Americans as criminals. Since life in the refugee camps is more difficult than a federal prison, I urge you to consider this alternative."

She clasped her hands like a novice about to take her vows.

"If you cannot accept the alternatives I have presented, I want you to know that I am prepared to go to prison. I am left with no choice. I cannot abandon the Central Americans.

"This is not an easy decision. It has not been made lightly. I have consulted with many and am now at peace. My commitment calls me to take all steps, Judge Carroll, not to count the cost. It is the price of living out the integrity of conscience. It is the price of living out my faith."

She didn't expect her words to sway the judge. He had not even bothered to look up from his notebook when she spoke. The court's rulings, she felt, showed no compassion for the plight of the refugees, no respect for the motivation of the defendants. To Carroll it was a cut-and-dried case of alien smuggling. She was ready to go to jail.

The following day, however, the judge surprised the defendants with a show of leniency. Darlene, John Fife, Father Quiñones, Socorro Aguilar, Phil Willis-Conger, and Peggy Hutchinson received five years' probation; Tony Clark and Wendy LeWin, three. They were not going to jail, but they would have to meet regularly with probation officers, informing them of their comings and goings; they could not vote; they could not run for public office.

The judge left the group with a warning "to follow proper procedure," to work within the law. "Admittedly it's time-consuming," Carroll said. "It doesn't have the kind of attraction that a trial such as this has, the media attention, the applause, and that kind of thing. But the legal system has worked for two hundred years."

Darlene was outraged by what she thought was Carroll's patronizing tone. After months in the courtroom the defendants were being slapped on the wrist like children. If Carroll thought she was going to stop counseling refugees, he had another thing coming. She would continue her work in the sanctuary movement, even with a probation officer breathing down her neck.

When she heard that Don Reno had told a reporter that he cared more about the reform of the defendants than he did about INS procedures, Darlene could barely contain her anger. Phil Willis-Conger beat her to the punch. He jumped on a bench and gave Reno a Nazi salute.

In the summer of 1987 Darlene startled family and friends with a decision she had been considering for some time. She had decided to sever her relationship with Rome. After twenty-one years she was leaving religious life.

She believed that her decision did not negate more than two decades of service to the School Sisters of Saint Francis. Still, she worried that the sisters who had stood beside her during the sanctuary trial would feel betrayed. She wanted her community to understand that she still cared for them deeply. She would no longer be a School Sister, but she would always be their sister.

If she had initially considered leaving the order because of conflicts with the congregation, in the end her reason for returning to secular life was the same one cited by thousands of nuns before her. She no longer wanted to be affiliated with the hierarchy of the Roman Catholic church.

"The relationship of 'sister' with the institutional Church has become personally oppressive to me," she wrote to her community in August. "I cannot accept or teach directly or indirectly by my institutional association the Church's dogmatic and repressive stance against women, its teachings regarding sex and procreation, and its oppression of lesbians and gays. And so the faith that led me to ask to be received as a School Sister of Saint Francis twenty years ago now urges me to seek dispensation from canonical vows.

"This decision will not surprise some of you. It was

in the summer of 1984 that I started asking the questions out loud. However, with the indictment in January 1985 I decided to put the issue 'on hold' until after the trial. There was not the physical or psychological space to give to a discernment process amid the pressures and tensions of a public trial.

"After twenty-one years as a School Sister of Saint Francis, it has been a painful discernment process for me. I also know that it is not easy for you to hear because of our relationship. I wish it could be different, but I know it to be right and just. You may very well be disappointed. You may even feel angry or betrayed. It has taken me six months of grieving, and I'm not through yet.

"I want to be as faithful as possible to you, my God, and the struggle for justice. Even though I'm not in canonical relationship to you, I'm open to associate relationship or any new forms of membership we can create. But to pursue the journey, to walk and speak on behalf of all oppressed, I need to be free of the canonical association of the institutional Church.

"I'm grateful for the years we have shared life so closely; especially I'm thankful for the relationships, the ministry opportunities, and the personal challenges that have come through these involvements. I know that I would not be at the place where I am today if it were not for the support and witness that School Sisters of Saint Francis gave me and the sanctuary movement throughout the trial.

"What I ask of you is that we continue to be sisters together—sisters in the struggle for justice, right relationships in a world turned upside down."

After the trial Darlene decided to head east to contemplate her decision. She had heard about a women's center and retreat house in Plainville, Massachusetts, run by two women known for their commitment to peace and justice. For a few months, at least, she would try to relax. She had much to think about, from her career plans to her financial status. Like most former nuns she did not have a pension. Under federal regulations nuns had not been allowed to join the Social Security system until 1972. After two decades of working she had no money in the bank.

The first year of secular life, she had been warned, was like the aftermath of a divorce. Being on her own brought up feelings of confusion and vulnerability as she contemplated her former life. She missed her friends in community; she felt misunderstood by some leaders of the order, who could not comprehend her feelings toward the hierarchy. Still, Darlene enjoyed her independence and meeting women from all religious traditions. A few months after she arrived, she threw a "coming-out-of-the-convent" party for her new friends in Plainville. She baked the food; a guest brought a bottle of Blue Nun.

She decided to put down roots in Cambridge, Massachusetts, a college town with a strong activist tradition. Although job hunting was a new experience, she quickly found two part-time positions teaching English as a second language. Most of her students were refugees from Guatemala, El Salvador, and Haiti. The more than thirty thousand Central Americans in Boston made up one of the largest immigrant groups in the city. Many lacked working papers; some needed homes. The stories of refugees who had migrated east were new to Darlene. Their terror was not.

In January 1991 the sanctuary defendants lost their last appeal. Darlene and seven others argued that the prosecution had violated their religious freedom. They maintained that they should have been allowed to offer evidence that they believed refugees had a right to enter and reside in the United States under the terms of international law and the 1980 Refugee Act. But the U.S. Supreme Court was not convinced. It rejected their appeal without comment. Michael Altman was devastated; Darlene was not surprised.

December 1990, however, had brought good news for Central American refugees. The Justice Department had agreed to settle a lawsuit brought against the INS five years earlier by more than eighty immigrant rights and church groups, including the Baptist, Methodist, Presbyterian, and Unitarian churches. The landmark settlement came in conjunction with a law granting temporary legal status to Salvadoran refugees who had arrived in the United States during the 1980s.

The settlement required the readjudication of some 150,000 cases in which asylum was denied. As many as 350,000 refugees who had never applied would be encouraged to seek hearings for the first time. The government agreed to give $200,000 to churches and organizations to help them inform refugees of their new rights. The INS agreed to hire all new agents to process asylum applications, a staff that would be trained by human-rights activists about conditions in Central America.

The suit had charged that the United States had routinely violated the Refugee Act of 1980, which mandated that ideological factors should not be considered in the decision whether to grant asylum to refugees. The plaintiffs claimed that Salvadorans and Guatemalans had been routinely denied asylum because of the U.S. government's close ties to military rulers in those countries. Ninety-seven percent of Salvadoran and 99 percent of Guatemalan requests for asylum had been denied between 1980 and 1989. Rather than going to trial and facing public scrutiny of its record, the government agreed to a settlement.

In another December victory for the sanctuary movement, a federal district judge limited the government's authority to send undercover informants to spy on religious gatherings. The INS could never again dispatch agents like Jesus Cruz to bug Bible-study classes, tape worship services, or take down the license-plate numbers of parishioners. Such actions, the judge ruled, were a violation of the First Amendment.

Darlene was euphoric when she heard all the news. The settlement, she felt, was a vindication for the Tucson Eleven and their refugee "co-conspirators." With the court decision it was clear that the movement had been much more than a symbolic protest.

The full effect of the settlement remains to be seen. But hundreds of thousands of refugees, like Maria, Francisco, and Ana, are no longer being deported to face death squads—at least for now. After a decade of struggle, they have finally found a sanctuary.

CHAPTER 6

SURVIVING THE REVOLUTION:

SISTERS OF THE FUTURE

which me will survive
all these liberations.

AUDRE LORDE

Darlene Nicgorski's decision to leave her order was not surprising. She had suggested early on that religious life might be a chapter in a longer story.

But when Mary Aileen Dame told me she, too, was renouncing her vows after almost four decades, I was startled. The last straw for her: the decision of the Sister of Mercy congregations in the United States to merge back into a single union. She had wanted to remain in her autonomous community.

Why did this incident trigger her departure when she had survived more dramatic differences with her congregation? Mary Aileen knows the Mercy union might seem like a small matter to outsiders. She is not completely sure why the pressure to amalgamate was the breaking point. She says it may take her years to come to terms with her decision.

When I told Donna Quinn that two more of her sisters were leaving, she was disturbed. I, too, was saddened that the convent had lost two of the women it needed most. Still, while Darlene moved on to an independent life, she became more active than ever in groups of women. She was elected to the board of the

National Association of Religious Women, which now welcomed laywomen. She continued to work for refugee rights. Mary Aileen was one of the thousands of nuns whose postcanonical life hardly changed at all. Her friends from the convent continued to be her community; she was as passionate as ever about her mission for justice.

The two women remind me of the early Christians, who prayed together in their homes; of the twelfth-century Beguines, who ministered to the sick; of the nineteenth-century "walking sisters," who housed orphans in their convent. These sisters don't need the Church to sanctify their communities of faith.

Still, the Catholic church provided the structure for communities of sisters, and it is no accident that strong women emerged from its convents. While its repressive rules devastated some nuns psychologically, it gave the survivors a higher education and a passport to Third World cultures—opportunities available to few women in the 1950s. It allowed them—indeed forced them—to take on leadership roles in schools and hospitals at home and abroad. For more than 150 years the social-service network of the Catholic church was operated, and often owned, by communities of religious women. They used their own money to build and staff colleges, schools, hospitals, orphanages, and homes for the elderly. While they were accountable to bishops, they operated independently.

Even the vows liberated nuns. While some sisters gave the vow of poverty lip service, others devoted their lives to living among the marginalized. Although superiors taught that the vow of obedience meant unquestioning adherence to authority, many sisters instinctively interpreted it as a response to conscience. When chastity was forced upon women by men who rejected female sexuality, it was oppressive. But when chosen by women it was often a liberating option that freed sisters from familial responsibility and allowed them to focus full attention on their work.

The convent also provided community. While the extended family was disintegrating in America in the 1950s and more women were isolated in suburbia, nuns had the comfort of their sisters. Even in the outposts of the Third World they tried to find communities of likeminded women. The support of their sisters gave them strength to persevere.

Religious life gave sisters grounding in faith. Many rejected the tenets of their traditional religious training early on, but their education inspired a new theology based on principles of equality. In time the Father God was joined by the Mother God. The Divine Office evolved into feminist prayer services that celebrated the divine within. This new faith motivated nuns to follow their own convictions despite opposition from the Church.

Ironically the oppressiveness of the Church may have been the most liberating factor of all. Authoritarian superiors, priests, and bishops inspired rebelliousness. Nuns felt oppressed and thus they reached out to others in similar circumstances. Their activism was not based on other people's manifestos, but on their own experiences. Darlene had responded to refugees before the sanctuary movement had a name. Mary Aileen had made her own "preferential option for the poor" long before the bishops met in Medellín.

As progressive nuns internalized their values, however, the convent became less alluring. When nuns left their motherhouses to move into their own houses, their communities were made up of sisters of like mind. The order may have been their extended family, but their primary loyalty was to the few women who shared their values. The more they disagreed with official Church teachings, the less eager they were to retain their ties with the institution. Loyalists like Donna were committed to staying in the order to fight sexism in the Church. But others felt that continued affiliation would legitimize practices they abhorred.

So the identity of nuns has changed as many have rejected the institution that spawned them. Rome no longer defines sisters. They define themselves by their values, their commitment to community, their grounding in faith.

Today when I socialize with nuns and former nuns who have sustained their vision, I cannot tell them apart. Perhaps it is because many don't distinguish between themselves. Women are already experimenting with noncanonical orders, such as Sisters for Christian Community. Even some contemplative nuns, whose vocation depends upon cloistered community, question the need for papal approval. They are nuns not because they have Rome's imprimatur, but because they feel drawn to a life of prayer.

Yesterday's nuns reveled in the exclusivity of their vocation; today's sisters share their wisdom with the rest of us. Four years after I began this book, nuns' stories still inspire me. There are no women with whom I would rather talk about politics; there are no women with whom I would rather discuss God. Sisters embrace women of all faiths and welcome us into their communities. As a feminist I meet them at marches. As a Jew I join them in prayer.

What will the future hold for North American nuns?

It's a tough question to answer. Religious orders are experiencing a sharp decline in entrants. During the past twenty years the most dramatic drop occurred among sisters, whose population decreased from 167,167 in 1969 to 104,419 in 1989. Today's religious communities are also in financial straits as more nuns live into their eighties and nineties and the number of sisters bringing in income dwindles. A study sponsored by the National Conference of Catholic Bishops concluded that Catholic religious communities in the United States may fall $2.5 to $3.5 billion short in meeting the retirement needs of their members. Sisters were outraged when a priest proposed a solution to their retirement needs, modeled after programs that sponsor children in foreign countries. He called his plan BACON—"Buy a Catholic Old Nun"—and promised that sisters would pray for people who sent them checks.

While some observers believe that we are witnessing the final chapter in the history of women's religious communities, Sister Joan Chittister, prioress of Mount Saint Benedict Priory in Erie, Pennsylvania, and former president of the Leadership Conference of Women Religious, disagrees. Religious life in the late twentieth century, she acknowledges, has gone through a period of breakdown when "morale dropped, productivity deteriorated, and membership declined." It is nothing new. "Eighty-five percent of the religious orders founded before the year 1500 have ceased to exist," she notes. "Sixty-six percent of the religious orders founded before the year 1850 no longer exist. And in our own time, twenty-five percent of all religious of the world have left religious life." But breakdown precedes a period of transition, she maintains. "There is nothing wrong with death with dignity. But the communities that will flourish are those that will form around something of more sustaining value than a common philosophy."

Most of today's congregations, she believes, lack that sustaining identity and mission. "We have a crisis of significance and a crisis of spirituality." It is not enough anymore for sisters to have a common "task," such as teaching or nursing. Their role is not to provide a labor force for the Church. The entire community, she says, must develop a ministry to meet the needs of the marginalized of the world. The group must decide upon a common commitment based on gospel values, whether it is fighting hunger, working for women's rights, protesting the arms race, lobbying for economic justice, or caring for the environment. The postulants will come if communities have a compelling identity.

"Young women are just as intent on doing something worthwhile in their lives as in times past," she says. "If they see intensely spiritual people making profound contributions to life, giving their own lives becomes desirable. They will be attracted to communities that will enable them to accomplish what they couldn't on their own." She predicts that congregations will be smaller than in the past; their members will be older, but they can be as vibrant as their predecessors if they renew their vision: "It may be another ten to twenty years, but a phoenix will rise out of these ashes."

The phoenix is already ascending, according to Sister Marie Augusta Neal. She says that today's nuns, more than any other group, have successfully internalized the values inspired by Vatican II and the past one hundred years of progressive social teachings in the Catholic church. People focused on the hierarchy's insensitivity to women may have lost sight of such documents as the first labor encyclical of 1891, the papers of the Medellín

Conference, and the more recent U.S. bishops' pastoral letters calling for racial equality, peace, and economic justice. Such values, she says, are reflected in sisters' new constitutions and their choices of ministry.

(Unfortunately the first draft of the U.S. bishops' pastoral letter on women has not been equally impressive. Failing to call for full equality for women, it has elicited an onslaught of protest from sisters and the laity over both its content and the lack of input from women in its drafting. Consequently the bishops have postponed release of the final version until the summer of 1992.)

Sister Marie Augusta Neal believes that given the vitality in Catholic women's communities, we will see a resurgence of interest in religious life, particularly among immigrants from Latin America, Asia, and Africa, where vocations are on the rise. The number of sisters has fluctuated throughout history, she notes. In the 1930s the population of apostolic congregations declined; in the fifties young women flocked to the convent.

Sister of Notre Dame Mary Johnson, a doctoral student at the University of Massachusetts in Amherst, questions the criteria people use to determine the health of religious communities. Intrigued by descriptions in popular and scholarly circles of religious life as "declining" and "decaying," she has decided to study the cultural and societal factors that have influenced women who entered religious orders during the last twenty years.

"Why do we focus on median ages, number of entrants per year, and financial difficulties within orders as indicators of the state of religious life," she asks, "instead of looking at the quality of the ministry and the people performing it? There are indications of ageism and sexism in the way the 'decline' is being described, as if there were no new entrants, as if sisters are the only people facing hard financial choices, and as if sisters over sixty have nothing to contribute." Joan Chittister is among those who maintain that "when life and commitment converge, age is not a factor. In my own monastery, sisters the world calls 'retired' are working in the prisons and with the poor, visiting the isolated elderly, and tutoring the single-parent mothers."

Father Andrew M. Greeley, a sociologist who has studied American Catholics, expects to see life and commitment converge in radically new ways.

"Any institution that has been as responsible to human needs for fifteen hundred years as religious life is not going to vanish from the earth," he says. "But I suspect that we won't be seeing the large monolithic orders that we've known since the Council of Trent. I predict lots of small experiments, including mixed communities of men and women, celibates and married people, those who have made lifelong commitments and those who have made partial commitments."

The communities, he believes, will not seek Rome's blessing. "People attracted to new forms of religious life are not going to care about canonical mandates," he says. "They won't be anticanonical, but they will not expect approval from the traditional Church." Still, he predicts they will be firmly rooted in Catholicism. "We may very well have ecumenical communities. But I think most people will want the Catholic tradition and imagery. What will bind most is the Eucharist and the Sacraments."

A survey conducted by the National Sisters Vocation Conference, "Models of Membership in Religious

Life," bears out some of Andrew Greeley's conclusions, and Joan Chittister's as well. The conference surveyed women who chose not to enter canonical communities. Among the reasons they cited: They did not see a "good spirit among the sisters" they encountered, nor did they find them "living [the] radical poverty" they espoused. The women objected to the fact that communities did not allow a limited time commitment, and they worried that they might not find peer support among an aging population. They were also repelled by what they saw as a "masculine preference in the Church." A priestly vocation, they maintained, was more desirable than that of a nun.

Given these findings, the conference concluded that future models of religious life will most likely include canonical communities that allow nonvowed affiliate or associate membership, and noncanonical groups. "There is a steadily increasing number of communities forming that have no desire to attach themselves to an already formed canonical group and that do not desire to become canonical communities themselves," the conference noted. Such communities could include men, non-Catholics, and even non-Christians.

The most famous noncanonical group, the Sisters for Christian Community, is already in its third decade. The international community, now six hundred strong, is one of the few groups of religious women gaining membership. In addition to refugees from traditional Catholic orders, sisters include Lutherans, Baptists, and Episcopalians—even ordained priests. They live alone or in clusters and stay in touch with the community at large via newsletters and meetings.

"Communication creates community," says founder and sociologist Lillanna Kopp, who co-owns a home with two other sisters. "In the old days you could have two hundred sisters living side by side in traditional convents with no sense of community because they had no communication. Today we have local networks and regional networks. This network community is the model of the future."

Darlene Nicgorski agrees with Lillanna Kopp that religious orders will survive "only if sisters refuse to let Rome define them and their relationship to one another in community." Catherine O'Reilly is less interested in the form communities will take than in the ongoing call to religious life. She is convinced that there will always be women who feel drawn to a life of the spirit, a yearning that transcends political and sociological trends. Donna Quinn maintains that the need for a separate class of "religious" will becomes less important as more women find their voice in the Church. In the future, she says, young and old, rich and poor, will live together in community. Women who feel called to lead will become the new priests.

But if giving up religious congregations as we know them means losing the values and vision we have come to associate with sisters, it will be a loss for us all. What kind of structure will allow women to nurture their faith and follow their consciences? What will give women the financial freedom to pursue their work among the marginalized? Would commitment be necessary? Would Christian faith? Should members live communally? Could men apply?

The last time I met with Donna and her friends, nuns and former nuns among them, we discussed how to retain the values they had learned in religious life and how to share them with others. As her friends bantered back and forth, Donna was uncharacteristically quiet.

Her face then lit up. "Let's start our own community of sisters," she said. I would have smiled, except that I know this is a woman who starts communities for a living.

"Could sisters be Jewish?" I asked.

"Of course," she replied.

"Would we have to be celibate?"

"Of course not."

"What about poverty?"

"Simplicity."

"Would we have to live in Chicago?"

Now this gave her pause.

"We'll have to work out the details. But I think we should start simply. How about a vow of hospitality?" she asked, smiling at the thought. "That's a good one. I think that's where we'll begin."

NOTES

The four sisters were the primary sources for the material in the book, including conversations and interactions with third parties, such as the late Archbishop John Cardinal Cody. Friends, families, colleagues, "superiors," teachers, and lawyers provided extensive background information. The Center for Constitutional Rights in New York gave me access to the transcript of the sanctuary trial.

PREFACE

xvi NUNS WHO LEFT CONVENT: Gerelyn Hollingsworth, *Ex-Nuns: Women Who Have Left the Convent* (Jefferson, N.C.: McFarland & Co., 1985), p. vii.

xvi NUMBER OF SISTERS: *The Official Catholic Directory 1991* (Wilmette, Ill.: P. J. Kenedy & Sons, 1991), p. 1 (general summary). According to the *Directory*, there were 101,911 sisters in 1990.

xvii NUNS NOT JUST NUNS: Jeane Kirkpatrick quoted in Ana Carrigan, *Salvador Witness: The Life and Calling of Jean Donovan* (New York: Ballantine Books, 1984), p. 275.

CHAPTER ONE

7 HEALTH CARE IN NICARAGUA: See: Fernando Silva and Mayra Pasos, "Health Care for the Nation," i.1 Philip Zwerling and Connie Martin, *Nicaragua: A New Kind of Revolution* (Westport, Conn.: Lawrence Hill & Co., 1985), pp. 106–17.

7 NUNS IN LATIN AMERICA: Mary Jo Weaver, *New Catholic Women: A Contemporary Challenge to Traditional Religious Authority* (San Francisco: Harper & Row, 1985), p. 83. Weaver reports that in the early 1960s the Vatican asked 10 percent of American sisters to volunteer for service in Latin America; twenty thousand went.

7 SAVING REGION FROM "GODLESS COMMUNISM": Author's interview with Sister of Mercy Rose McMahon.

7 SENATORS ON TWENTY-FOUR-HOUR TOURS: Mary Aileen was referring to nine Republican Congressmen who went to Nicaragua for twenty hours. See: Stephen Kinzer, "House Delegation Leaves Nicaragua," *The New York Times*, March 16, 1986.

8 ADVERTISEMENT: Donna Quinn was one of ninety-seven nuns, priests, and laypeople who signed an ad, purchased by Catholics for Free Choice, calling for dialogue on abortion. See: *The New York Times*, October 7, 1984.

10 WALKER PERCY ON NUNS: Walker Percy, *Sign-Posts in A Strange Lane* (New York: Farrar, Straus and Giroux, 1991), p. 320. Percy wrote: "This is not to say that . . . Sister Scholastica has to shed both her name and her habit (in which I always thought she looked great, to tell you the truth) for a J. C. Penney pantsuit in which she does not look so great."

12 SEARCH, CONFISCATION, CHARGES: Author's interviews with defense attorney Michael Altman, prosecutor Don Reno, and defendant Darlene Nicgorski. See also: Stuart Taylor, Jr., "16 Indicted by U.S. in Bid to End Church Smuggling of Latin Aliens," *The New York Times*, January 15, 1985.

14 BOOKS BY NUNS AND FORMER NUNS: The most sentimental accounts of convent life are the biographies of founders commissioned by religious orders. The most sensational

story of convent life by an alleged former nun is Maria Monk, *Awful Disclosures by Maria Monk of the Hotel Dieu Nunnery of Montreal* (New York: Hoisington & Trow, 1836).

14 BOOKS ON MODERN NUNS: Among those I have found particularly valuable: Marcelle Bernstein, *The Nuns* (Philadelphia: J. B. Lippincott, 1976); Ann Patrick Ware, ed., *Midwives of the Future: American Sisters Tell Their Story* (Kansas City, Mo.: Leaven Press, 1985); Marie Augusta Neal, *Catholic Sisters in Transition from the 1960s to the 1980s* (Wilmington, Del.: Michael Glazier, 1984); Rosemary Curb and Nancy Manahan, *Lesbian Nuns: Breaking Silence* (Tallahassee, Fla.: Naiad Press, 1985; reprint ed. New York: Warner Books, 1986); Neal, *From Nuns to Sisters: An Expanding Vocation* (Mystic, Conn.: Twenty-Third Publications, 1990); Weaver, *New Catholic Women*; and Barbara Ferraro and Patricia Hussey with Jane O'Reilly, *No Turning Back: Two Nuns' Battle with the Vatican Over Women's Right to Choose* (New York: Poseidon Press, 1990; reprint ed., New York: Ivy Books, 1991).

14 NUNS INVISIBLE: See: Bernadette J. Brooten, "Early Christian Women and Their Cultural Context: Issues of Method in Historical Reconstruction," in Adela Yarbro Collins, ed., *Feminist Perspectives on Biblical Scholarship* (Chico, Calif.: Scholars Press, 1985), p. 68. Brooten points out, "Some ancient sources would lead us to believe that women either did not exist or that they were beings very marginal to life." See also: Weaver, *New Catholic Women*, p. 11. Sisters, says Weaver, "are almost totally absent when it comes to historical recognition."

14 SCHOLARS ON NUNS: Among the authors to whom I am indebted for their research on the history of women in the early church: Bernadette J. Brooten, Elizabeth Castelli, Elisabeth A. Clark, Mary Ewens, Jean Laporte, Elisabeth Schüssler Fiorenza, Jo Ann McNamara, Margaret R. Miles, Rosemary Radford Ruether, Jane Tibbetts Schulenburg, and Suzanne Fonay Wemple.

14 PIECING TOGETHER THE HISTORY: Brooten, "Early Christian Women," p. 67. Brooten notes that given the lack of

sources about women's lives, reconstructions of this period can never be firmly rooted in "certain and objective knowledge." The work of women's history, she writes, must be "based upon historical imagination."

15 THE VIRGINS, MIXED COMMUNITIES, BISHOPS' ATTITUDES: Jo Ann McNamara, *A New Song: Celibate Women in the First Three Christian Centuries* (New York: Harrington Park Press, 1985), pp. 57–58. Elisabeth Schüssler Fiorenza, *In Memory of Her: A Feminist Theological Reconstruction of Christian Origins* (New York: Crossroad Publishing Co., 1988), p. 313. Fiorenza writes that it appears that unmarried women were already living together in community in the beginning of the second century. Jean Laporte, *The Role of Women in Early Christianity* (Lewiston, N.Y.: The Edwin Mellen Press, 1982), pp. 70–71. Laporte states that the virgins were not a religious order until the second half of the third century.

15 THE WIDOWS: Laporte, *The Role of Women*, pp. 58–59, 65; Roger Gryson, *The Ministry of Women in the Early Church* (Collegeville, Minn.: The Liturgical Press, 1976), pp. 8–9, 38–40. The New Testament mentions only one order of unmarried women, "the widows," females over the age of sixty. They took vows of chastity and devoted their lives to prayer and the laying on of hands to heal the sick. Some early Church writings insist so vehemently that widows not be ordained that they suggest that they may have rivaled priests in stature.

15 CELIBACY NOT IMPOSED ON WOMEN: Neal, *From Nuns to Sisters*, p. 15; McNamara, *A New Song*, pp. 39, 44, 83, 90. McNamara states that Paul did not invent the idea of celibacy "and attempt to impose it on his congregation. The idea came from the Corinthian community." She writes that in the first and second centuries "the message that women should forsake husbands, homes, and children for the sake of sexual purity was not received well by the clergy."

15 CLEMENT VS. TERTULLIAN ON VIRGINITY: McNamara, *A New Song*, pp. 90–94; 99–104; Neal, *From Nuns to Sisters*, p. 15; Margaret R. Miles, *Fullness of Life: Historical Foundations for*

a New Asceticism (Philadelphia: The Westminster Press, 1981), p. 45.

15 VIRGINS' VOWS, CLOTHES, HABITS: Margaret R. Miles, "Patriarchy as Political Theology," in Leroy S. Rouner, ed., *Civil Religion and Political Theology* (Notre Dame: University of Notre Dame Press, 1986), pp. 178–79; Laporte, *The Role of Women*, pp. 72–73; McNamara, *A New Song*, pp. 116–17.

15 CYPRIAN ON THE BATHS: Margaret R. Miles, *Carnal Knowing: Female Nakedness and Religious Meaning in the Christian West* (Boston: Beacon Press, 1989), pp. 28–29; Cyprian, "The Dress of Virgins," quoted in Miles, "Patriarchy as Political Theology," pp. 179–80.

15 TERTULLIAN ON THE VEIL: Tertullian quoted in McNamara, *A New Song*, p. 121; Miles, *Carnal Knowing*, p. 70; Elizabeth Castelli, "Virginity and Its Meaning for Women's Sexuality in Early Christianity," *Journal of Feminist Studies in Religion* 2, no. 1 (Spring 1986): 71.

15 MYSTICAL MARRIAGE: McNamara, *A New Song*, p. 121; Laporte, *The Role of Women*, p. 105; Jane Tibbetts Schulenburg, "The Heroics of Virginity: Brides of Christ and Sacrificial Mutilation," in Mary Beth Rose, ed., *Women in the Middle Ages and the Renaissance: Literary and Historical Perspectives* (Syracuse N.Y.: Syracuse University Press, 1986), p. 31; Castelli, "Virginity and Its Meaning," p. 71.

16 BEGINNING OF MONASTIC LIFE: Laporte, *The Role of Women*, pp. 78–80; Jo Ann McNamara, "Matres Patriae/Matres Ecclesiae: Women of the Roman Empire," in Renate Bridenthal, Claudia Koonz, and Susan Stuard, eds., *Becoming Visible: Women in European History* (Boston: Houghton Mifflin, 1987), pp. 122–23; Castelli, "Virginity and Its Meaning," pp. 78–79.

16 DAUGHTERS OF ARISTOCRACY: Neal, *From Nuns to Sisters*, p. 18; McNamara, "Matres Patriae/Matres Ecclesiae," pp. 123, 137.

16 POSITIVE ASPECTS OF CELIBACY: Elizabeth Clark and Herbert Richardson, *Women and Religion: A Feminist Sourcebook of Christian Thought* (San Francisco: Harper & Row, Publishers, 1977), pp. 6–8; Rosemary Ruether, "Mothers of

the Church: Ascetic Women in the Late Patristic Age," in Ruether and Eleanor McLaughlin, eds., *Women of Spirit: Female Leadership in the Jewish and Christian Traditions* (New York: Simon and Schuster, 1979), pp. 73, 93–94. Reuther contends that asceticism was an attractive option in a society that married twelve-year-old girls to men forty years their senior to cement political and business relationships. Although religious life did not allow women to hold established positions of leadership in the Church, they were assured "equality with men on the plane of their spiritual kingdom."

16 NEGATIVE ASPECTS OF CELIBACY: Miles, *Carnal Knowing*, p. 17; Ruth P. Liebowitz, "Virgins in the Service of Christ: The Dispute Over an Active Apostolate for Women During the Counter-Reformation," in Ruether, *Women of Spirit*, p. 134; Castelli, "Virginity and Its Meaning," pp. 85–88. Castelli maintains that in both marriage and religious life a woman's sexuality was used as a bartering tool. The wife's body was given to her husband while the virgin's belonged to "the celestial Bridegroom." "The ideology of virginity," she writes, equates femininity with a passion that must be repressed. "For a woman to participate in the institution which calls for the negation of the feminine is . . . for her to participate in a profound self-abnegation, self-denial, even self-destruction."

16 HONORARY MALES: Miles, *Carnal Knowing*, p. 55. Miles notes that the "metaphor most frequently used for women who undertook to live an uncompromising Christian faith was that they had 'become male.' "

16 GROWTH OF MONASTERIES, MISSIONARY ACTIVITY, FAMILY FOUNDATIONS: Jane Tibbetts Schulenburg, "Women's Monastic Communities, 500–1100," in Judith Bennett et al., eds., *Sisters and Workers in the Middle Ages* (Chicago: The University of Chicago Press, 1989), pp. 212–20; Suzanne F. Wemple, "Sanctity and Power: The Dual Pursuit of Early Medieval Women," in Bridenthal, *Becoming Visible*, p. 133.

17 ABBESSES: Bernstein, *The Nuns*, pp. 141–43; Caroline Walker Bynum, "Religious Women in the Later Middle

Ages," in Jill Rait, ed., *Christian Spirituality: High Middle Ages and Reformation* (New York: Crossroad Publishing, 1987), p. 128; Wemple, "Sanctity and Power," pp. 134, 137; Suzanne Fonay Wemple, *Women in Frankish Society: Marriage and the Cloister 500 to 900* (Philadelphia: University of Pennsylvania Press, 1981), p. 160.

17 CENTERS OF LEARNING, CHARLEMAGNE: Wemple, "Sanctity and Power," p. 139; Bernstein, *The Nuns*, pp. 165–66.

17 CONVENT LIFESPAN, INVASIONS, RAPES: Miles, *Carnal Knowing*, pp. 64, 74; Schulenburg, "Women's Monastic Communities," pp. 221–23; Schulenburg, "The Heroics of Virginity," pp. 31–32, 46–50, 62. Schulenburg writes that a woman's virginity "was the single most essential prerequisite for a life of Christian perfection; and through it they would be granted entry into heaven."

18 DECLINE IN RELIGIOUS LIFE, END OF DOUBLE MONASTERY: Neal, *From Nuns to Sisters*, p. 19–20; Schulenburg, "Women's Monastic Communities," pp. 224–25; Susan Stuard, "The Dominion of Gender: Women's Fortunes in the High Middle Ages," in Bridenthal, *Becoming Visible*, p. 159.

18 PAPAL BULL OF ENCLOSURE: "Periculoso," quoted in Neal, *From Nuns to Sisters*, pp. 20–21.

18 HILDEGARD OF BINGEN: Margaret Wade Labarge, *A Small Sound of the Trumpet: Women in Medieval Life* (Boston: Beacon Press, 1986), pp. 101–102; Stuard, "The Dominion of Gender," p. 160.

19 THE BEGUINES: Both quotations on Beguines from Fiona Bowie, ed., *Beguine Spirituality: An Anthology* (London: SPCK, 1989), pp. 11–42.

20 SEMICLOISTERED COMMUNITIES: Saint Vincent de Paul quoted in Neal, *From Nuns to Sisters*, pp. 21–26; William Monter, "Protestant Wives, Catholic Saints, and the Devil's Handmaid: Women in the Age of Reformations," in Bridenthal, *Becoming Visible*, p. 210; Liebowitz, "Virgins in the Service of Christ," pp. 144–45. Quotation on enclosure from H. J. Schroeder, ed., *The Canons and Decrees of the Council of Trent* (Rockford, Ill. Tan Books and Publishers, 1978), p. 221.

20 FIRST NUNS IN THE UNITED STATES: Mary Ewens, "Women

in the Convent," in Karen Kennelly, ed., *American Catholic Women: A Historical Exploration* (New York: Macmillan Publishing Co., 1989), p. 19; Mary Ewens, "The Leadership of Nuns in Immigrant Catholicism," in Rosemary Radford Ruether and Rosemary Skinner Keller, eds., *Women & Religion in America: Volume One: The Nineteenth Century* (San Francisco: Harper & Row, Publishers, 1981), pp. 101–107.

21 EUROPEAN VS. AMERICAN CONGREGATIONS, BISHOPS' ATTITUDES TOWARD CLOISTER: John Carroll quoted in Ewens, "Women in the Convent," pp. 18–21.

21 CONDITAE A CHRISTO, SISTERS OF LORETTO: Mary Ewens, "Political Activity of American Sisters Before 1970," in Madonna Kolbenschlag, *Between God and Caesar: Priests, Sisters and Political Office in the United States* (New York: Paulist Press, 1985), pp. 42–43; Neal, *From Nuns to Sisters*, p. 21; Margaret Brennan, "Enclosure: Institutionalising the Invisibility of Women in Ecclesiastical Communities," in Elisabeth Schüssler Fiorenza and Mary Collins, eds., *Women Invisible in Church and Theology* (Edinburgh: T & T Clark Ltd, 1985), p. 43; Ewens, "Women in the Convent," pp. 22–23.

21 ELIZABETH SETON: Ewens, "Women in the Convent," pp. 21–22.

22 NUNS, INCOME, SLAVES: Nun's quotation about slaves in Ewens, "Women in the Convent," p. 22; Hollingsworth, *Ex-Nuns*, p. 87.

22 BLACK SISTERS: Ewens, "Women in the Convent," p. 29; Debra Campbell, "Reformers and Activists," in *American Catholic Women*, pp. 154, 156; Hollingsworth, *Ex-Nuns*, p. 87.

22 NINETEENTH–CENTURY NUNS, ANTI–CATHOLIC PREJUDICE: Ewens, "The Leadership of Nuns," pp. 101–107, 132, 137; Ewens, "Women in the Convent," p. 25; Hollingsworth, *Ex-Nuns*, pp. 90–95, 103; Bernstein, *The Nuns*, pp. 224–26.

23 BOOKS ABOUT EX-NUNS: Hollingsworth, *Ex-Nuns*, pp. 90–93.

23 EXPANDING VOCATIONS, CIVIL WAR NURSES: Ewens, "The

Leadership of Nuns," p. 138; Soldier's quotation in Ewens, "Women in the Convent," p. 26; Hollingsworth, *Ex-Nuns*, p. 95.

24 TWENTIETH-CENTURY DECLINE IN INFLUENCE: Lorine M. Getz, "Women Struggle for an American Catholic Identity," in Rosemary Radford Ruether and Rosemary Skinner Keller, eds., *Women and Religion in America: Volume Three, 1900–1968:* (San Francisco: Harper & Row, Publishers, 1986), p. 178; Brennan, "Enclosure: Institutionalising the Invisibility," p. 43.

25 INTERNATIONAL STATISTICS: Felician A. Foy, ed., *1991 Catholic Almanac* (Huntington, Ind.: Our Sunday Visitor Publishing Division, 1990), p. 364. The Almanac cites as its primary sources the *Yearbook of the Church* (1988) and *Annuario Pontificio* (1990).

27 NUNS AS NEW LEADERS: Author's interviews with reverends Harvey Cox and Andrew M. Greeley.

27 VATICAN AND FEMINISM: Rosemary Radford Ruether, *Women-Church: Theology and Practice of Feminist Liturgical Communities* (San Francisco: Harper & Row, Publishers, 1985), pp. 4, 283.

27 VATICAN RULE: *Code of Canon Law: Latin-English Edition* (Washington, D.C.: Canon Law Society of America, 1983), pp. 225–255.

28 IMMACULATE HEART SISTERS, AGNES MARY MANSOUR, ARLENE VIOLET: Weaver, *New Catholic Women*, 93–100.

28 CHARLES E. CURRAN: See: Annie Lally Milhaven, "Dissent Within the U.S. Church: An Interview with Charles Curran," in Mary C. Segers, ed., *Church Polity and American Politics: Issues in Contemporary Catholicism* (New York: Garland Publishing, 1990), pp. 275–301.

28 LEONARDO BOFF: See: Harvey Cox, *The Silencing of Leonardo Boff: The Vatican and the Future of World Christianity* (Oak Park, Ill.: Meyer Stone Books, 1988).

CHAPTER TWO

34 LITTLE OFFICE: Text and translation provided by Sister M. Christina Branswell, Archivist, Sisters of Mercy, Windham, New Hampshire.

41 PRAYER ON COMMUNISM: Author's interview with Sister of Mercy Rose McMahon.

41 VOLUNTEERING FOR FAITH: Weaver, *New Catholic Women*, p. 83.

43 CATHERINE MCAULEY, FRANCES WARDE: Isabelle Keiss and Joanna Regan, *Tender Courage: A Reflection on the Life and Spirit of Catherine McAuley, First Sister of Mercy* (Chicago: Franciscan Herald Press, 1988), pp. 32–35; Frances Warde quoted in Kathleen Healy, *Frances Warde: American Founder of the Sisters of Mercy* (New York: The Seabury Press, 1973), pp. 31–43, 108–110, 118, 148–53, 273–76, 467, 518.

51 KEEPING POOR SUBMISSIVE: Penny Lernoux, "The Long Path to Puebla," in John Eagleson and Philip Scharper, eds., *Puebla and Beyond: Documentation and Commentary* (Maryknoll: Orbis Books, 1979), pp. 1–11.

51 THEOLOGY NO LONGER FOR PRIVILEGED: Quoted in Harvey Cox, *The Silencing of Leonardo Boff*, pp. 11–12.

51 BASE COMMUNITIES, ALLIANCE BETWEEN CHURCH AND RUL-ING CLASS RUPTURED, PROGRESSIVES VS. CONSERVATIVES: Lernoux, "The Long Path," pp. 11–12; Penny Lernoux, *Cry of the People: The Struggle for Human Rights in Latin America* (New York: Penguin Books, 1982), pp. 42–44.

52 CAMILO TORRES: Lernoux, *Cry of the People*, pp. 29–30.

54 ECCLESIAE SANCTAE: Vatican Congregation for Religious and Secular Institutes, *Ecclesiae Sanctae: Norms for Implementing the Decree on Renewal of Religious Life*, in Austin Flannery, ed., *Vatican Council II: The Conciliar and Post-Conciliar Documents* (Northport, N.Y.: Costello Publishing, 1975), pp. 626–33.

60 NUNS AND MEDICINE: Bernstein, *The Nuns*, pp. 184–85; Weaver, *New Catholic Woman*, pp. 32–34.

62 MARY DALY: Daly, *The Church and the Second Sex* (New York: Harper & Row, Publishers, 1968); Daly, *Beyond God the Father: Toward a Philosophy of Women's Liberation* (Bos-

ton: Beacon Press, 1985), pp. 19–20, 33–34; and Daly *Gyn/Ecology: The Metaethics of Radical Feminism* (Boston: Beacon Press, 1978), pp. 1–2, 134–293.

68 BISHOPS OPPOSED SOMOZA: Philip J. Williams, *The Catholic Church and Politics in Nicaragua and Costa Rica* (Pittsburgh: University of Pittsburgh Press, 1989), pp. 40–41.

68 CATHOLIC PRIESTS AMONG LEADERS: Williams, *The Catholic Church and Politics*, pp. 68–69. Father Ernesto Cardenal became minister of culture and Father Miguel D'Escoto foreign minister. Father Fernando Cardenal was director of the country's literacy campaign. Said Ernesto Cardenal, "My obedience to the revolution is my obedience to God."

69 NUMBER OF VOLUNTEERS, MISSIONARIES: Nicaraguan Embassy, Washington, D.C.; Catholic Mission Association, Washington, D.C.

72 MARY HARTMAN: See: Melissa Everett, *Bearing Witness, Building Bridges: Interviews with North Americans Living and Working in Nicaragua* (Philadelphia: New Society Publishers, 1986).

73 OBANDO OPPONENT OF SANDINISTAS: Author's interview with Jesuit Father César Jerez of the University of Central America in Managua. See: Williams, *The Catholic Church and Politics*, pp. 78–79, 90–93; Laura Nuzzi O'Shaughnessy and Luis H. Serra, *The Church and Revolution in Nicaragua* (Athens, Ohio: Ohio University Center for International Studies, 1986), pp. 15–42.

73 LUZ BEATRIZ ARELLANO: See Arellano's article, "Women's Experience of God in Emerging Spirituality," in Virginia Fabella and Mercy Amba Oduyoye, eds., *With Passion and Compassion: Third World Women Doing Theology* (Maryknoll, N.Y.: Orbis Books, 1989), pp. 135–50.

78 ABORTION IN NICARAGUA: Mary Chapman, "Abortion in Nicaragua: A Debate Whose Time Has Come," *Links* 3, no. 3 (May/June, 1986): 3.

79 OBANDO'S FEAR OF MARXISM: Author's interview with Jerez; Williams, *The Catholic Church and Politics*, pp. 94–95.

CHAPTER THREE

86   BLACK TEEN UNEMPLOYMENT: U.S. Department of Labor, *Geographic Profile of Employment and Unemployment* (Washington D.C.: U.S. Department of Labor, 1989), p. 104. The unemployment rate for black male teenagers in the city of Chicago was 41.9 percent, compared with 26.9 percent for all teenagers in the area.

86   SAINT MARTIN DE PORRES: Author's interview with Sister Connie Driscoll.

93   CATHERINE OF SIENA: Raymond of Capua, *The Life of Catherine of Siena*, ed. Conleth Kearns (Wilmington: Michael Glazier, 1980), pp. 29–34, 43–45, 54–57, 62–63. Raymond was Catherine's spiritual director and confessor. See also: Mary Ann Fatula, *Catherine of Siena's Way* (Wilmington: Michael Glazier, 1987), pp. 25–39.

97   AUGUSTINE'S RULE: Quoted in Laporte, *The Role of Women*, pp. 92–100; Mary Paschala O'Connor, *Five Decades: History of the Congregation of the Most Holy Rosary Sinsinawa, Wisconsin 1849–1899* (Sinsinawa, Wisc.: The Sinsinawa Press, 1954), p. 87.

99   EDUCATION OF NUNS: Bertrande Meyers, *The Education of Sisters* (New York: Sheed & Ward, 1941), pp. 27–36; Weaver, *New Catholic Women*, pp. 80–82; Neal, *From Nuns to Sisters*, pp. 28–29, 121. Neal notes that the Sister Formation Conference, founded in 1953, helped upgrade educational programs for sisters in cooperation with Catholic colleges and universities. This changed nuns' lives dramatically.

100   SAINT DOMINIC: Barbara Cahill, *Dominic the Preacher* (London: Darton, Longman and Todd, Ltd., 1988), p. 15; *New Catholic Encyclopedia*, 1967 ed. "Dominicans," pp. 974, 984.

100   SAMUEL MAZZUCHELLI, HISTORY OF ORDER: O'Connor, *Five Decades*, pp. 1–12, 24–25; 196; 330; community history prepared for author by Sister Marie Laurence Kortendick, archivist, Sinsinawa Dominicans.

102   TEILHARD DE CHARDIN: Ellen Lukas and Mary Lukas, *Teil-*

hard (New York: McGraw-Hill Book Co., 1981), pp. 172–74, 304.

102 CATHERINE OF SIENA: Quotation in Raymond of Capua, *The Life of Catherine of Siena*, pp. 63, 147; Rudolph M. Bell, *Holy Anorexia* (Chicago: University of Chicago Press, 1985), pp. 22–53. Bell suggests that Catherine was suffering from an eating disorder.

104 EARLY ACTIVISTS: Bernstein, *The Nuns*, pp. 162–65; Ewens, "Political Activity of American Sisters Before 1970," pp. 54–55; Mel Piehl, *Breaking Bread: The Catholic Worker and the Origin of Catholic Radicalism in America* (Philadelphia: Temple University Press, 1982), p. 96; Francine du Plessix Gray, *Divine Disobedience: Profiles in Catholic Radicalism* (New York: Alfred A. Knopf, 1970), p. 120; Maureen McCormack, "Uprooting and Rerooting," in Ware, *Midwives of the Future*, p. 108. See also: Mary Luke Tobin, *Hope Is an Open Door* (Nashville: Abingdon, 1981).

107 IMMACULATE HEART SISTERS, GLENMARY NUNS: *New Catholic Women*, pp. 92–94.

110 WOMEN'S ORGANIZATIONS: Weaver, *New Catholic Women*, pp. 83–86, 128–29; Ewens, "Women in the Convent," in *American Catholic Women*, p. 44.

111 MARGARET TRAXLER: See: Robert McClory, "The Church, Abortion and Sister Margaret Traxler," *Chicago* (December 1985): 199–252.

112 CODY REFUSES TO MEET COUNCIL, FUNDING CUT FOR LIAISON GROUP, STATISTICS ON WOMEN IN DIOCESE: Statistics compiled by Chicago Catholic Women. See also: James Robison, "Catholic Women Seek Voice in Archdiocese," *Chicago Tribune*, June 2, 1975.

115 ARCHDIOCESAN NEWSPAPER ACCOUNT: "Strange Stories Appearing in Chicago Newspapers," *The New World*, June 6, 1975.

116 PROTESTANT WOMEN ORDAINED, APOSTOLIC LETTER: Barbara Brown Zikmund, "Winning Ordination for Women in Mainstream Protestant Churches," in *Women and Religion in America: Volume Three: 1900–1968*, 339–48; Weaver, *New Catholic Women*, pp. 110–11.

119 1976 ORDINATION DECREE: Ruether, *Women-Church*, p. 139.

119 THERESA KANE ADDRESSES POPE: "Excerpts from Nun's Greeting and Pope's Remarks," *The New York Times*, October 8, 1979.

121 CATHOLIC BISHOPS ON HATCH AMENDMENT, CHURCH ON ABORTION: Barbara Varro, "The New Sisters," *Chicago Sun-Times*, February 6, 1983; *The New Catholic Encyclopedia*, "Abortion," pp. 28–30; Joseph Berger, "Catholics and Abortion: Issue Is Right to Dissent," *The New York Times*, March 3, 1986.

122 NUNS NOT PRO-ABORTION: Donna Quinn quoted in Varro, "The New Sisters," p. 8.

122 JOSEPH SCHEIDLER: Quoted in Varro, "The New Sisters," p. 8.

123 RICH WHITE MALES: Donna Quinn quoted in "Serenely Silent No Longer, Two Angry Nuns Battle Their Bishops Over the Issue of Abortion," *People*, August 16, 1982, p. 90.

124 RESPONSE TO PHIL DONAHUE SHOW: Weaver, *New Catholic Women*, pp. 129–30.

124 THE MALE CLERGY: Donna Quinn quoted in Varro, "The New Sisters," p. 14.

124 WOMEN-CHURCH CONFERENCE: For a complete text of Rosemary Radford Ruether's speech, see Ruether, *Women-Church*, pp. 69–74.

132 BREAKING SILENCE: Curb and Manahan, *Lesbian Nuns: Breaking Silence*. Contains stories of present and former nuns.

134 SISTERS FOR CHRISTIAN COMMUNITY: Weaver, *New Catholic Women*, p. 95.

136 O'CONNOR ON ELECTION, FERRARO ON ABORTION: Peter Johnson, "Nuns Paying a Price for Stance," *USA Today*, November 5, 1985.

138 HAMER THREATENS NUNS WITH DISMISSAL: "Cardinal Insists Nuns Retract Abortion View," *The New York Times*, August 25, 1985; McClory, "The Church, Abortion, and Sister Margaret Traxler," p. 199; Brett Harvey, "Holy War: The Nuns Who Defied the Pope On Abortion," *Village Voice*, January 27, 1987, p. 22.

138 PRIESTS RETRACT NAMES FROM AD: "Cardinal Insists Nuns Retract Abortion View"; Harvey, "Holy War," p. 22.

138 A RIGHT TO SPEAK: Donna Quinn quoted in "Shutting the Door on Dissent," *Time*, January 7, 1985, p. 83.

139 NUNS ISSUE STATEMENT FROM WASHINGTON: "Shutting the Door," p. 83.

139 NATIONAL CATHOLIC REPORTER CRITIQUE: "Don't Sign the Abortion Ad," *National Catholic Reporter*, September 27, 1985, p. 27.

140 JOSEPH T. GILL CRITIQUE: "Excommunication Time," *The Wanderer*, February 20, 1986.

141 REPERCUSSIONS FOR SIGNERS: Peter Johnson, "Nuns Paying a Price for Stance," *USA Today*, November 5, 1985.

142 INTERACTION WITH HAMER: The account of this confrontation is based on Donna Quinn's recollection.

144 HAMER SOFTENS STANCE: Johnson, "Nuns Paying a Price."

146 ELEVEN NUNS NOT CLEARED: Ferraro, *No Turning Back*, p. 277.

146 HUSSEY AND FERRARO MEET PAPAL NUNCIO, ORDER ISSUES PRESS RELEASE, NUNS SET CONDITIONS FOR DIALOGUE: Ferraro, *No Turning Back*, pp. 287–302, 307–310.

147 HAMER SAYS OTHER NUNS MADE PUBLIC DECLARATIONS: Ari L. Goldman, "2 Nuns at Eye of Dispute on Abortion," *The New York Times*, July 27, 1986; Harvey, "Holy War," p. 23.

147 NUNS ISSUE STATEMENT CONTRADICTING HAMER: Goldman, "2 Nuns"; Harvey, "Holy War," p. 23.

147 LEADERS CRITICIZE NUNS, ORDER RESISTS DISMISSING: Ferraro, *No Turning Back*, pp. 312–13; E. J. Dionne, Jr., "Vatican Report Threatens Pro-Choice Nuns," *The New York Times*, July 22, 1986.

147 TWO SIGNERS CRITICIZE NUNS: *NCAN Newsletter* 18, no. 2 (Spring 1988).

147 LEADERS BEGIN DISMISSAL PROCESS, DISMISSAL HALTED: Ferraro, *No Turning Back*, pp. 318, 320.

148 TWO NUNS LEAVE: Ferraro, *No Turning Back*, pp. 320–23.

149 SUSANNA WESLEY: Ruth A. Tucker and Walter Liefeld, *Daughters of the Church: Women and Ministry from New Testament Times to the Present* (Grand Rapids, Mich.: Academie

Books, 1987), pp. 236–38. In response to criticism of her preaching to women, Wesley wrote, "I cannot conceive why any should reflect upon you, because your wife endeavors to draw people to church, and to restrain them from profaning the Lord's day, by reading to them, and other persuasions. For my part, I value no censure upon this account."

CHAPTER FOUR

156 TWO THOUSAND CONTEMPLATIVES: This figure is an estimate based on numbers published in *The Official Catholic Directory 1991*. No organization of nuns keeps detailed statistics on contemplatives, and some communities will not reveal numbers of sisters, so it is difficult to come up with a reliable figure.

156 BACKGROUND ON CONTEMPLATIVES: Julia Lieblich, "The Cloistered Life," *The York Times Magazine*, July 1983, pp. 12–21.

177 CLARE AS A GIRL, JOINING FRANCIS, CONVENT LIFE: Madge Karecki, "Clare: Poverty and Contemplation in Her Life and Writings," in John A. Nichols and Lillian Thomas Shank, eds., *Medieval Religious Women, Volume 2: Peaceweavers* (Kalamazoo, Mich.: Cistercian Publications, 1987), pp. 167–70.

178 DEPENDING ON DIVINE PROVIDENCE: Excerpt from Clare's rule, quoted in Karecki, "Clare," p. 171.

178 FOURTH LATERAN COUNCIL, PRIVILEGE OF POVERTY, CARDINAL'S RULE: Karecki, "Clare," p. 172; Fidelis Hart, "Following in the Footprints of the Poor Christ: Clare's Spirituality," in Nichols, *Medieval Religious Women*, pp. 180–81; Frances Ann Thom, "Clare of Assisi: New Leader of Women," in *Medieval Religious Women*, p. 198.

179 CLARE AND MYSTICISM: Witness quoted in Thom, "New Leader," pp. 204–205; Caroline Walker Bynum, *Jesus as Mother: Studies in the Spirituality of the High Middle Ages* (Berkeley: University of California Press, 1982), p. 185. Bynum notes that mysticism can be a substitute for clerical status.

179 CLARE'S NEGLECT OF HEALTH: Hart, "Following the Poor Christ," pp. 181, 192; Thom, "New Leader," pp. 197, 203.

179 TERESA'S GIRLHOOD: Teresa quoted in Teresa of Jesus, *The Autobiography of Saint Teresa of Avila*, ed. E. Allison Peers (Garden City, N.Y.: Image Books, 1960), pp. 67, 69, 71–75.

180 FITTING INTO CONVENT, CONVERSION: Jodi Bilinkoff, *The Avila of Saint Teresa: Religious Reform in a Sixteenth-Century City* (Ithaca, N.Y.: Cornell University Press, 1989), pp. 114–17. Teresa quoted in *The Autobiography*, p. 105.

181 TERESA'S VISIONS: God on angels quoted in Mary Hester Valentine, *Saints for Contemporary Women* (Chicago: The Thomas More Press, 1987), p. 80; Teresa on hell quoted in Laurin Hartzog, "Teresa of Jesus: The Saint and Her Spirituality," in Nichols, *Medieval Religious Women*, pp. 323, 326–27; Bilinkoff, *The Avila of St. Teresa*, pp. 120–21.

181 FOUNDING DISCALCED ORDER, LIFE IN CONVENT: Valentine, *Saints*, pp. 81–82; Teresa on sisters and particular friendships quoted in Bilinkoff, *The Avila of St. Teresa*, pp. 123–127, 131, 150.

182 PRAYER, THE INTERIOR CASTLE, MYSTICAL MARRIAGE, TERESA'S DISCOURSE: Hartzog, "Teresa of Jesus," p. 318; Teresa of Avila, *Interior Castle* (New York: Doubleday, 1961), pp. 10–11; Teresa and prosecutor quoted in Alison Weber, *Teresa of Avila and the Rhetoric of Femininity* (Princeton, N.J.: Princeton University Press, 1990), pp. 11, 18–19, 39, 114, 160.

182 TERESA'S TRAVELS: Keith J. Egan, "Teresa of Jesus: Foundations of Mystical Prayer," in Nichols, *Medieval Religious Women*, p. 332.

183 REVISED CONSTITUTION: Author's interview with Sister Catherine Quinn, co-vicar for religious, New York, and Sister Joan Bourne, president of the Association of Contemplative Nuns. See also: Richard Ostling, "Surprise and Pain in the Cloister," *Time*, April 8, 1985, p. 67.

201 CONTEMPLATIVE SISTERS WHO LEFT: Statistics provided by the National Sisters Vocation Conference, Chicago, Illi-

nois. The Conference has not conducted a new survey of contemplatives, and contemplative groups do not keep such statistics.

CHAPTER FIVE

203 THE BREAK-IN: Author's interview with Margarita Barrios, a pseudonym; author's viewing of a copy of the agents' videotape of the break-in.

207 POLITICAL ASYLUM: Ann Crittenden, *Sanctuary: A Story of American Conscience and the Law in Collison* (New York: Weidenfeld & Nicolson, 1988), p. 20. Crittenden reports that from mid-1980 to mid-1985, 626 Salvadorans were granted political asylum in the United States out of ten thousand who had applied.

209 HISTORY OF SCHOOL SISTERS: M. Francis Borgia, *He Sent Two: The Story of the Beginning of the School Sisters of St. Francis* (Milwaukee: The Bruce Publishing Co., 1965), pp. 22–25, 36–37, 60–69, 97–101, 187; historical summary written by the School Sisters of Saint Francis; *New Catholic Encyclopedia*, "Franciscans—Sisters," p. 52.

218 REPRESSION IN GUATEMALA: Renny Golden and Michael McConnell, *Sanctuary: The New Underground Railroad* (Maryknoll, N.Y.: Orbis Books 1986), p. 24.

219 GUATEMALA, 1980 STATISTICS: Provided by Darlene Nicgorski.

228 FAMILY WOULD BE DENIED ASYLUM: Golden, *Sanctuary: The New Underground Railroad*, p. 13.

229 BACKGROUND OF SANCTUARY MOVEMENT: Arizona Sanctuary Defense Fund's prepared history of the movement. Crittenden, *Sanctuary*, pp. 16–17; Miriam Davidson, *Convictions of the Heart: Jim Corbett and the Sanctuary Movement* (Tucson: The University of Arizona Press, 1988), pp. 6–16.

230 JIM CORBETT BEGINS UNDERGROUND RAILROAD: Wayne King, "Trail Opening in Arizona Sanctuary Case," October 21, 1985; Golden, *Sanctuary: The New Underground Railroad*, pp. 37–40.

231 NUMBER OF SANCTUARY CONGREGATIONS, CHURCH SUPPORT

OF MOVEMENT: Golden, *Sanctuary: The New Underground Railroad*, pp. 53–54.

231 REFUGEE ACT, GENEVA CONVENTION: Crittenden, *Sanctuary*, pp. 20–22; "Legal Justification for the Sanctuary Movement: The Rest of the Story," paper by Defense Attorney A. Bates Butler III, Tucson, Arizona, April 1985.

231 POLITICAL ASYLUM, THE U.N. HIGH COMMISSION: Golden, *Sanctuary: The New Underground Railroad*, pp. 41–45.

234 SANDRA AND FRANCISCO: Nieto-Nuñez is a pseudonym.

236 CHICAGO TASK FORCE V. CORBETT AND TUCSON: Miriam Davidson, "Sanctuary Movement Under Fire," *The Christian Science Monitor*, October 22, 1985.

238 JESUS CRUZ'S HISTORY: Author's interview with prosecutor Don Reno.

241 DOROTHEE SÖLLE: See Sölle, *The Strength of the Weak: Toward a Christian Feminist Identity* (Philadelphia: The Westminster Press, 1984).

241 DOROTHY DAY: Piehl, *Breaking Bread*, p. 14. See: Dorothy Day, *The Long Loneliness: An Autobiography* (San Francisco: Harper & Row, Publishers, 1981).

244 CHARGES, CONFISCATION: Author's interviews with defense attorney Michael Altman, prosecutor Don Reno, and defendant Darlene Nicgorski. See also: Taylor, "16 Indicted by U.S. in Bid to End Church Smuggling of Latin Aliens."

245 AGENTS MARK JOURNALS: Author's interview with Darlene Nicgorski. See also: Wayne King, "Records Show U.S. Suspected Radical Ties in Group Aiding Illegal Aliens," *The New York Times*, November 3, 1985.

245 TWO SANCTUARY WORKERS ARRESTED: Davidson, *Convictions of the Heart*, p. 87. In February 1984 Stacey Lynn Merkt, Sister Diane Muhlenkamp, and Jack Fischer, a reporter for the *Dallas Times-Herald*, were arrested with three Salvadorans.

245 MILLION-DOLLAR LEGAL DEFENSE: Figure provided by the Arizona National Sanctuary Defense Fund.

246 THE TUCSON ELEVEN: Author's interview with defendants; "The Defendants," *Arizona Daily Star*, October 20, 1985.

247 PRETRIAL STIPULATIONS, BIAS CHARGE, CHANGE ·IN DEFENSE

STRATEGY: Author's interviews with Altman, defense attorney William J. Risner, and Reno; Mark Turner, "Sanctuary Trial Pits Federal Law vs. Church Duty," *Arizona Daily Star*, October 20, 1985; Turner, "Defense Dealt Another Loss in Sanctuary Case," *Arizona Daily Star*, October 25, 1985; Turner, "Last Major Defense Barred in Sanctuary Case," *Arizona Daily Star*, October 29, 1985.

251 DON RENO'S HISTORY: Author's interview with Reno; Gene Varn, "Lawyer Brings Mixed Background Into Sanctuary-Case Prosecution," *Arizona Republic*, October 21, 1985.

252 ALTMAN'S OPENING ARGUMENT: Transcript provided by Michael Altman; Gene Varn, "Nun Labeled U.S. Heroine by Defense," *Arizona Republic*, November 21, 1985.

254 CRUZ TESTIMONY: Jay Mathews, "Sanctuary's Point Being Made," *Washington Post*, January 30, 1986.

255 CRUZ ILLEGALLY TRANSPORTED ALIENS WHILE WORKING FOR INS: Author's interviews with Reno and Risner.

255 CRUZ CAUGHT LYING, CARROLL'S RESPONSE: Author's interview with Reno; Mathews, "Sanctuary's Point"; Gene Varn, " 'Perjury' Spurs Bid to Kill Sanctuary Case," *Arizona Republic*, January 22, 1986.

257 JUDGE LIMITS USE OF LANGUAGE TO DESCRIBE VIOLENCE: Michael Altman, "The Arizona Sanctuary Case," in *Litigation* 16, no. 4 (Summer 1990): 23–54.

259 THE CATHOLIC CHURCH ON SANCTUARY: "Convicted Nun Scores Bishops on Sanctuary," *National Catholic Reporter*, May 16, 1986. After the trial Darlene saw a confidential 1983 U.S. Catholic Conference legal memorandum on the sanctuary movement. It said that lawyers hired by the Church advised that the defendants' actions were illegal. "Unfortunately, the bishops as a group took the legal opinion of corporate lawyers instead of following the Spirit," Darlene said.

263 NIETO-NUÑEZ TESTIFIES: "Salvadorans Testify in Alien Smuggling Case," *The New York Times*, February 2, 1986. Daniel R. Browning, "Sanctuary Witness Gives Jury Details Previously Excluded," *Arizona Daily Star*, January 31, 1986.

268 THE VERDICTS: "6 Convicted, 5 Cleared of Plot to Smug-

gle in Aliens for Sanctuary," *The New York Times*, May 2, 1986.

279 NUNS AND SOCIAL SECURITY: John Deedy, *American Catholicism: And Now Where?* (New York: Plenun Press, 1987), p. 197.

279 COURT UPHOLDS CONVICTIONS: "8 Lose Last Appeal in Sanctuary Case," *Arizona Republic*, January 15, 1991.

280 REFUGEES GIVEN TEMPORARY LEGAL STATUS: Andrew Blake, "INS to Revamp Rules on Salvadoran, Guatemalan Asylum," *Boston Globe*, December 20, 1990; Blake, "Relief in Sight for Salvadoran Refugees," *Boston Globe*, December 31, 1990; Demetria Martinez and Bill Kenkelen, "Landmark Action Ends Refugee Deportation," *National Catholic Reporter*, December 28, 1990.

281 GOVERNMENT'S RIGHT TO SEND INFORMANTS INTO CHURCHES LIMITED: Demetria Martinez, "Ruling on Government Spying Seen as Victory for Sanctuary Movement," *National Catholic Reporter*, December 21, 1990; Lisa Morrell and Dee Ralles, "Curbs on Spying in Churches Hailed," *Arizona Republic*, December 12, 1990.

CHAPTER SIX

286 DROP IN VOCATIONS: Foy, *1991 Catholic Almanac*, p. 64.

286 BISHOPS' STUDY ON RETIREMENT: Joseph Berger, "Retiring Priests and Nuns Lack Adequate Funds," *The New York Times*, May 30, 1986.

286 PRIEST PROPOSES NUN SPONSORSHIP PROGRAM: Deedy, *American Catholicism*, pp. 202–203.

286 JOAN CHITTISTER: Quotations from author's interview with Sister Joan Chittister and Chittister, *Women, Ministry and the Church* (New York: Paulist Press, 1983), pp. 27–35; Chittister, *Winds of Change: Women Challenge the Church* (Kansas City: Sheed & Ward, 1986), pp. 123–29; *Womanstrength: Modern Church, Modern Women* (Kansas City: Sheed & Ward, 1990), pp. 84–93, 148, 151–52, 155; Chittister, "Religious Life Neither Age Nor Numbers," *National Catholic Reporter*, May 19, 1989.

287 MARIE AUGUSTA NEAL: Author's interview with Sister

Marie Augusta Neal. See also: Neal, "The Context of Medellín and Puebla: World Church Movement Toward Social Justice," in Edward L. Cleary, ed., *Born of the Poor: The Latin American Church Since Medellín* (Notre Dame: University of Notre Dame Press, 1990), pp. 171–76.

289 ANDREW GREELEY: Author's interview with Father Andrew M. Greeley. See also: Greeley, *The Catholic Myth: The Behaviors and Beliefs of American Catholics* (New York: Charles Scribner's Sons, 1990), p. 201.

289 SURVEY CONDUCTED: Carol Ann Jokerst and Gertrude Wemhoff, *Models of Membership in Religious Life* (Chicago: National Sisters Vocation Conference and Religious Formation Conference, 1983).

290 LILLANNA KOPP: Author's interview with Sister Lillanna Kopp. See also: Kopp, *Sudden Spring: 6th Stage Sisters* (Waldport, Ore.: Sunspot Publications, 1983).

INDEX